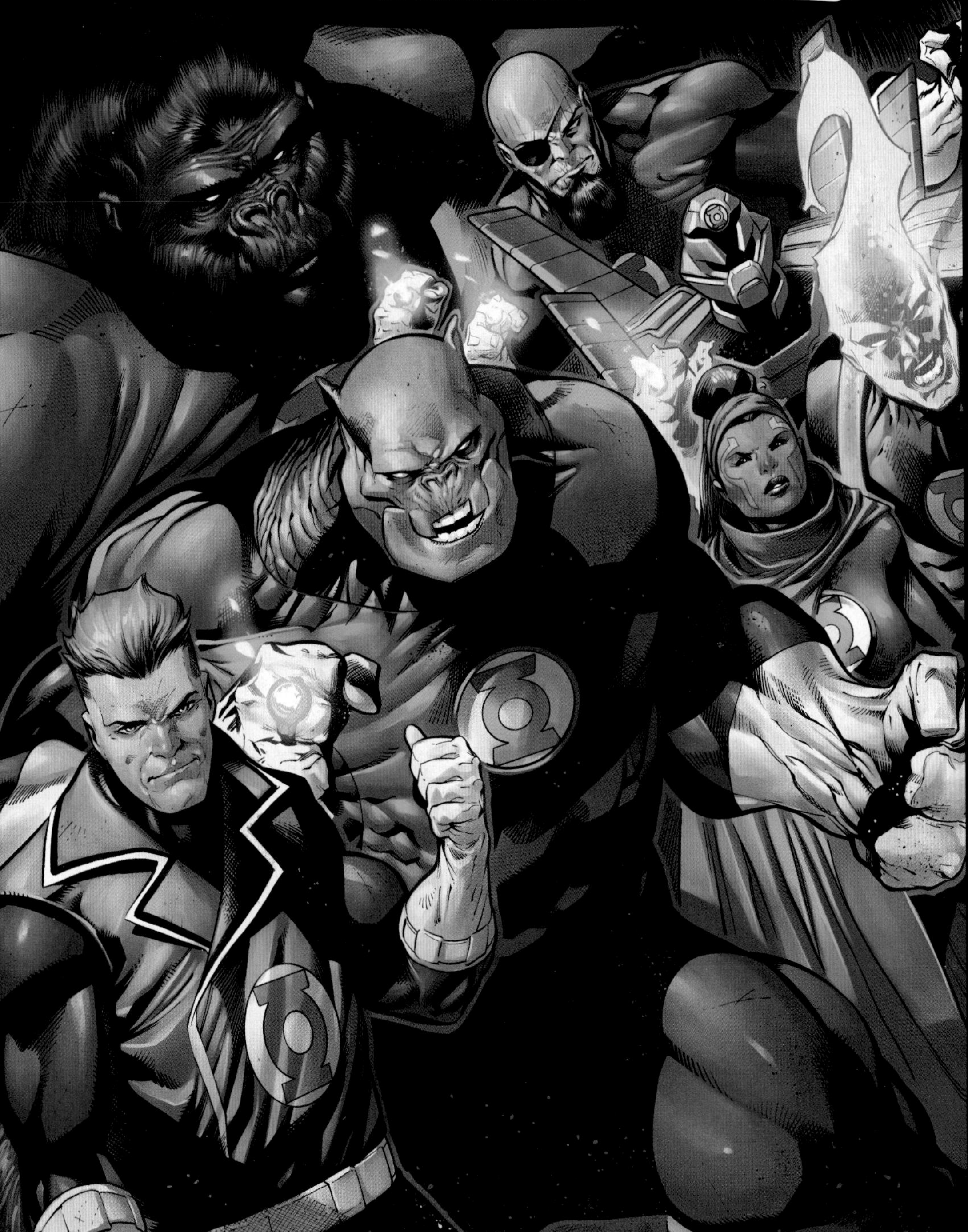

HAL JORDAN AND THE GREEN LANTERN CORPS

VOL.6 ZOD'S WILL

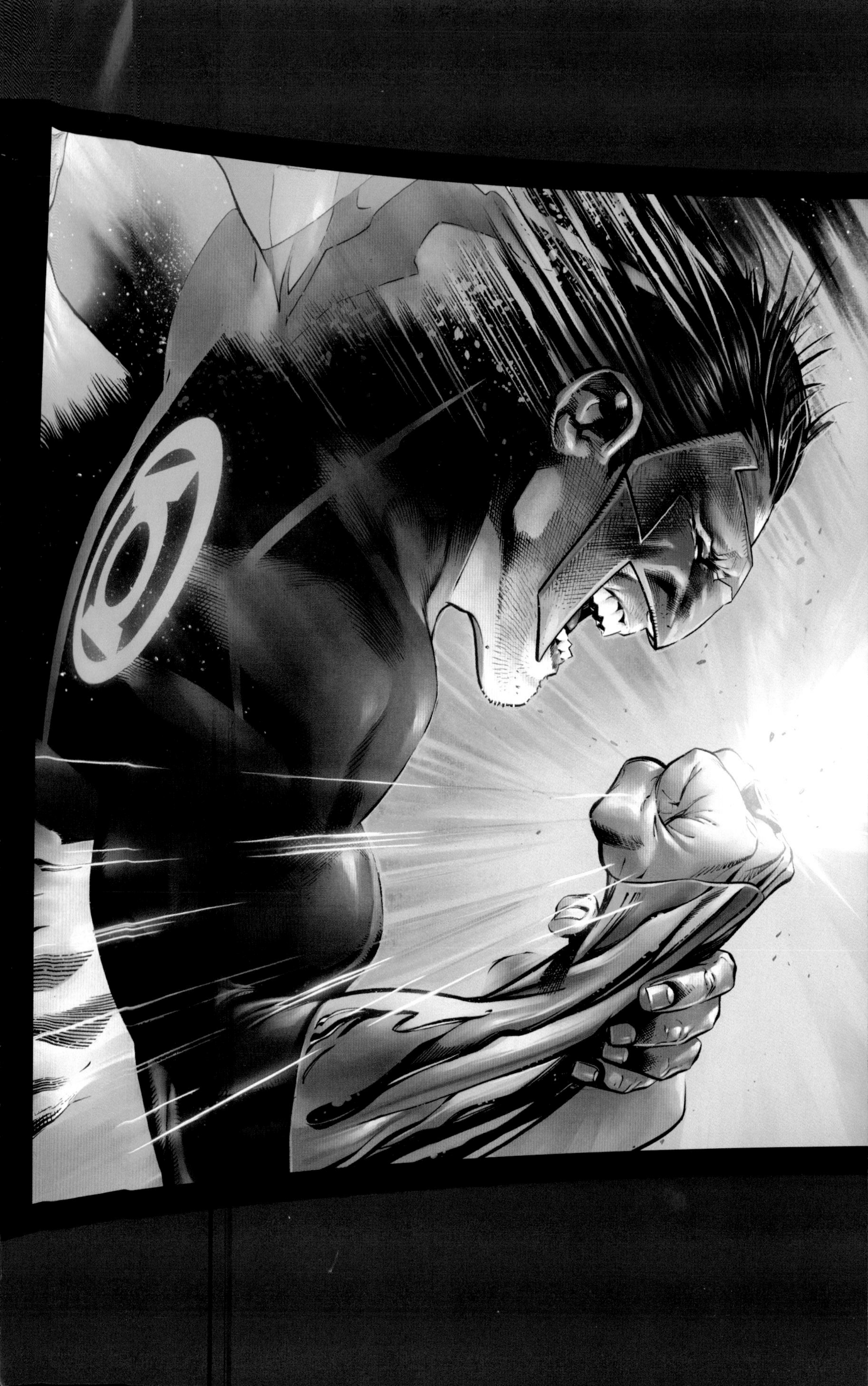

HAL JORDAN AND THE GREEN LANTERN CORPS
VOL.6 ZOD'S WILL

ROBERT VENDITTI
writer

RAFA SANDOVAL
ETHAN VAN SCIVER ✱ BRANDON PETERSON
pencillers

JORDI TARRAGONA
ETHAN VAN SCIVER ✱ BRANDON PETERSON
inkers

TOMEU MOREY
JASON WRIGHT
colorists

DAVE SHARPE
letterer

TYLER KIRKHAM and ARIF PRIANTO
collection cover artists

SUPERMAN created by **JERRY SIEGEL** and **JOE SHUSTER**
By special arrangement with the Jerry Siegel family

MIKE COTTON   BRIAN CUNNINGHAM Editors - Original Series ✳ **ANDREW MARINO** Assistant Editor - Original Series
JEB WOODARD Group Editor - Collected Editions ✳ **TYLER-MARIE EVANS** Editor - Collected Edition
STEVE COOK Design Director - Books ✳ **MONIQUE NARBONETA** Publication Design

BOB HARRAS Senior VP - Editor-in-Chief, DC Comics
PAT McCALLUM Executive Editor, DC Comics

DIANE NELSON President ✳ **DAN DiDIO** Publisher ✳ **JIM LEE** Publisher ✳ **GEOFF JOHNS** President & Chief Creative Officer
AMIT DESAI Executive VP - Business & Marketing Strategy, Direct to Consumer & Global Franchise Management
SAM ADES Senior VP & General Manager, Digital Services ✳ **BOBBIE CHASE** VP & Executive Editor, Young Reader & Talent Development
MARK CHIARELLO Senior VP - Art, Design & Collected Editions ✳ **JOHN CUNNINGHAM** Senior VP - Sales & Trade Marketing
ANNE DePIES Senior VP - Business Strategy, Finance & Administration ✳ **DON FALLETTI** VP - Manufacturing Operations
LAWRENCE GANEM VP - Editorial Administration & Talent Relations ✳ **ALISON GILL** Senior VP - Manufacturing & Operations
HANK KANALZ Senior VP - Editorial Strategy & Administration ✳ **JAY KOGAN** VP - Legal Affairs ✳ **JACK MAHAN** VP - Business Affairs
NICK J. NAPOLITANO VP - Manufacturing Administration ✳ **EDDIE SCANNELL** VP - Consumer Marketing
COURTNEY SIMMONS Senior VP - Publicity & Communications ✳ **JIM (SKI) SOKOLOWSKI** VP - Comic Book Specialty Sales & Trade Marketing
NANCY SPEARS VP - Mass, Book, Digital Sales & Trade Marketing ✳ **MICHELE R. WELLS** VP - Content Strategy

HAL JORDAN AND THE GREEN LANTERN CORPS VOL. 6: ZOD'S WILL

DC Comics, 2900 West Alameda Ave., Burbank, CA 91505
Printed by Times Printing, LLC, Random Lake, WI, USA. 8/17/18. First Printing.
ISBN: 978-1-4012-8444-2

Library of Congress Cataloging-in-Publication Data is available.

MIX
Paper from
responsible sources
FSC® C015572
www.fsc.org

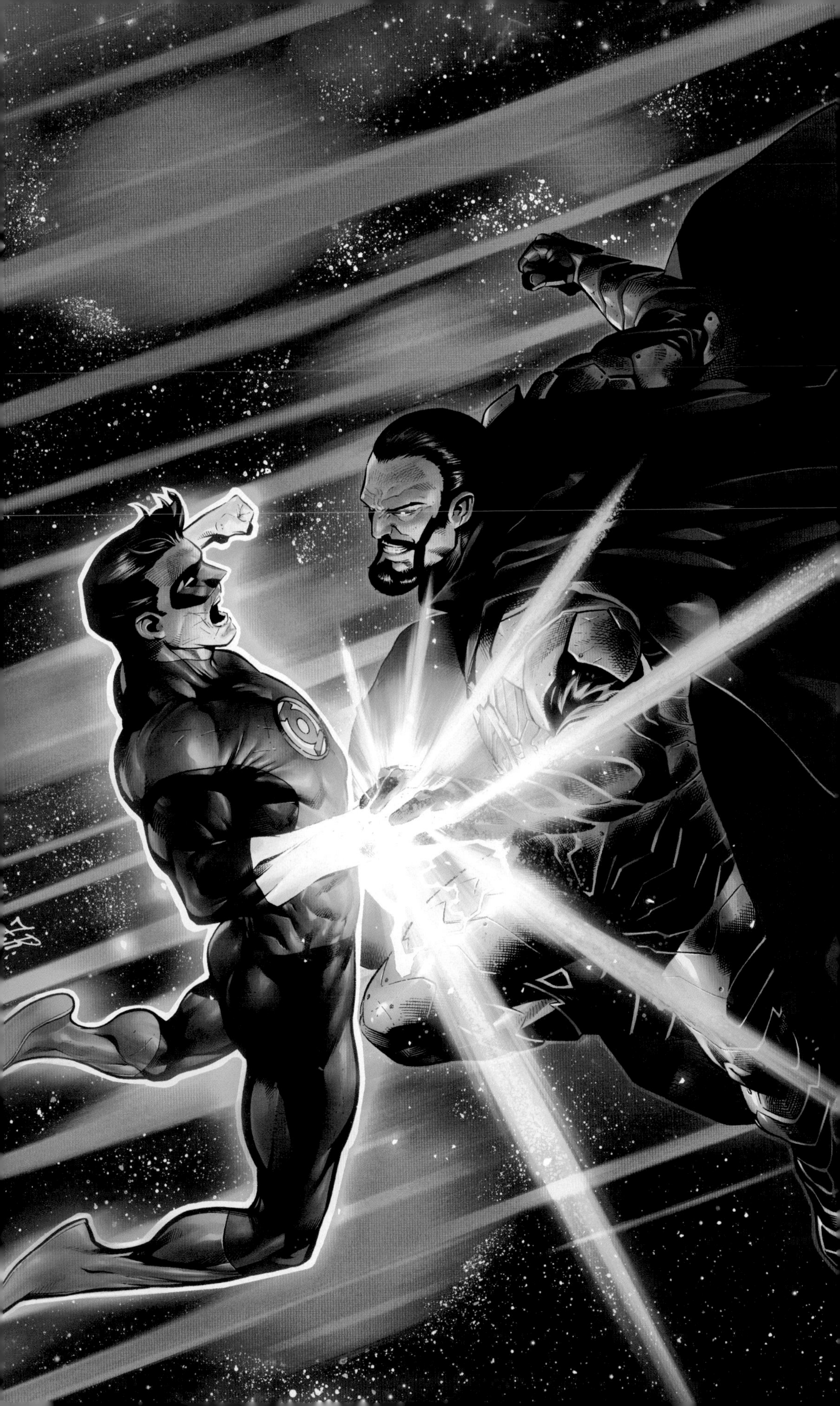

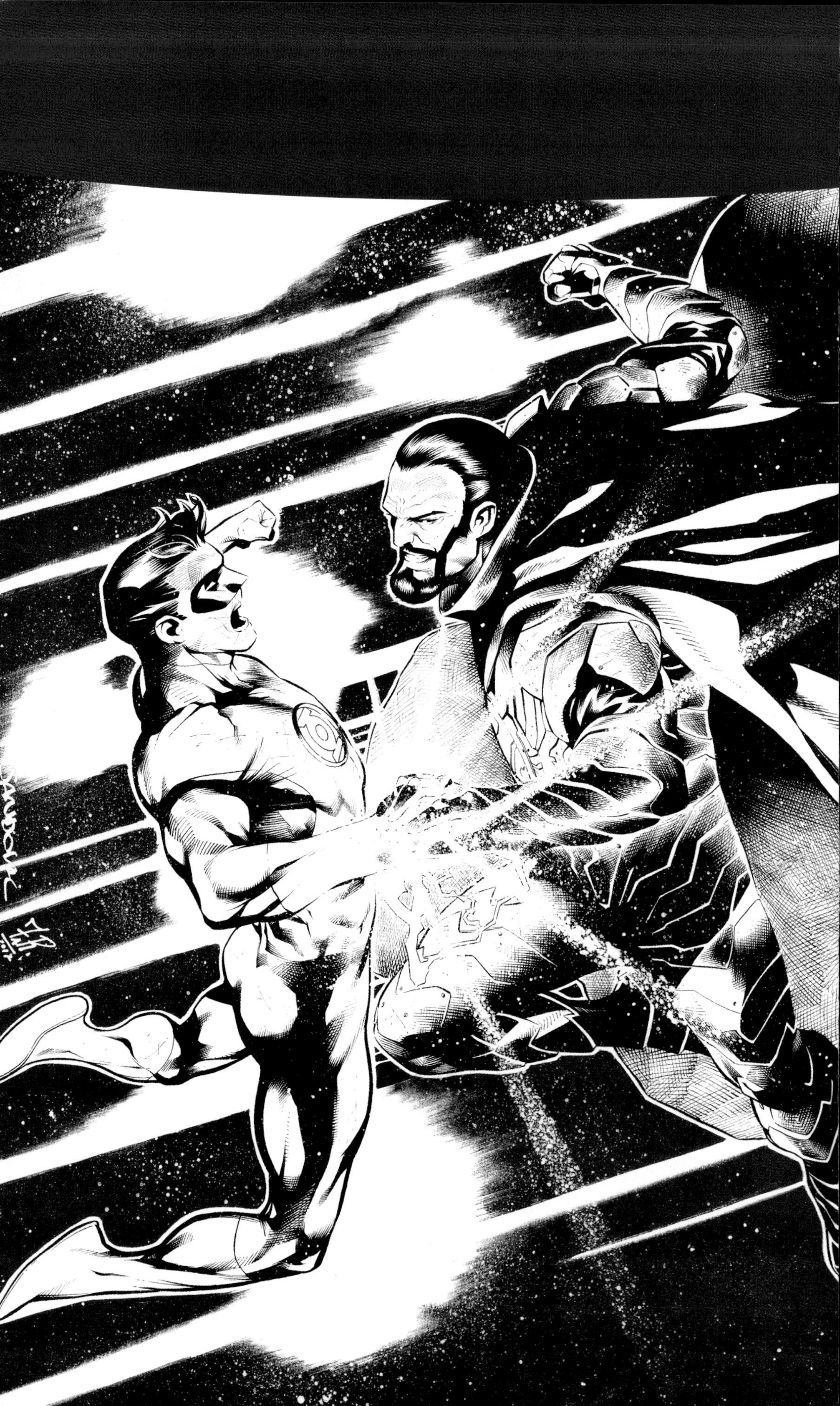

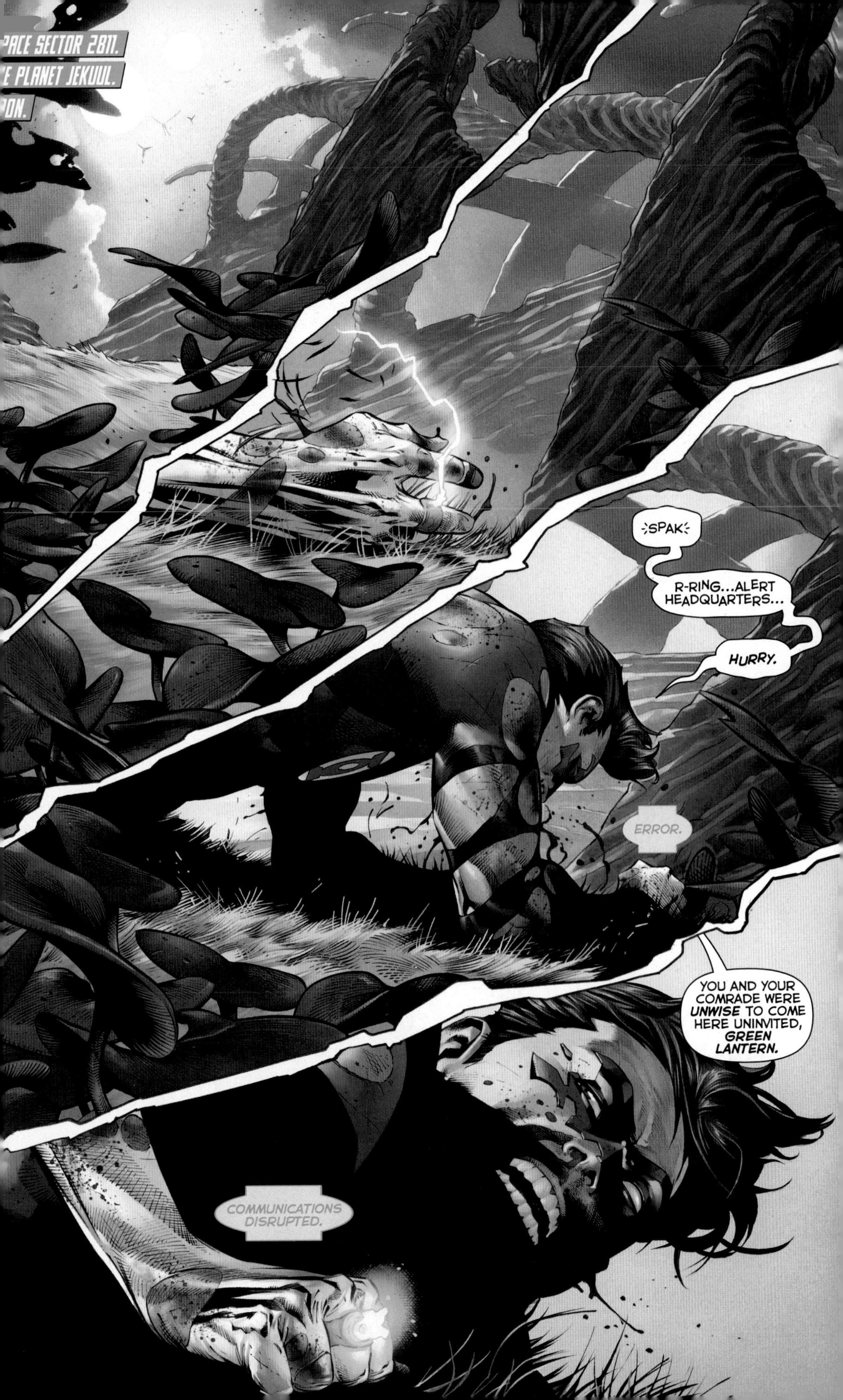

PACE SECTOR 2811.
E PLANET JEKUUL.
ON.
SPAK
R-RING...ALERT HEADQUARTERS...
HURRY.
ERROR.
YOU AND YOUR COMRADE WERE UNWISE TO COME HERE UNINVITED, GREEN LANTERN.
COMMUNICATIONS DISRUPTED.

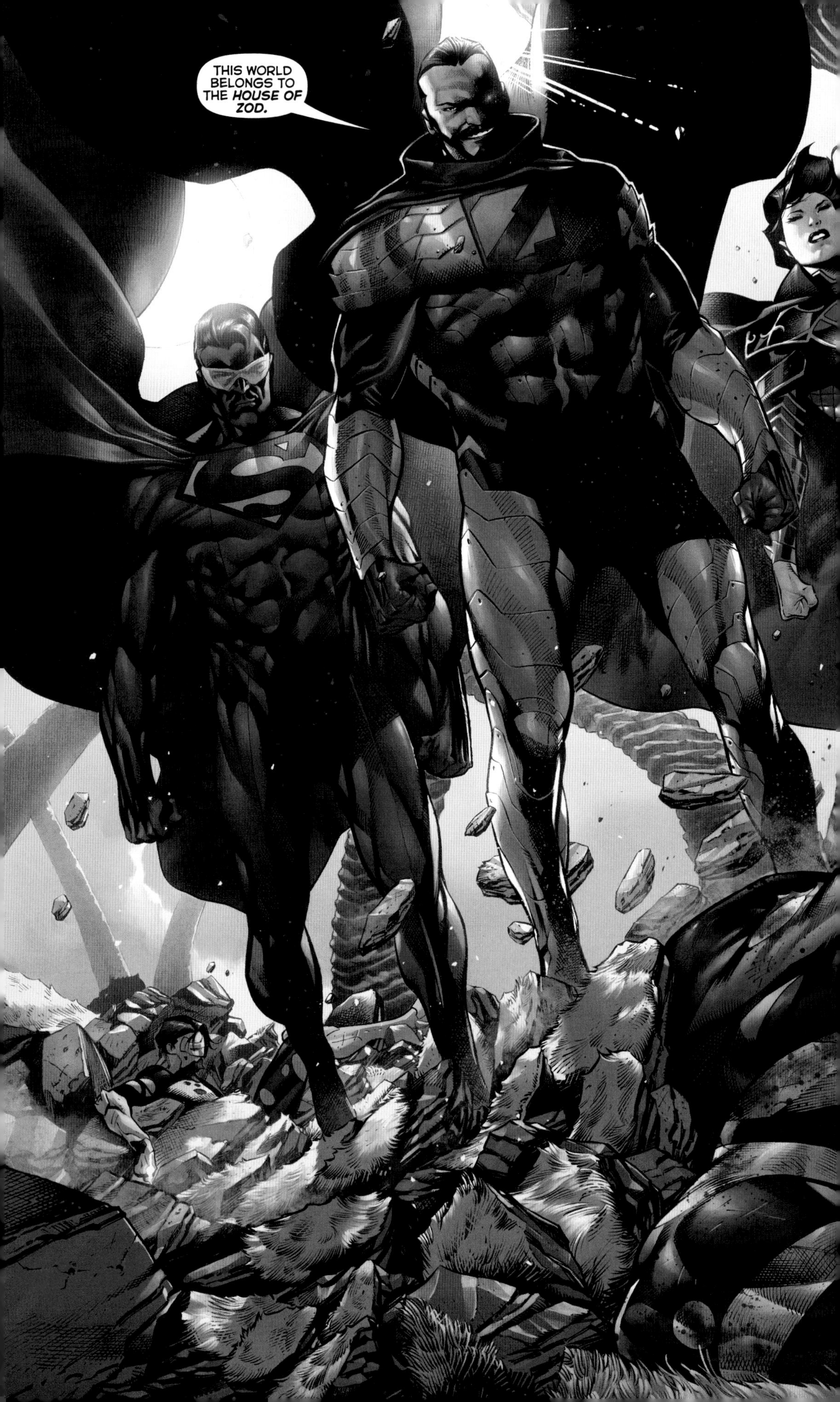
THIS WORLD BELONGS TO THE HOUSE OF ZOD.

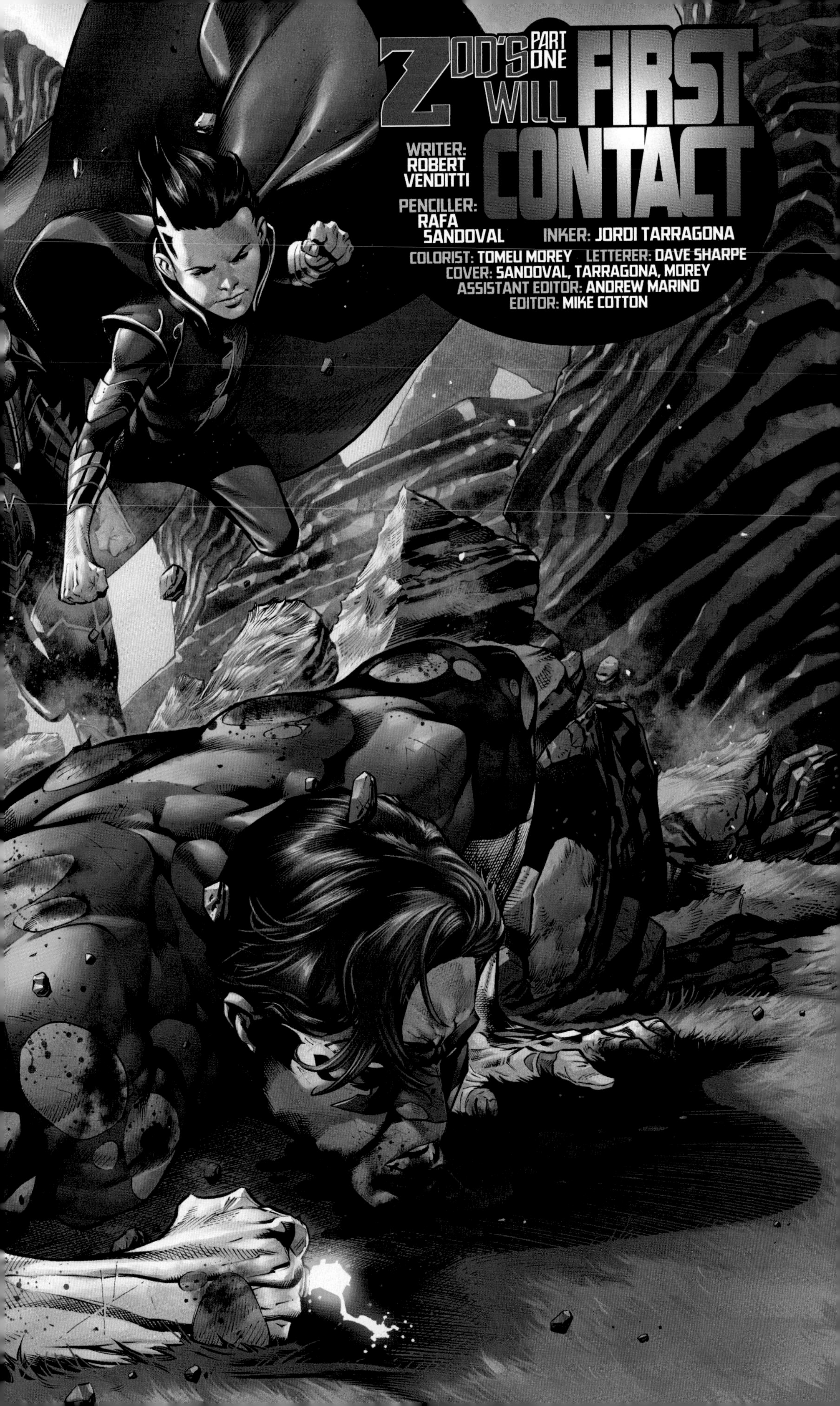
ZOD'S WILL PART ONE
FIRST CONTACT
WRITER: ROBERT VENDITTI
PENCILLER: RAFA SANDOVAL
INKER: JORDI TARRAGONA
COLORIST: TOMEU MOREY LETTERER: DAVE SHARPE
COVER: SANDOVAL, TARRAGONA, MOREY
ASSISTANT EDITOR: ANDREW MARINO
EDITOR: MIKE COTTON

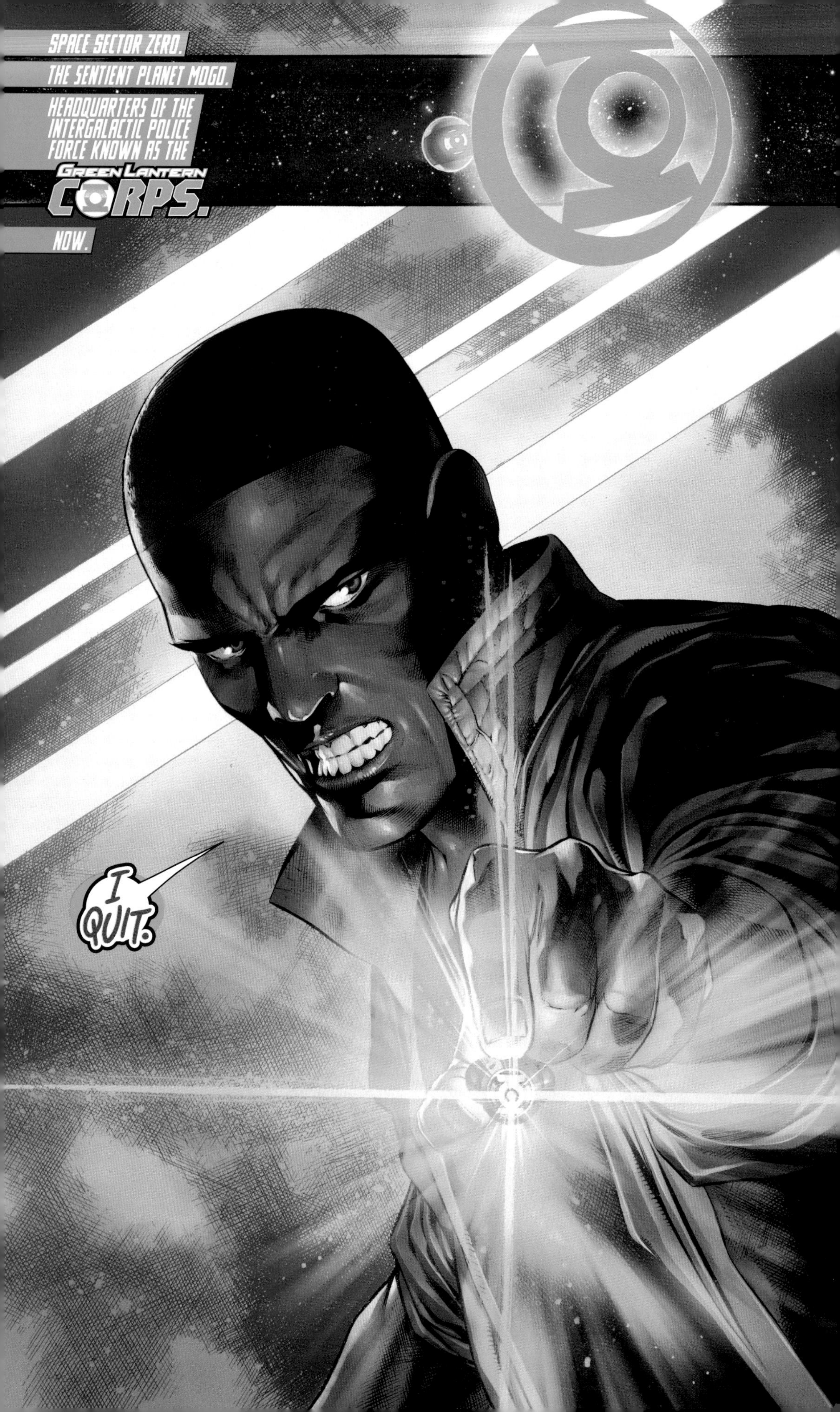
SPACE SECTOR ZERO.
THE SENTIENT PLANET MOGO.
HEADQUARTERS OF THE INTERGALACTIC POLICE FORCE KNOWN AS THE
GREEN LANTERN CORPS.
NOW.
I QUIT.

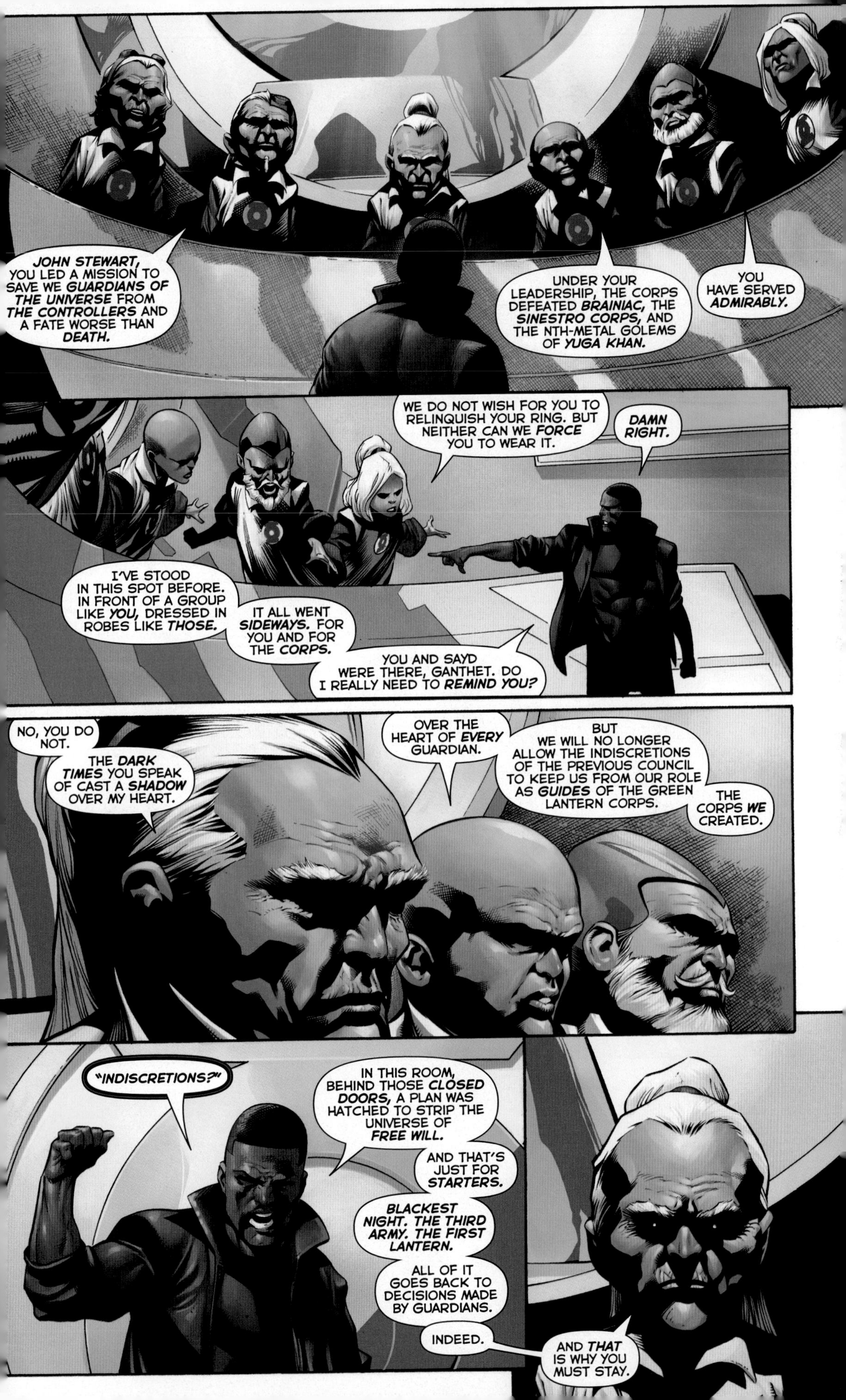

JOHN STEWART, YOU LED A MISSION TO SAVE WE GUARDIANS OF THE UNIVERSE FROM THE CONTROLLERS AND A FATE WORSE THAN DEATH.
UNDER YOUR LEADERSHIP, THE CORPS DEFEATED BRAINIAC, THE SINESTRO CORPS, AND THE NTH-METAL GOLEMS OF YUGA KHAN.
YOU HAVE SERVED ADMIRABLY.
WE DO NOT WISH FOR YOU TO RELINQUISH YOUR RING. BUT NEITHER CAN WE FORCE YOU TO WEAR IT.
DAMN RIGHT.
I'VE STOOD IN THIS SPOT BEFORE. IN FRONT OF A GROUP LIKE YOU, DRESSED IN ROBES LIKE THOSE.
IT ALL WENT SIDEWAYS. FOR YOU AND FOR THE CORPS.
YOU AND SAYD WERE THERE, GANTHET. DO I REALLY NEED TO REMIND YOU?
NO, YOU DO NOT.
THE DARK TIMES YOU SPEAK OF CAST A SHADOW OVER MY HEART.
OVER THE HEART OF EVERY GUARDIAN.
BUT WE WILL NO LONGER ALLOW THE INDISCRETIONS OF THE PREVIOUS COUNCIL TO KEEP US FROM OUR ROLE AS GUIDES OF THE GREEN LANTERN CORPS.
THE CORPS WE CREATED.
"INDISCRETIONS?"
IN THIS ROOM, BEHIND THOSE CLOSED DOORS, A PLAN WAS HATCHED TO STRIP THE UNIVERSE OF FREE WILL.
AND THAT'S JUST FOR STARTERS.
BLACKEST NIGHT. THE THIRD ARMY. THE FIRST LANTERN.
ALL OF IT GOES BACK TO DECISIONS MADE BY GUARDIANS.
INDEED.
AND THAT IS WHY YOU MUST STAY.

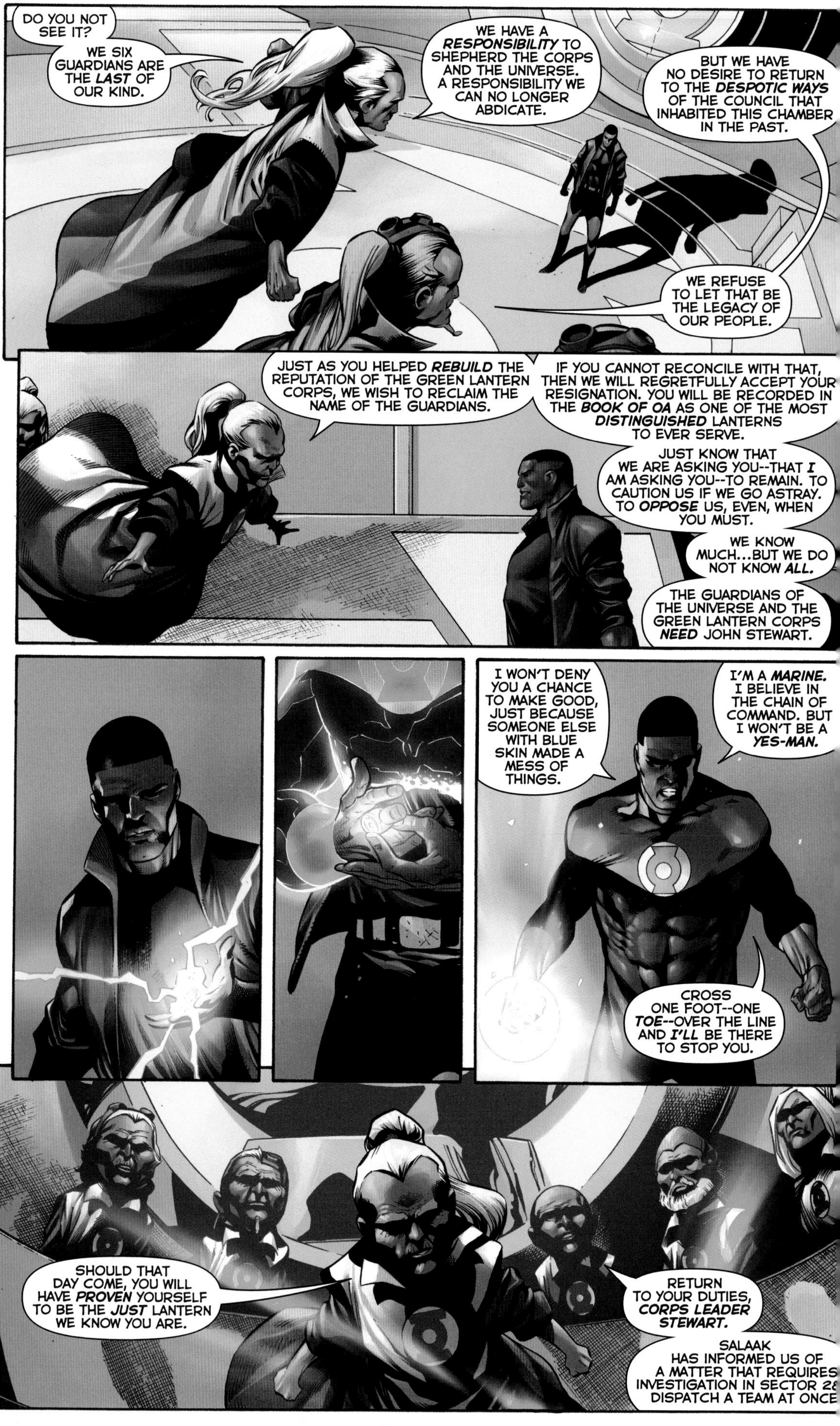
DO YOU NOT SEE IT?
WE SIX GUARDIANS ARE THE LAST OF OUR KIND.
WE HAVE A RESPONSIBILITY TO SHEPHERD THE CORPS AND THE UNIVERSE. A RESPONSIBILITY WE CAN NO LONGER ABDICATE.
BUT WE HAVE NO DESIRE TO RETURN TO THE DESPOTIC WAYS OF THE COUNCIL THAT INHABITED THIS CHAMBER IN THE PAST.
WE REFUSE TO LET THAT BE THE LEGACY OF OUR PEOPLE.
JUST AS YOU HELPED REBUILD THE REPUTATION OF THE GREEN LANTERN CORPS, WE WISH TO RECLAIM THE NAME OF THE GUARDIANS.
IF YOU CANNOT RECONCILE WITH THAT, THEN WE WILL REGRETFULLY ACCEPT YOUR RESIGNATION. YOU WILL BE RECORDED IN THE BOOK OF OA AS ONE OF THE MOST DISTINGUISHED LANTERNS TO EVER SERVE.
JUST KNOW THAT WE ARE ASKING YOU--THAT I AM ASKING YOU--TO REMAIN. TO CAUTION US IF WE GO ASTRAY. TO OPPOSE US, EVEN, WHEN YOU MUST.
WE KNOW MUCH...BUT WE DO NOT KNOW ALL.
THE GUARDIANS OF THE UNIVERSE AND THE GREEN LANTERN CORPS NEED JOHN STEWART.
I WON'T DENY YOU A CHANCE TO MAKE GOOD, JUST BECAUSE SOMEONE ELSE WITH BLUE SKIN MADE A MESS OF THINGS.
I'M A MARINE. I BELIEVE IN THE CHAIN OF COMMAND. BUT I WON'T BE A YES-MAN.
CROSS ONE FOOT--ONE TOE--OVER THE LINE AND I'LL BE THERE TO STOP YOU.
SHOULD THAT DAY COME, YOU WILL HAVE PROVEN YOURSELF TO BE THE JUST LANTERN WE KNOW YOU ARE.
RETURN TO YOUR DUTIES, CORPS LEADER STEWART.
SALAAK HAS INFORMED US OF A MATTER THAT REQUIRES INVESTIGATION IN SECTOR 2
DISPATCH A TEAM AT ONCE

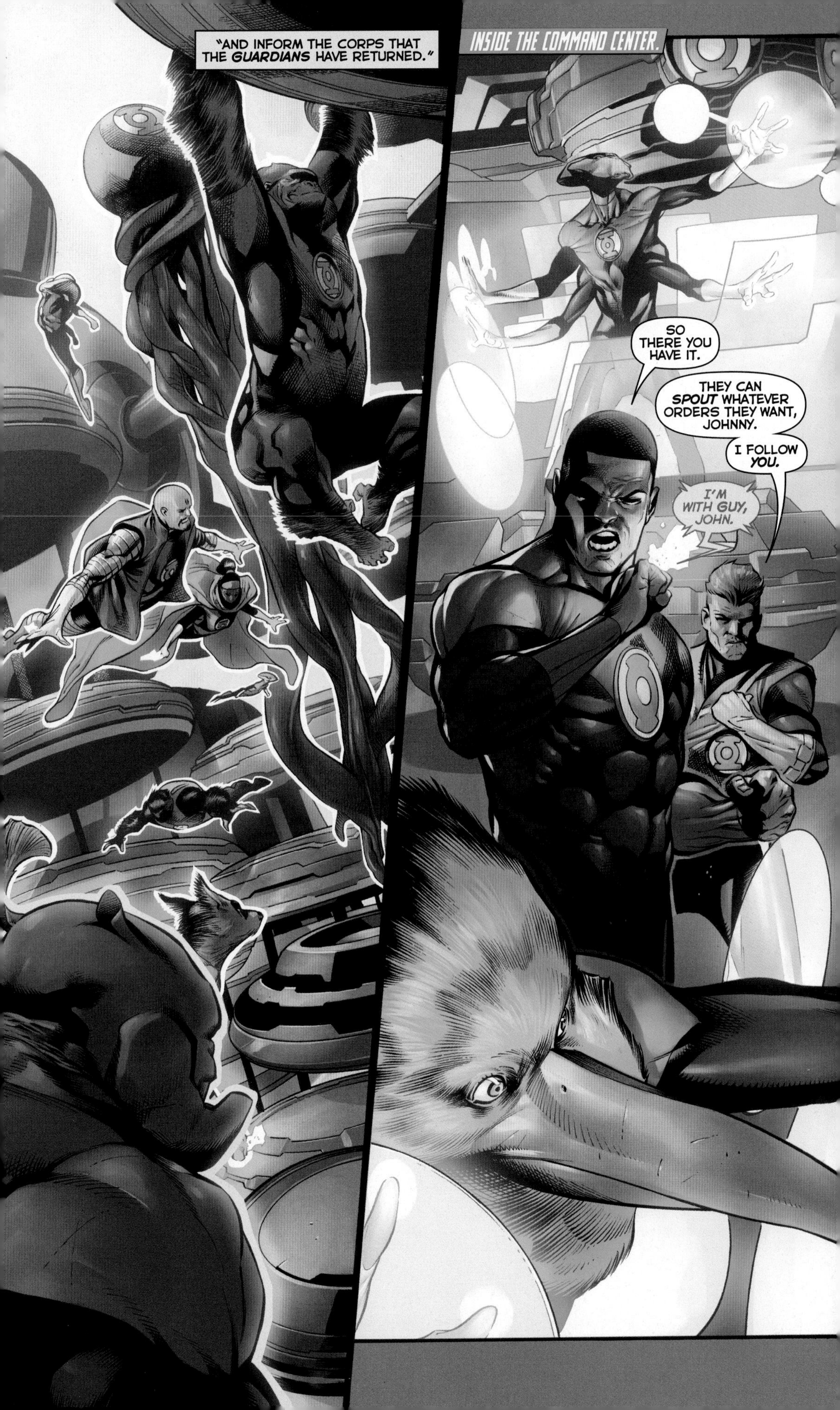
"AND INFORM THE CORPS THAT THE *GUARDIANS* HAVE RETURNED."
INSIDE THE COMMAND CENTER.
SO THERE YOU HAVE IT.
THEY CAN *SPOUT* WHATEVER ORDERS THEY WANT, JOHNNY.
I FOLLOW *YOU.*
I'M WITH GUY, JOHN.

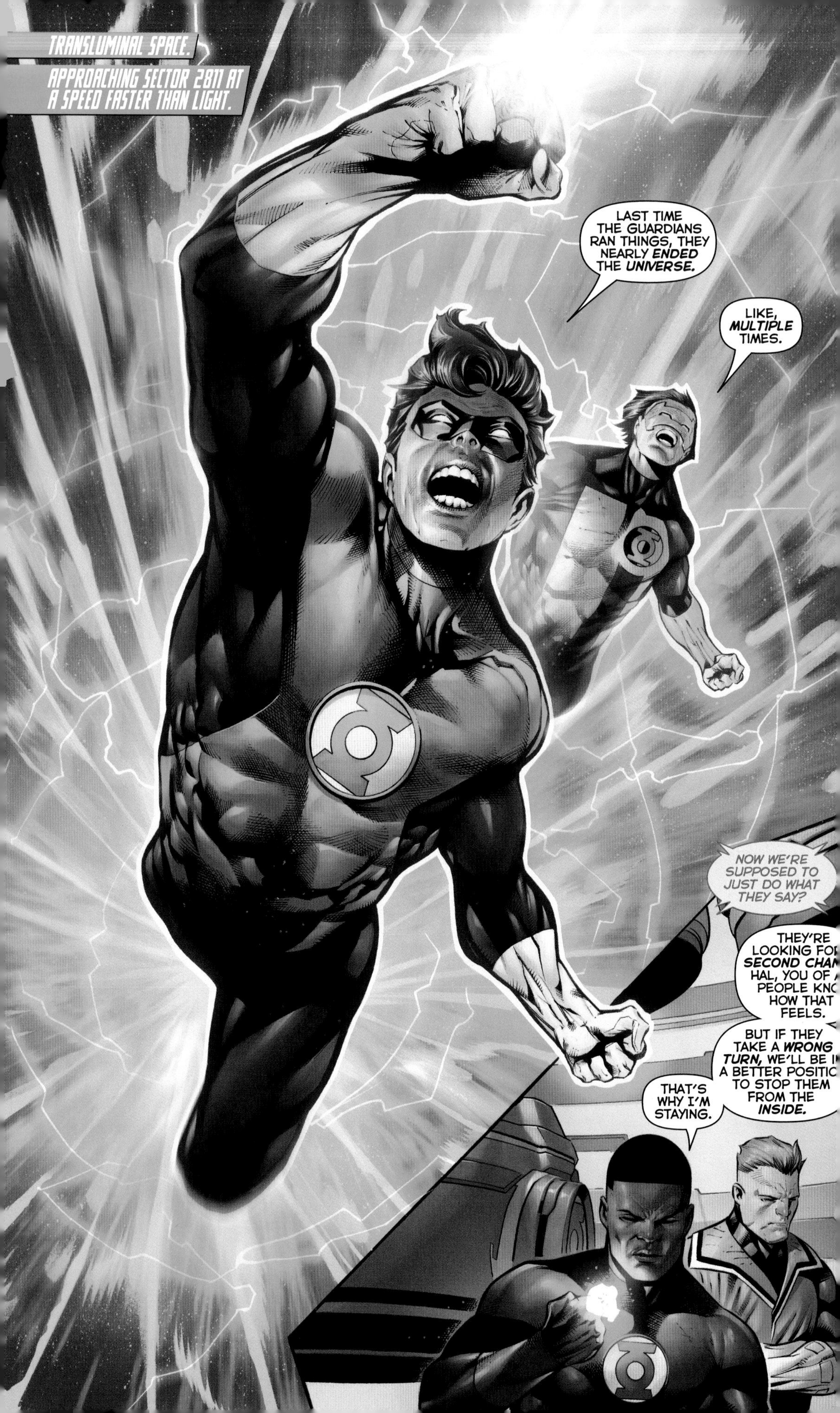
TRANSLUMINAL SPACE.
APPROACHING SECTOR 2811 AT A SPEED FASTER THAN LIGHT.
LAST TIME THE GUARDIANS RAN THINGS, THEY NEARLY ENDED THE UNIVERSE.
LIKE, MULTIPLE TIMES.
NOW WE'RE SUPPOSED TO JUST DO WHAT THEY SAY?
THEY'RE LOOKING FOR SECOND CHAN HAL, YOU OF PEOPLE KN HOW THAT FEELS.
BUT IF THEY TAKE A WRONG TURN, WE'LL BE A BETTER POSITIC TO STOP THEM FROM THE INSIDE.
THAT'S WHY I'M STAYING.

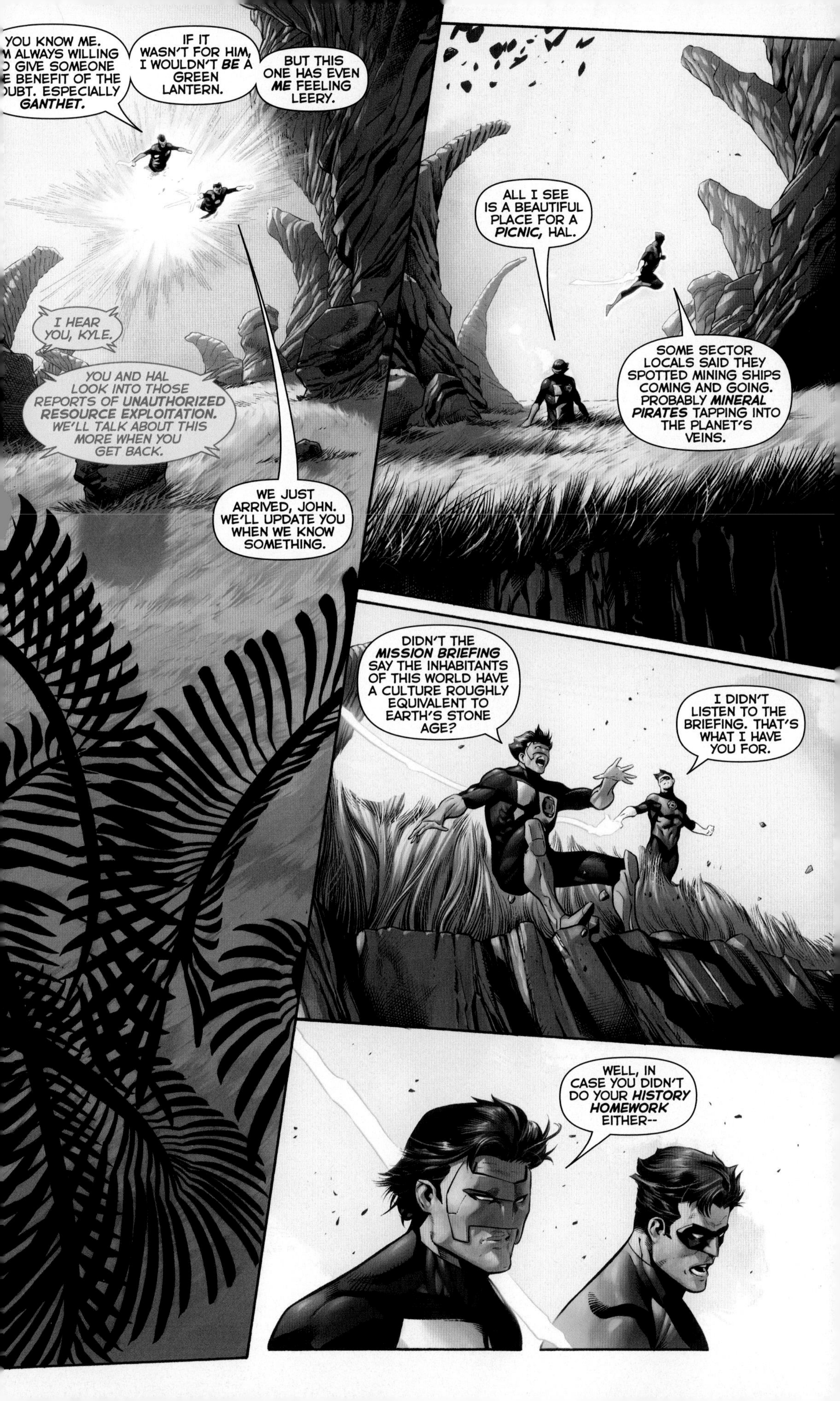
YOU KNOW ME. 'M ALWAYS WILLING O GIVE SOMEONE E BENEFIT OF THE OUBT. ESPECIALLY GANTHET.
IF IT WASN'T FOR HIM, I WOULDN'T BE A GREEN LANTERN.
BUT THIS ONE HAS EVEN ME FEELING LEERY.
I HEAR YOU, KYLE.
YOU AND HAL LOOK INTO THOSE REPORTS OF UNAUTHORIZED RESOURCE EXPLOITATION. WE'LL TALK ABOUT THIS MORE WHEN YOU GET BACK.
WE JUST ARRIVED, JOHN. WE'LL UPDATE YOU WHEN WE KNOW SOMETHING.
ALL I SEE IS A BEAUTIFUL PLACE FOR A PICNIC, HAL.
SOME SECTOR LOCALS SAID THEY SPOTTED MINING SHIPS COMING AND GOING. PROBABLY MINERAL PIRATES TAPPING INTO THE PLANET'S VEINS.
DIDN'T THE MISSION BRIEFING SAY THE INHABITANTS OF THIS WORLD HAVE A CULTURE ROUGHLY EQUIVALENT TO EARTH'S STONE AGE?
I DIDN'T LISTEN TO THE BRIEFING. THAT'S WHAT I HAVE YOU FOR.
WELL, IN CASE YOU DIDN'T DO YOUR HISTORY HOMEWORK EITHER--

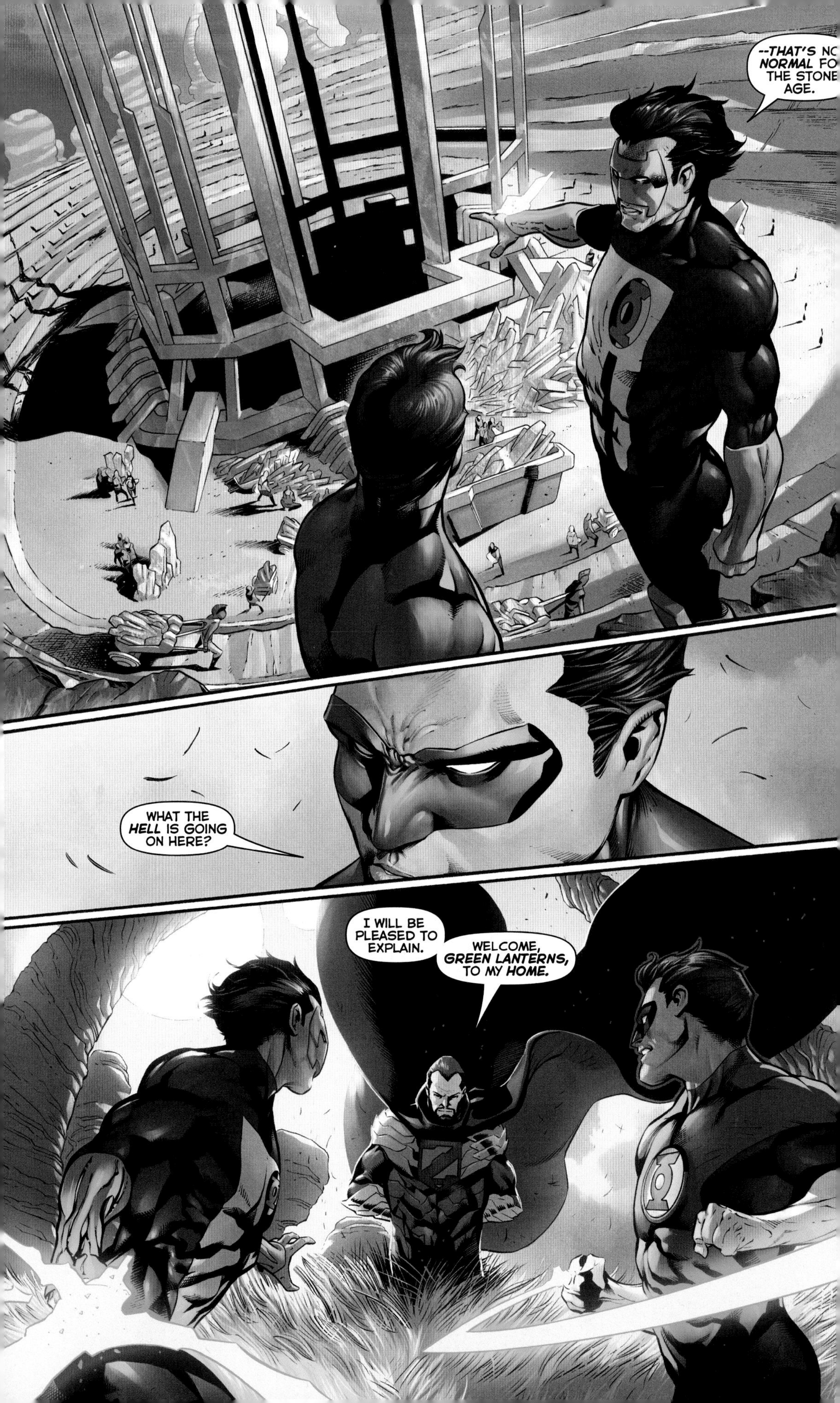
--THAT'S NC NORMAL FO THE STONE AGE.
WHAT THE HELL IS GOING ON HERE?
I WILL BE PLEASED TO EXPLAIN.
WELCOME, GREEN LANTERNS, TO MY HOME.

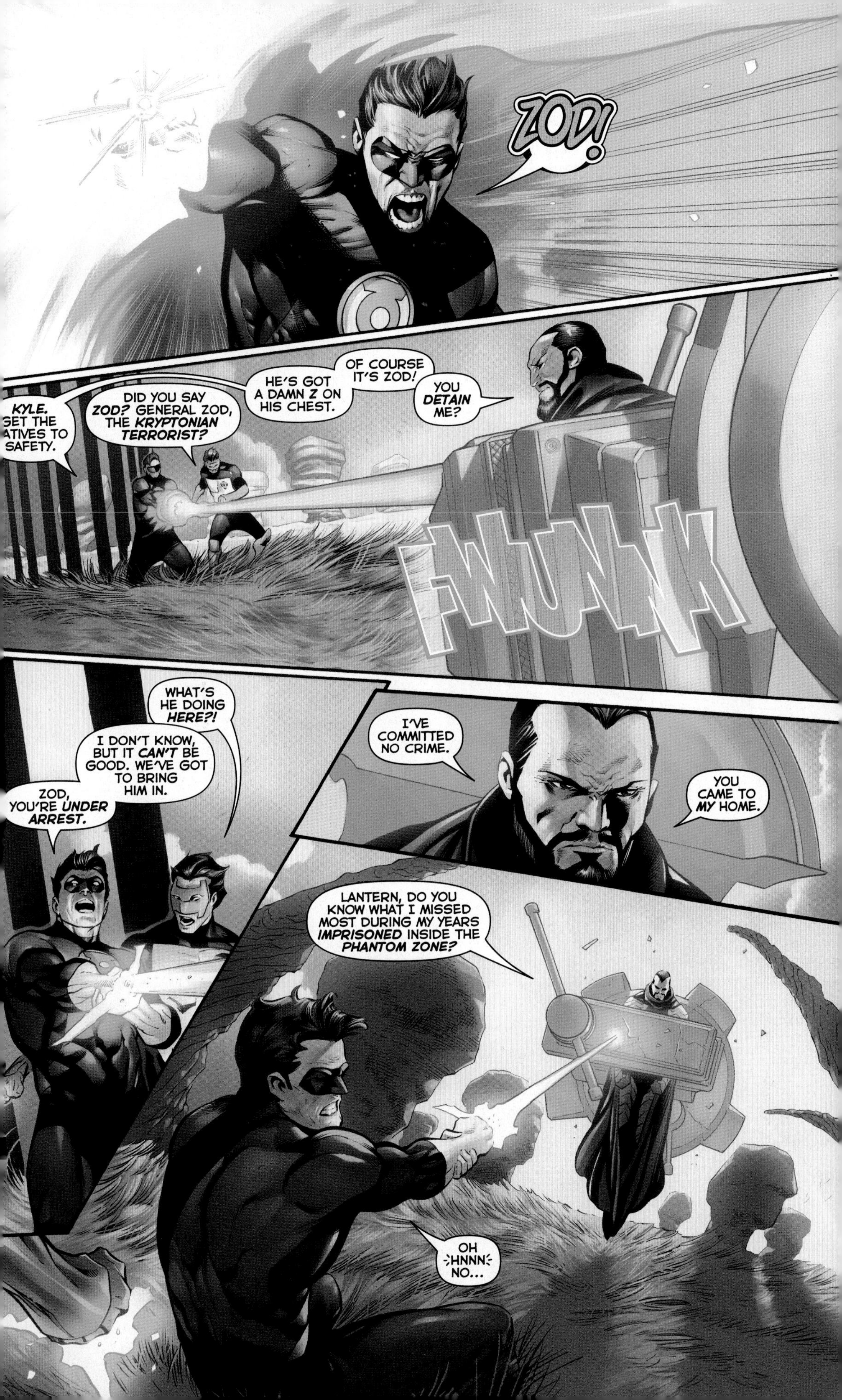
ZOD!
KYLE. GET THE ATIVES TO SAFETY.
DID YOU SAY ZOD? GENERAL ZOD, THE KRYPTONIAN TERRORIST?
HE'S GOT A DAMN Z ON HIS CHEST.
OF COURSE IT'S ZOD!
YOU DETAIN ME?
FWHUNNK
WHAT'S HE DOING HERE?!
I DON'T KNOW, BUT IT CAN'T BE GOOD. WE'VE GOT TO BRING HIM IN.
ZOD, YOU'RE UNDER ARREST.
I'VE COMMITTED NO CRIME.
YOU CAME TO MY HOME.
LANTERN, DO YOU KNOW WHAT I MISSED MOST DURING MY YEARS IMPRISONED INSIDE THE PHANTOM ZONE?
OH HNNN NO...

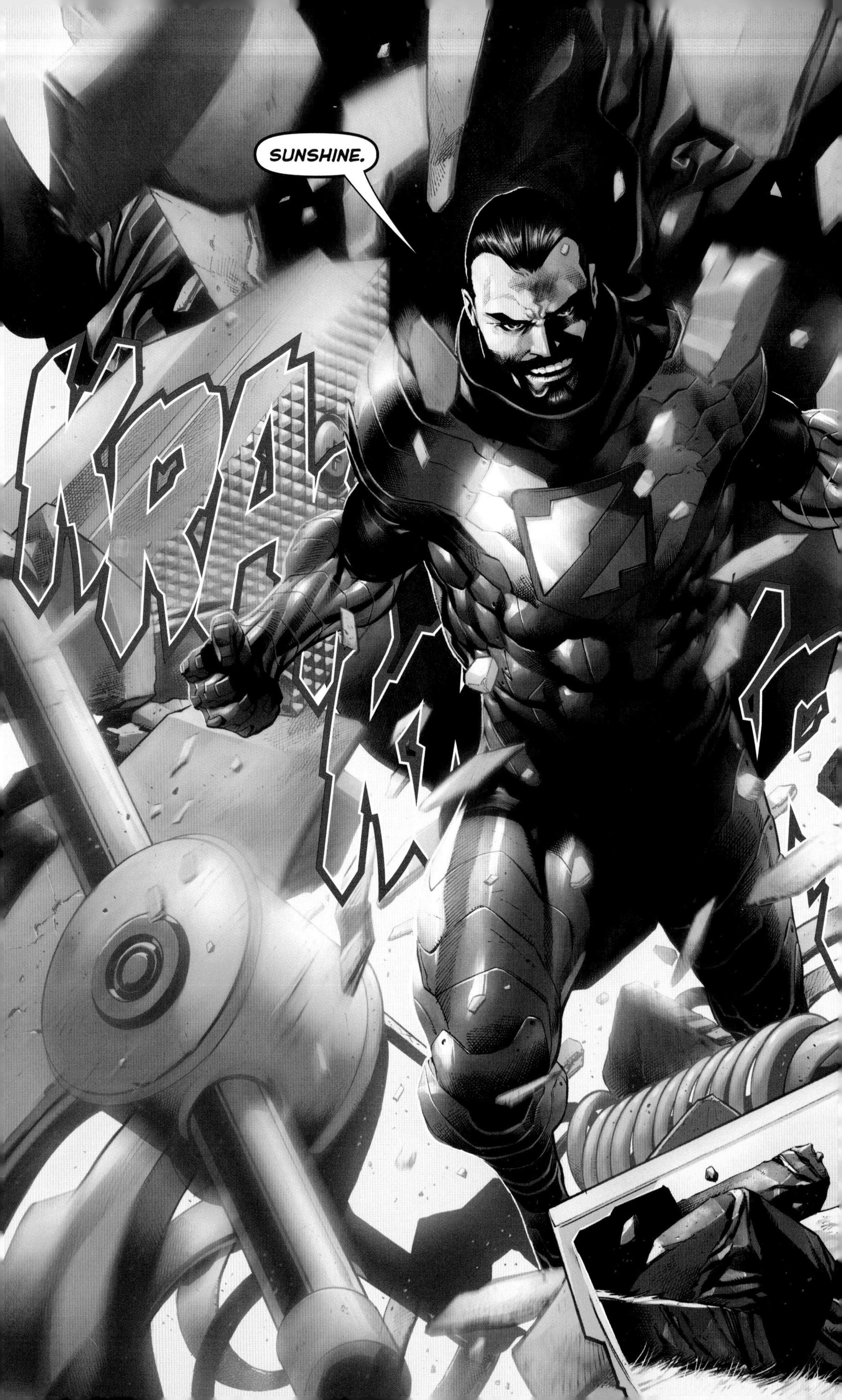
SUNSHINE.

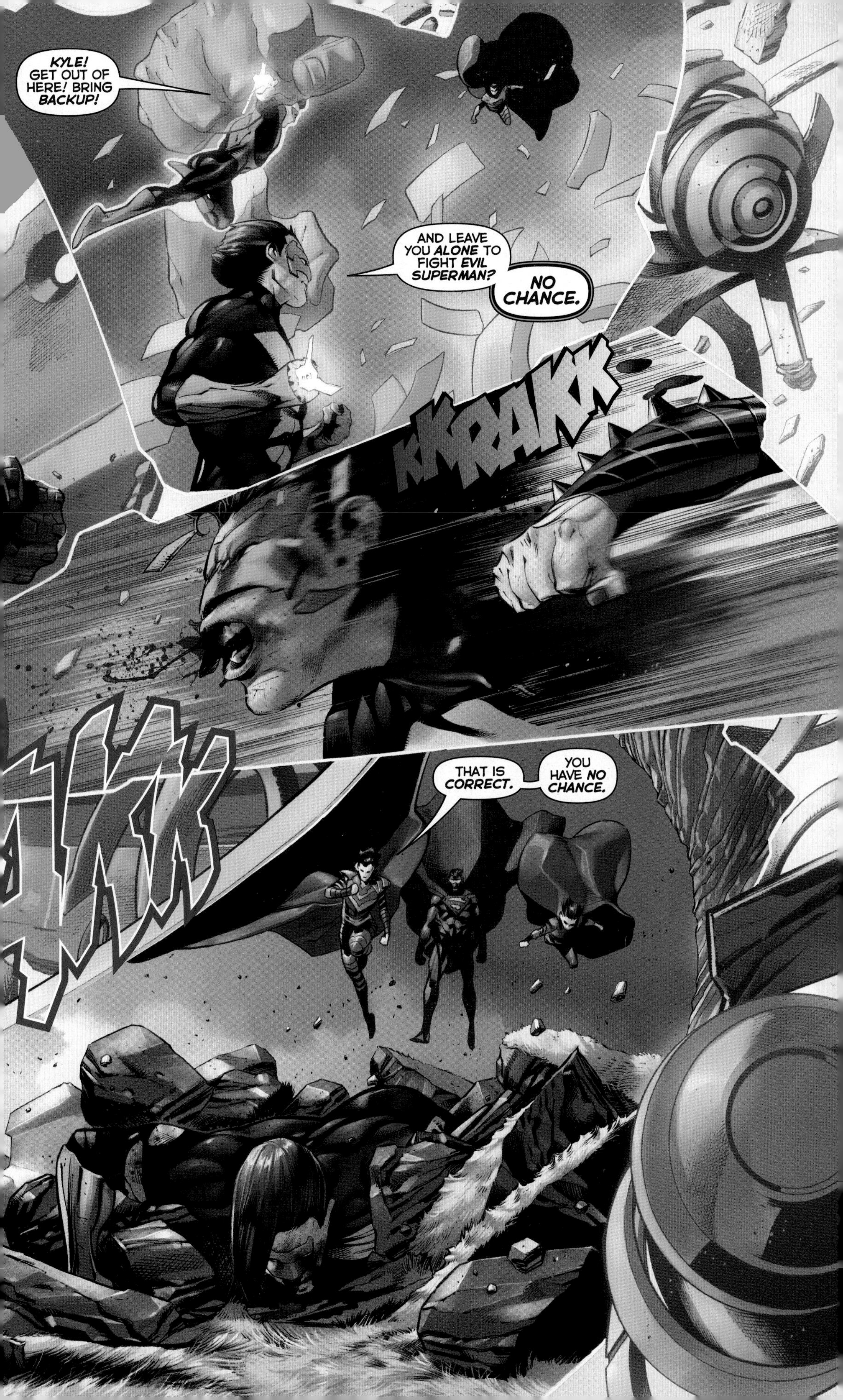
KYLE! GET OUT OF HERE! BRING BACKUP!
AND LEAVE YOU ALONE TO FIGHT EVIL SUPERMAN?
NO CHANCE.
KKRAKK
THAT IS CORRECT.
YOU HAVE NO CHANCE.

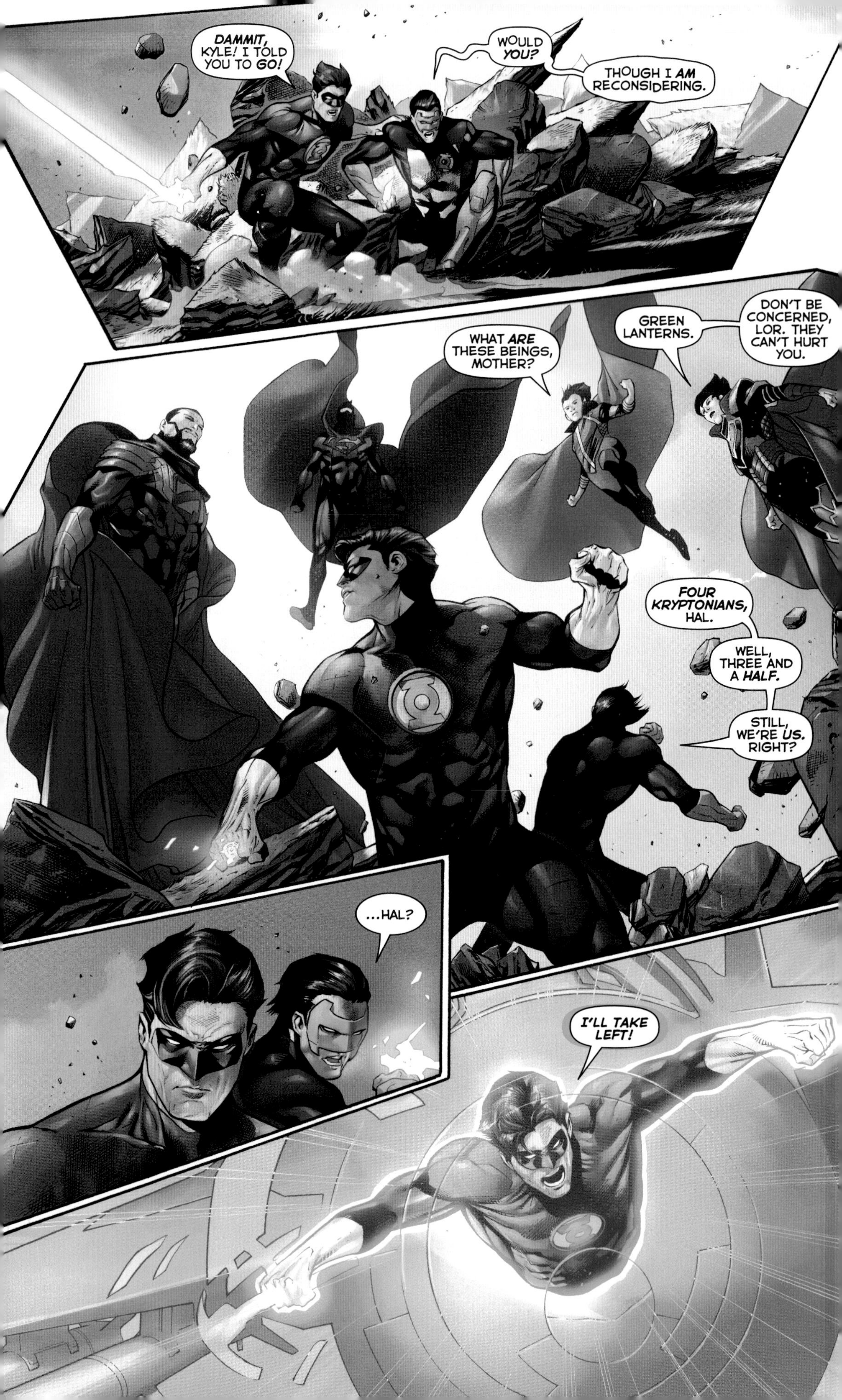

DAMMIT, KYLE! I TOLD YOU TO GO!
WOULD YOU?
THOUGH I AM RECONSIDERING.
WHAT ARE THESE BEINGS, MOTHER?
GREEN LANTERNS.
DON'T BE CONCERNED, LOR. THEY CAN'T HURT YOU.
FOUR KRYPTONIANS, HAL.
WELL, THREE AND A HALF.
STILL, WE'RE US. RIGHT?
...HAL?
I'LL TAKE LEFT!

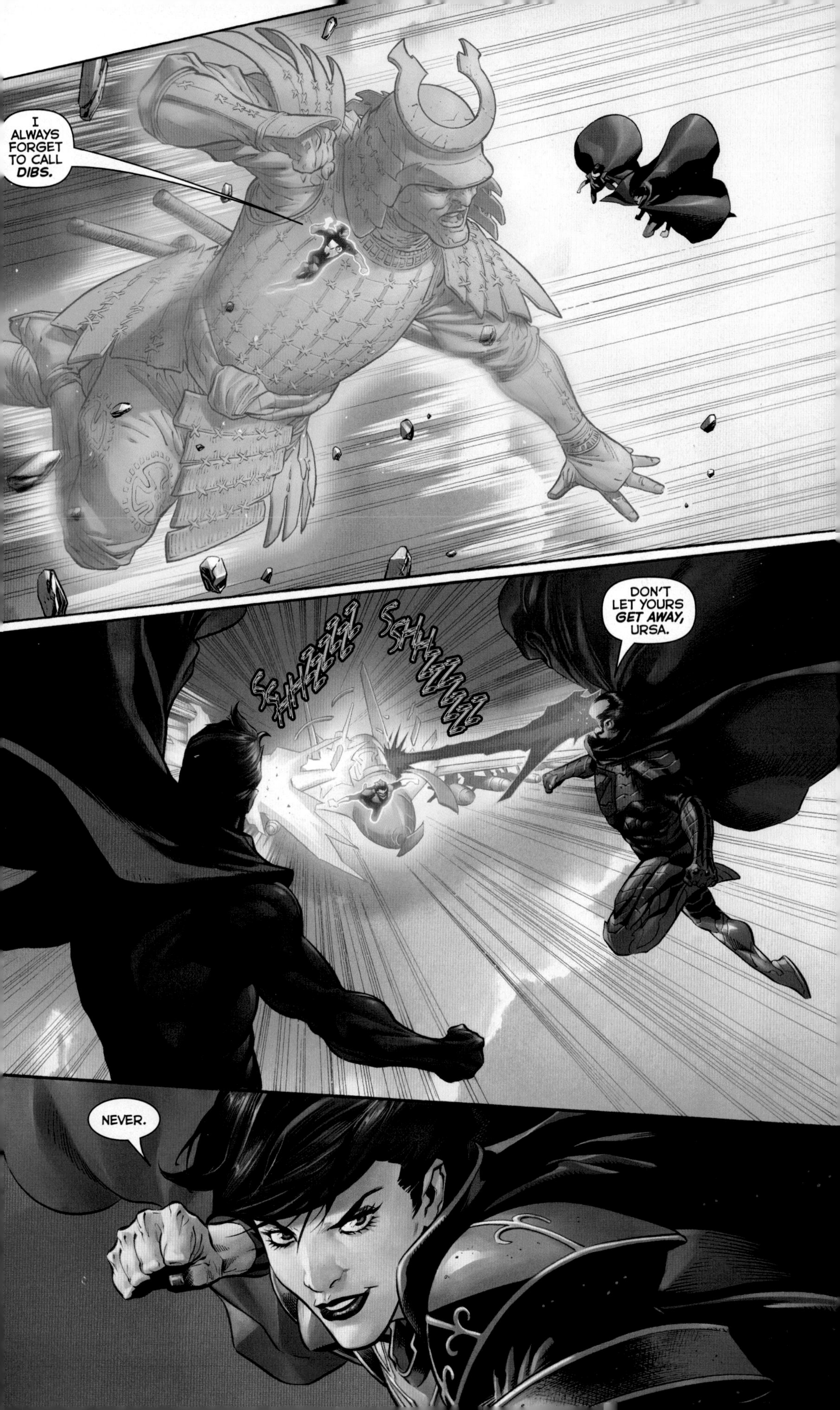
I ALWAYS FORGET TO CALL DIBS.
SSHHZZZZ SSHHZZZZZ
DON'T LET YOURS GET AWAY, URSA.
NEVER.

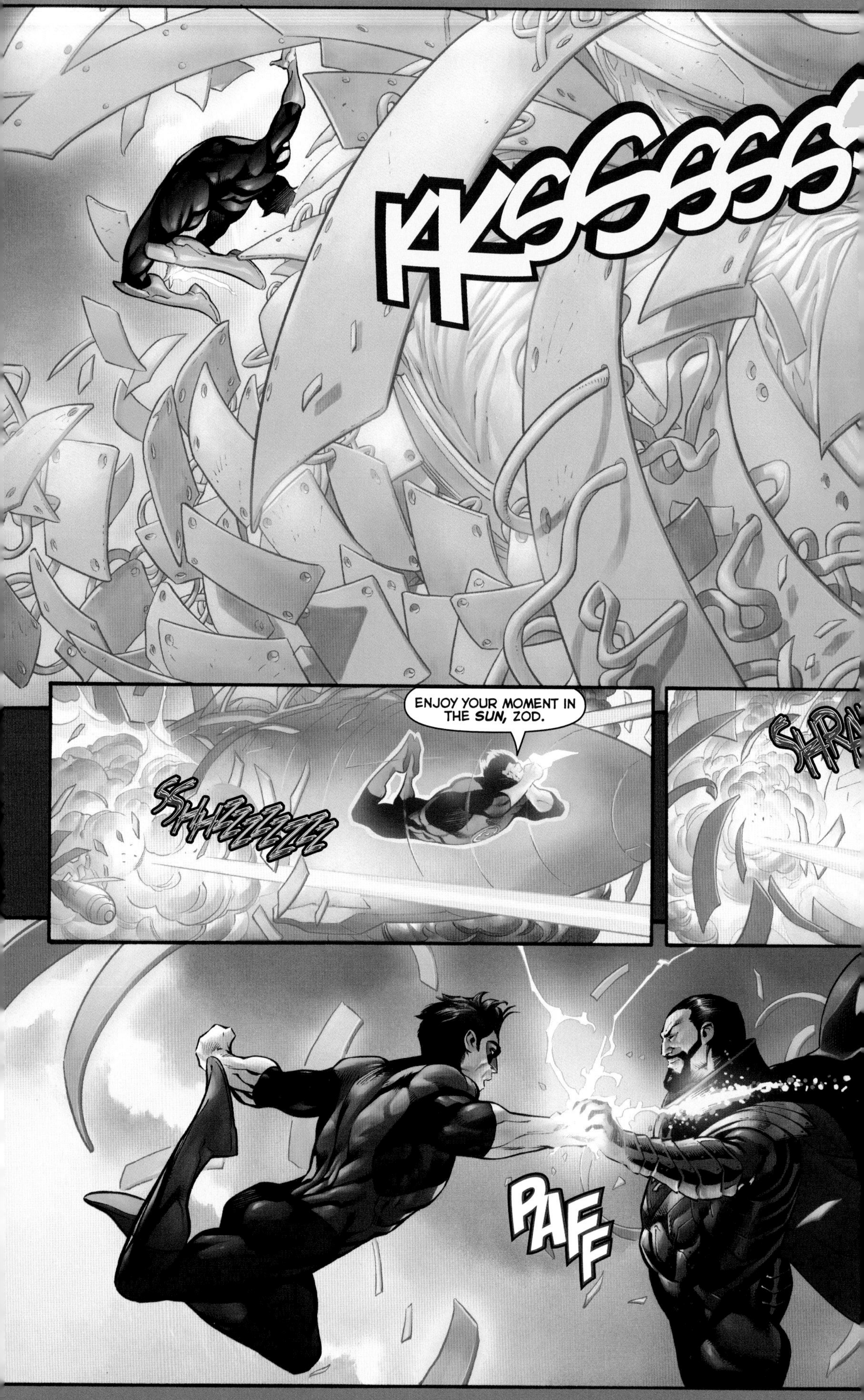
KKSSSSS
ENJOY YOUR MOMENT IN THE SUN, ZOD.
SSHHZZZZZZ
PAFF

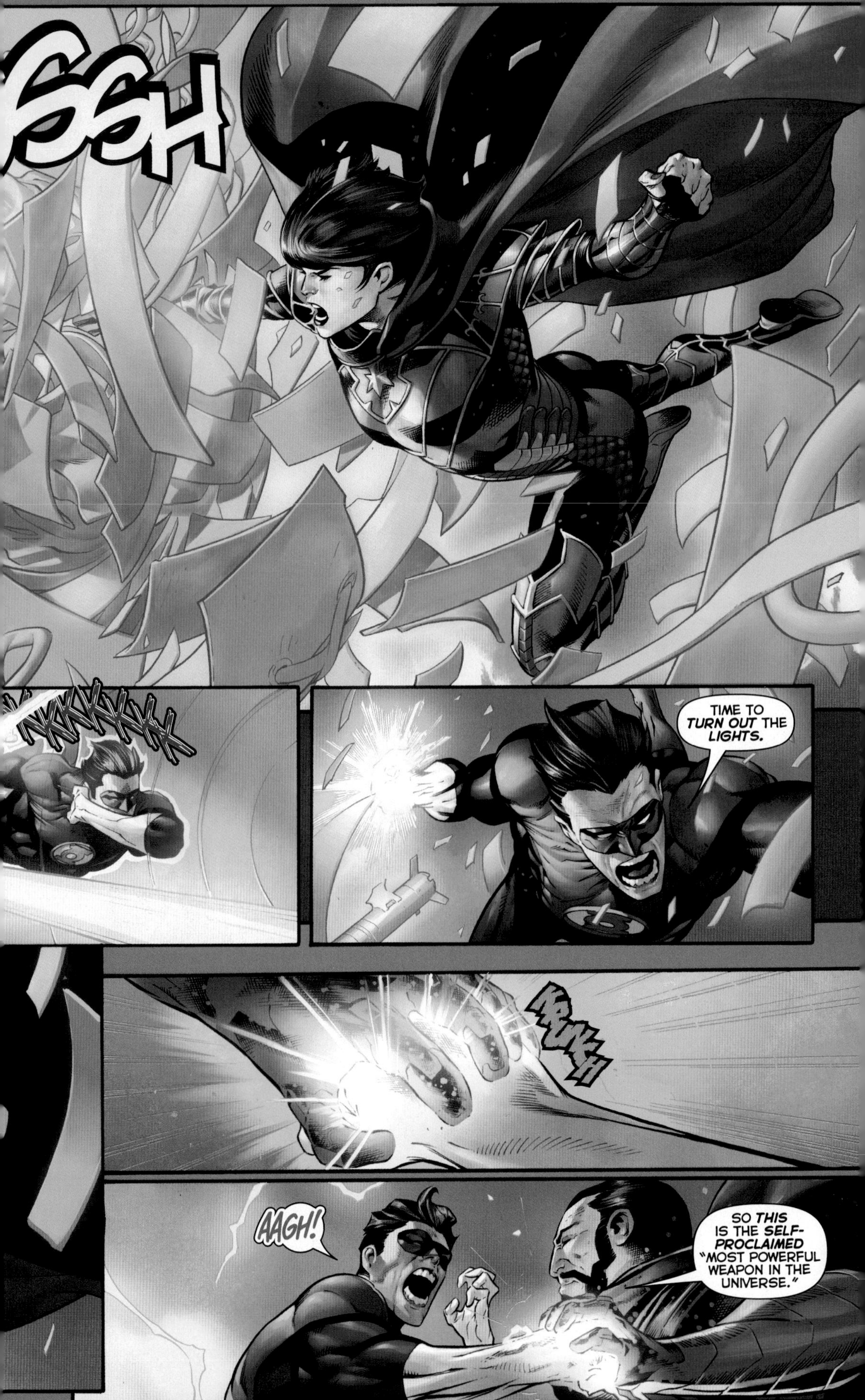
SSH
TIME TO TURN OUT THE LIGHTS.
AAGH!
SO THIS IS THE SELF-PROCLAIMED "MOST POWERFUL WEAPON IN THE UNIVERSE."

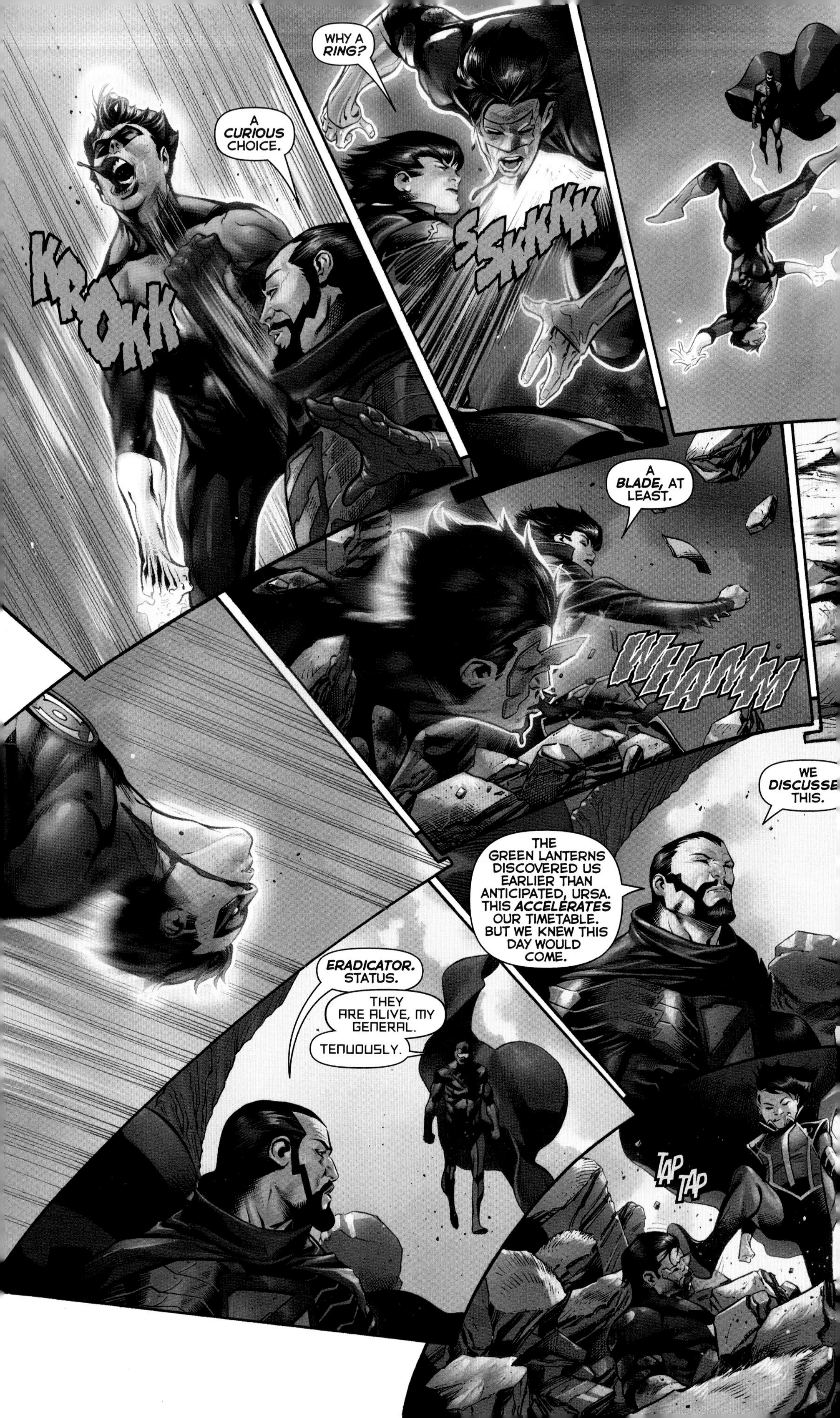
A CURIOUS CHOICE.
KROOKK
WHY A RING?
SSHKKK
A BLADE, AT LEAST.
WHAMM
WE DISCUSSE THIS.
THE GREEN LANTERNS DISCOVERED US EARLIER THAN ANTICIPATED, URSA. THIS ACCELERATES OUR TIMETABLE. BUT WE KNEW THIS DAY WOULD COME.
ERADICATOR. STATUS.
THEY ARE ALIVE, MY GENERAL.
TENUOUSLY.
TAP TAP

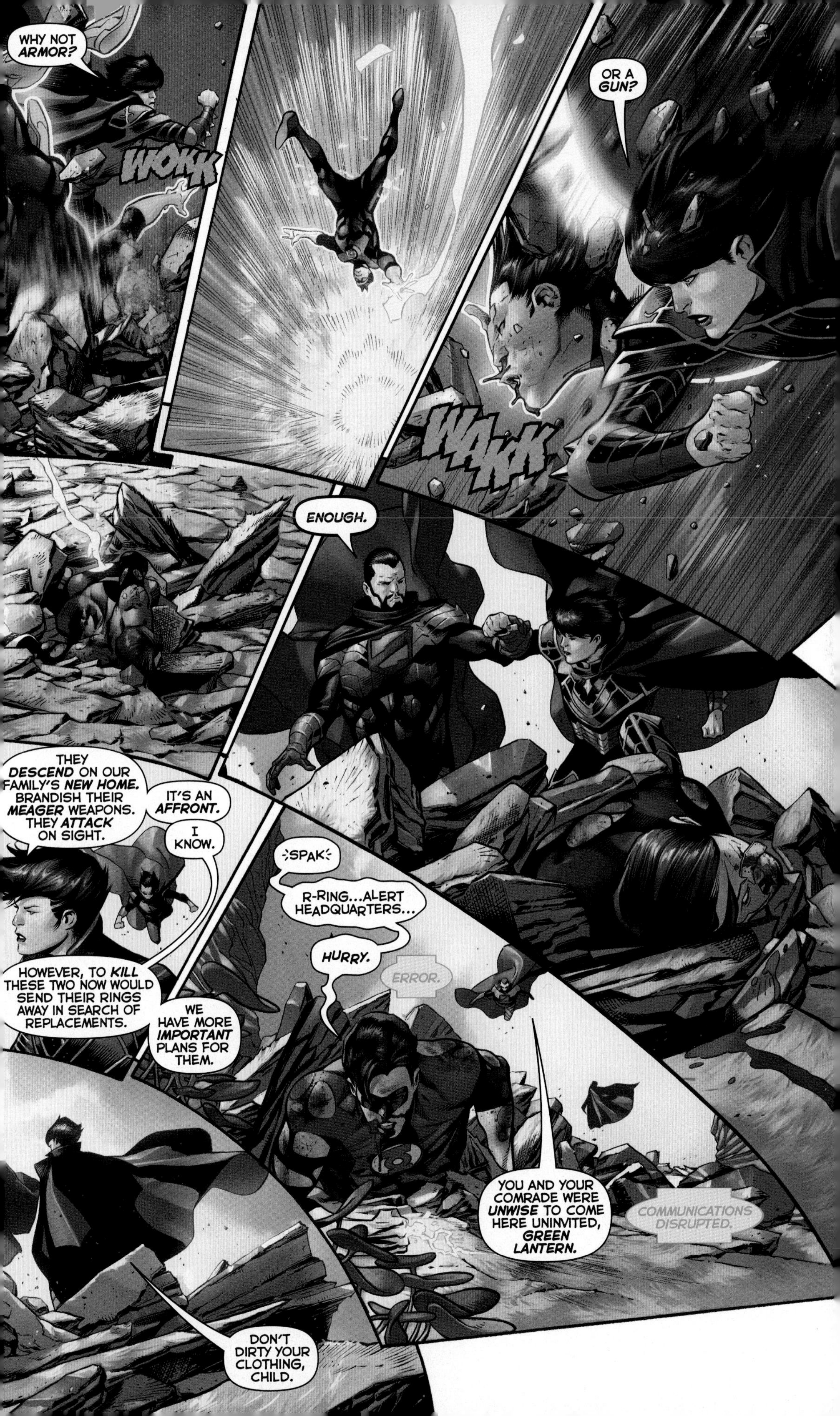

WHY NOT ARMOR?
WOKK
OR A GUN?
WAKK
ENOUGH.
THEY DESCEND ON OUR FAMILY'S NEW HOME. BRANDISH THEIR MEAGER WEAPONS. THEY ATTACK ON SIGHT.
IT'S AN AFFRONT.
I KNOW.
HOWEVER, TO KILL THESE TWO NOW WOULD SEND THEIR RINGS AWAY IN SEARCH OF REPLACEMENTS.
WE HAVE MORE IMPORTANT PLANS FOR THEM.
SPAK
R-RING...ALERT HEADQUARTERS...
HURRY.
ERROR.
YOU AND YOUR COMRADE WERE UNWISE TO COME HERE UNINVITED, GREEN LANTERN.
COMMUNICATIONS DISRUPTED.
DON'T DIRTY YOUR CLOTHING, CHILD.

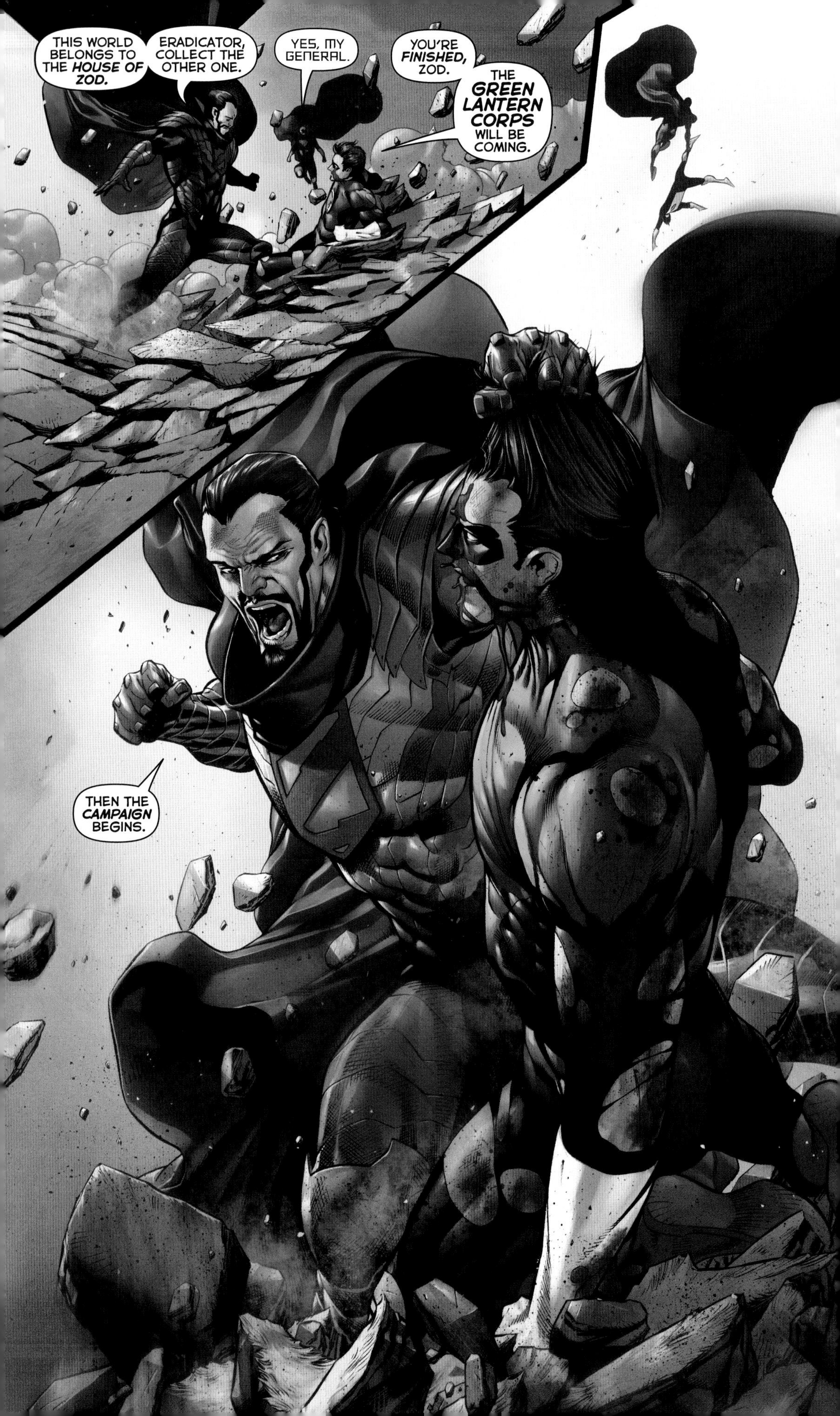
THIS WORLD BELONGS TO THE HOUSE OF ZOD.
ERADICATOR, COLLECT THE OTHER ONE.
YES, MY GENERAL.
YOU'RE FINISHED, ZOD.
THE GREEN LANTERN CORPS WILL BE COMING.
THEN THE CAMPAIGN BEGINS.

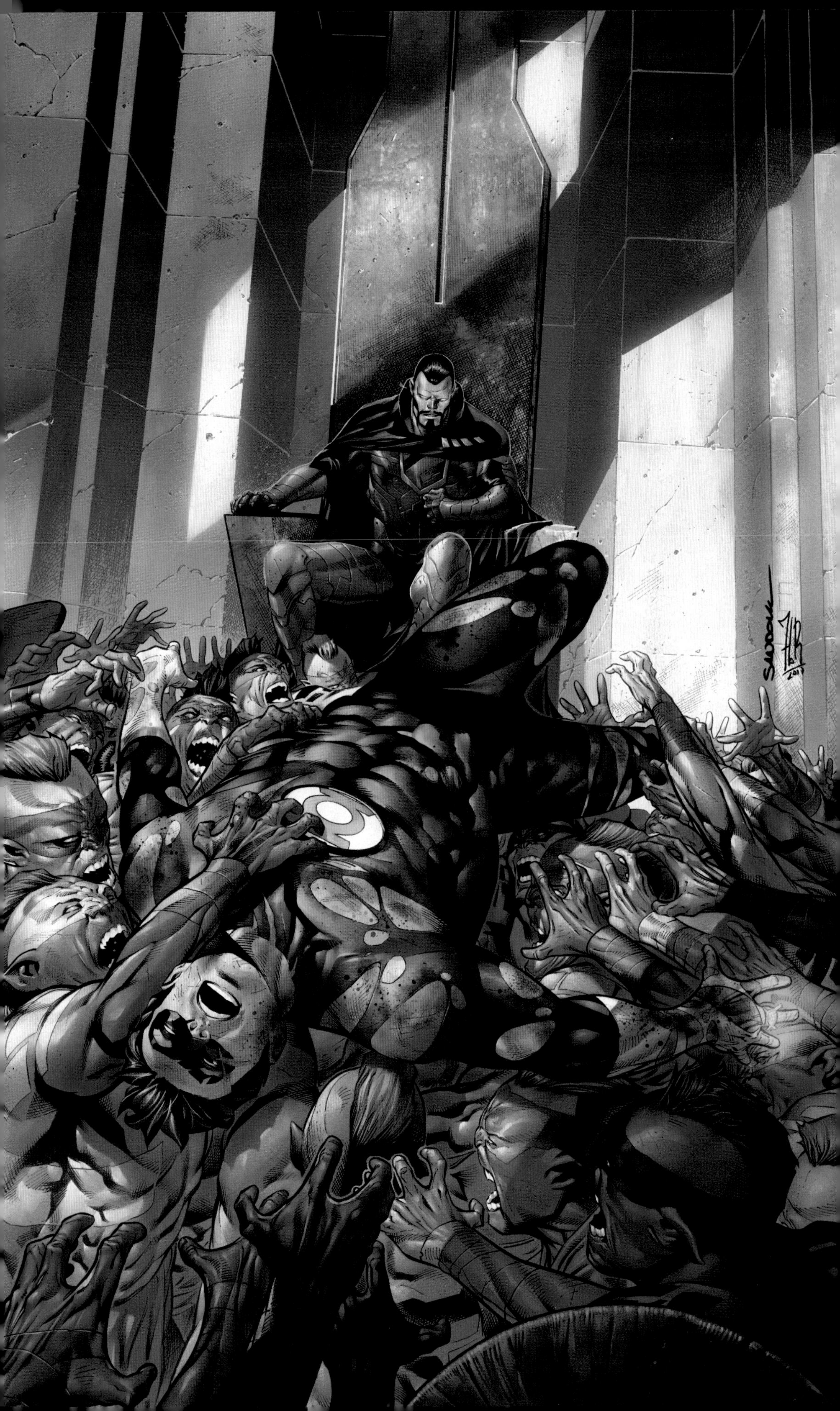

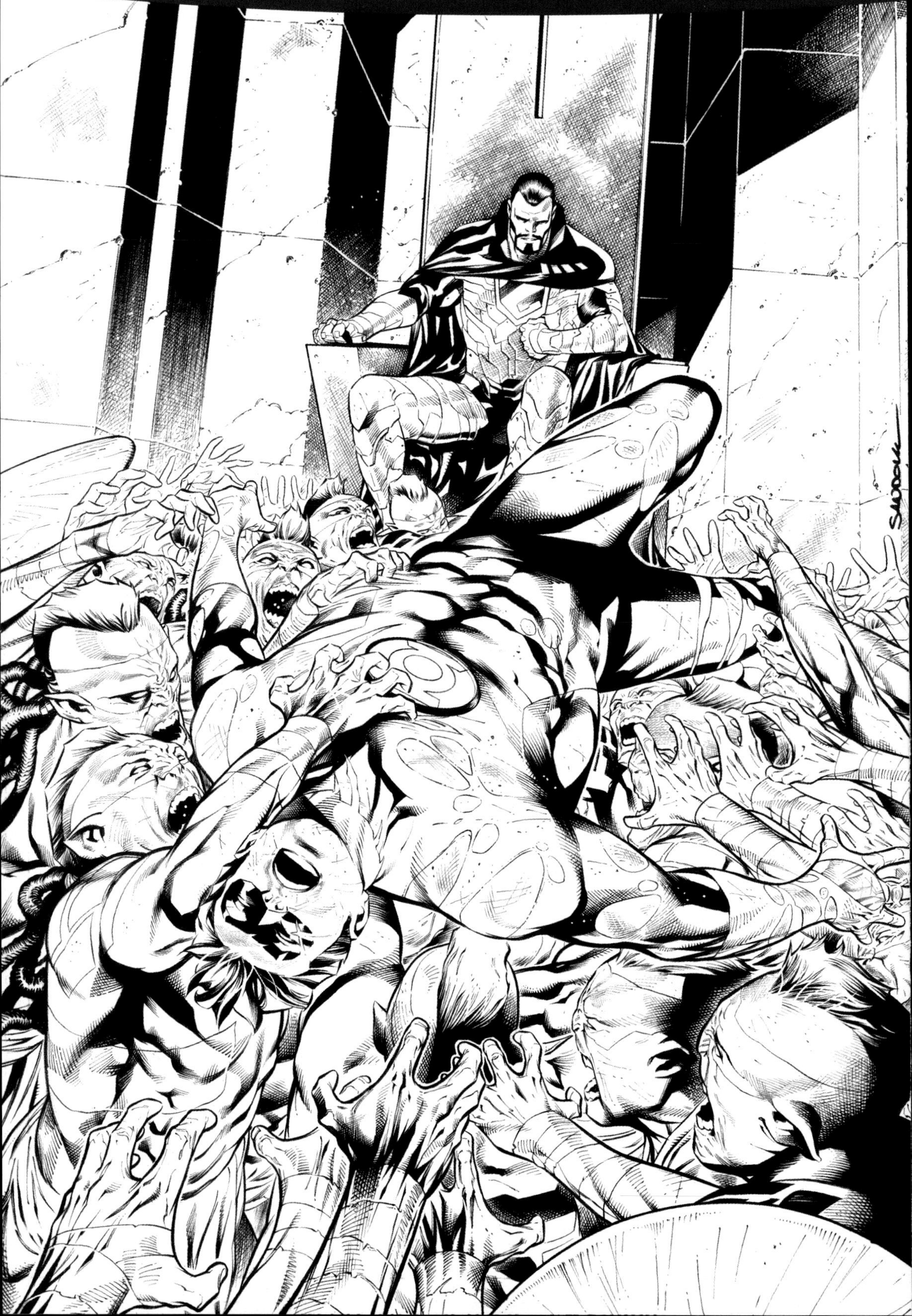

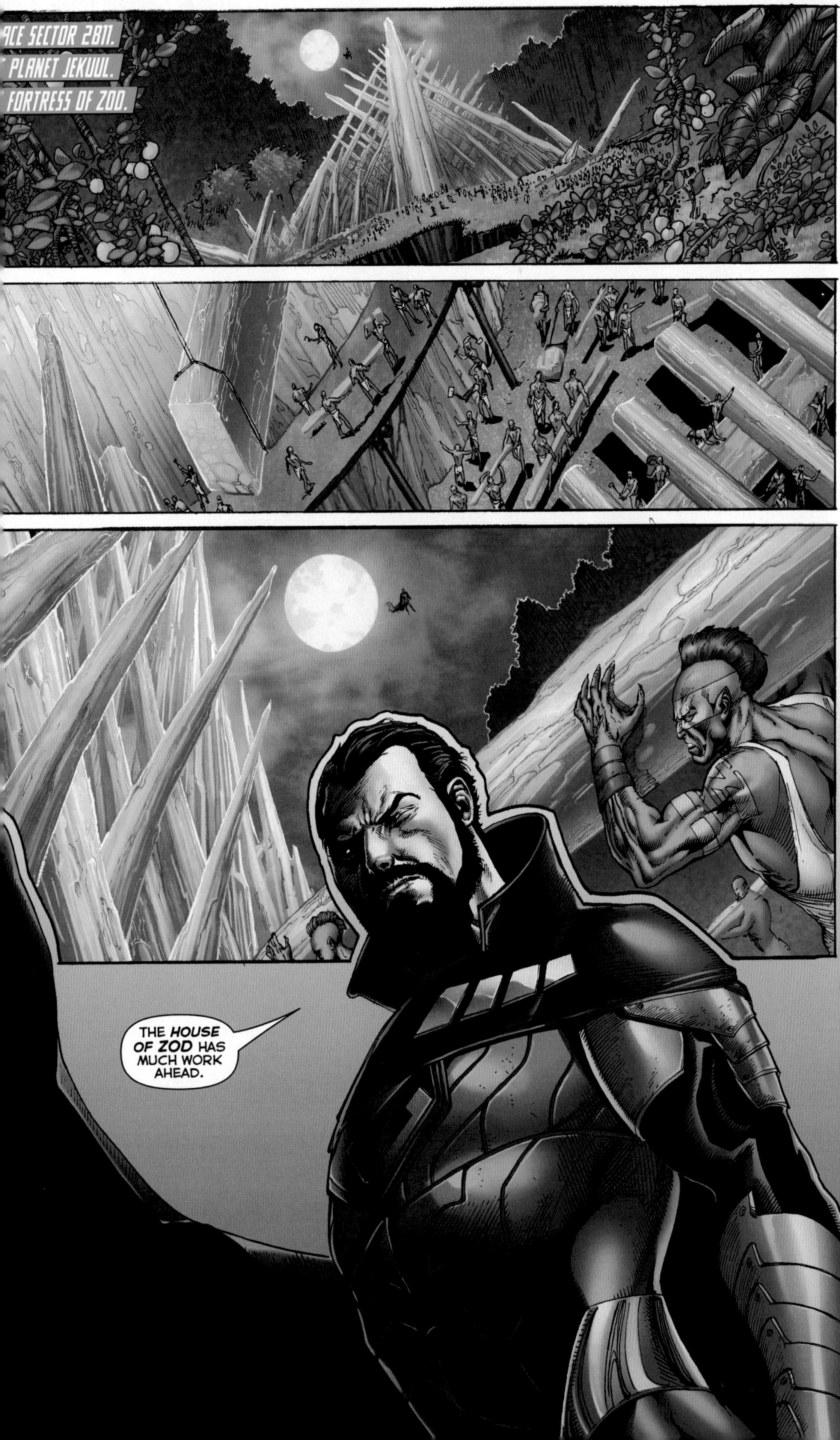
ACE SECTOR 2811.
PLANET JEKUUL.
FORTRESS OF ZOD.
THE HOUSE OF ZOD HAS MUCH WORK AHEAD.

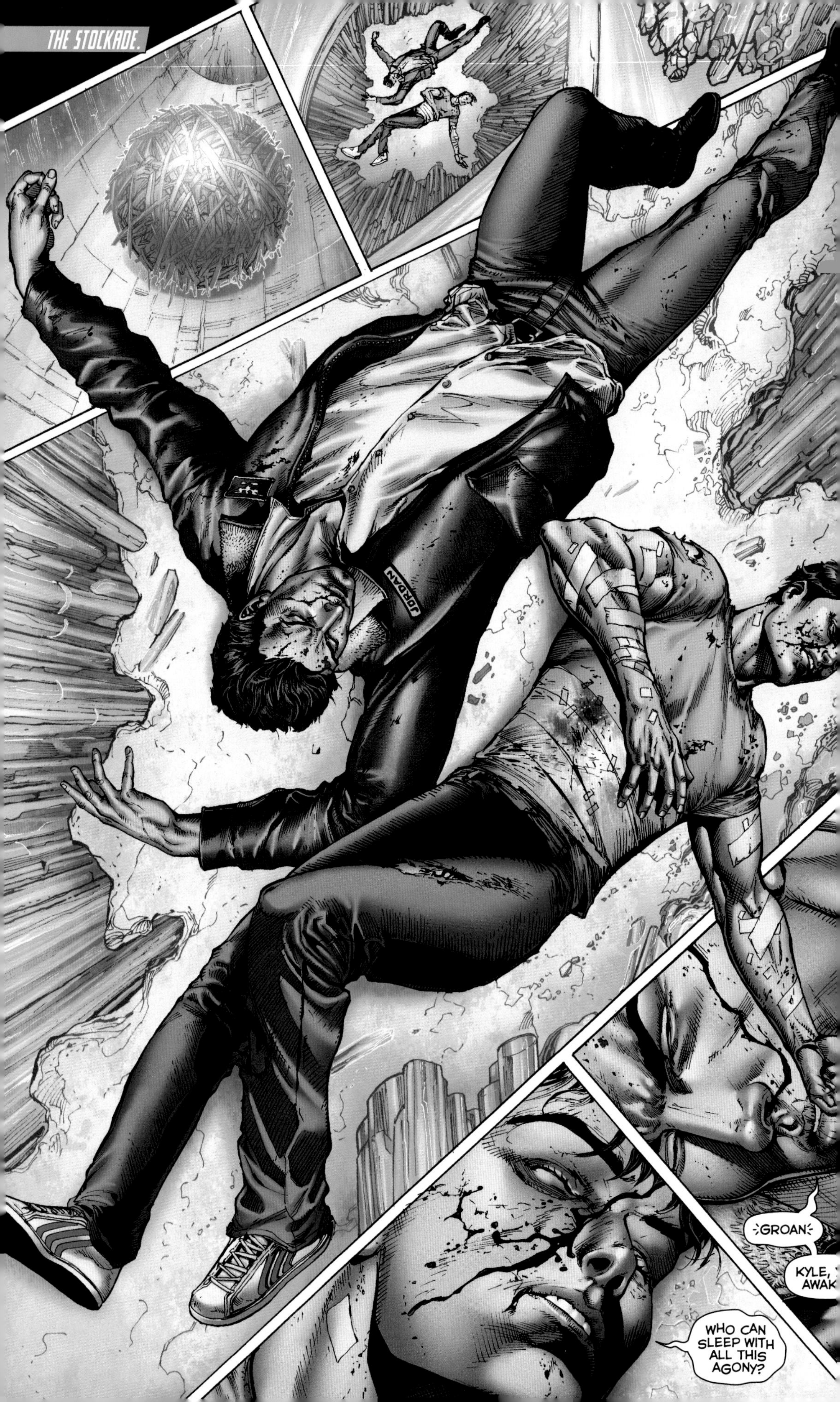
THE STOCKADE.
JORDAN
GROAN
KYLE, AWAK
WHO CAN SLEEP WITH ALL THIS AGONY?

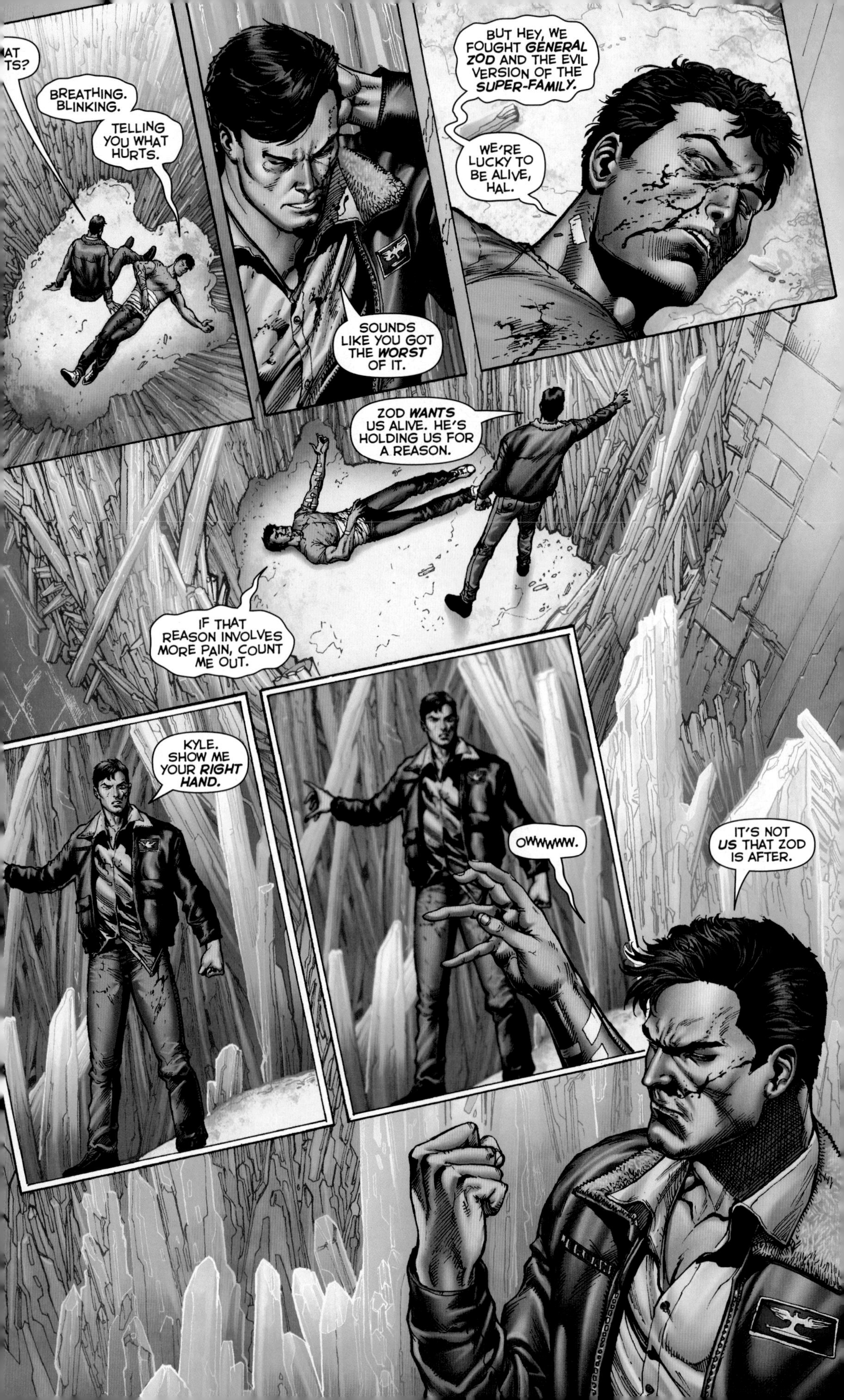
AT
TS?
BREATHING. BLINKING.
TELLING YOU WHAT HURTS.
SOUNDS LIKE YOU GOT THE WORST OF IT.
BUT HEY, WE FOUGHT GENERAL ZOD AND THE EVIL VERSION OF THE SUPER-FAMILY.
WE'RE LUCKY TO BE ALIVE, HAL.
ZOD WANTS US ALIVE. HE'S HOLDING US FOR A REASON.
IF THAT REASON INVOLVES MORE PAIN, COUNT ME OUT.
KYLE. SHOW ME YOUR RIGHT HAND.
OWWWWW.
IT'S NOT US THAT ZOD IS AFTER.

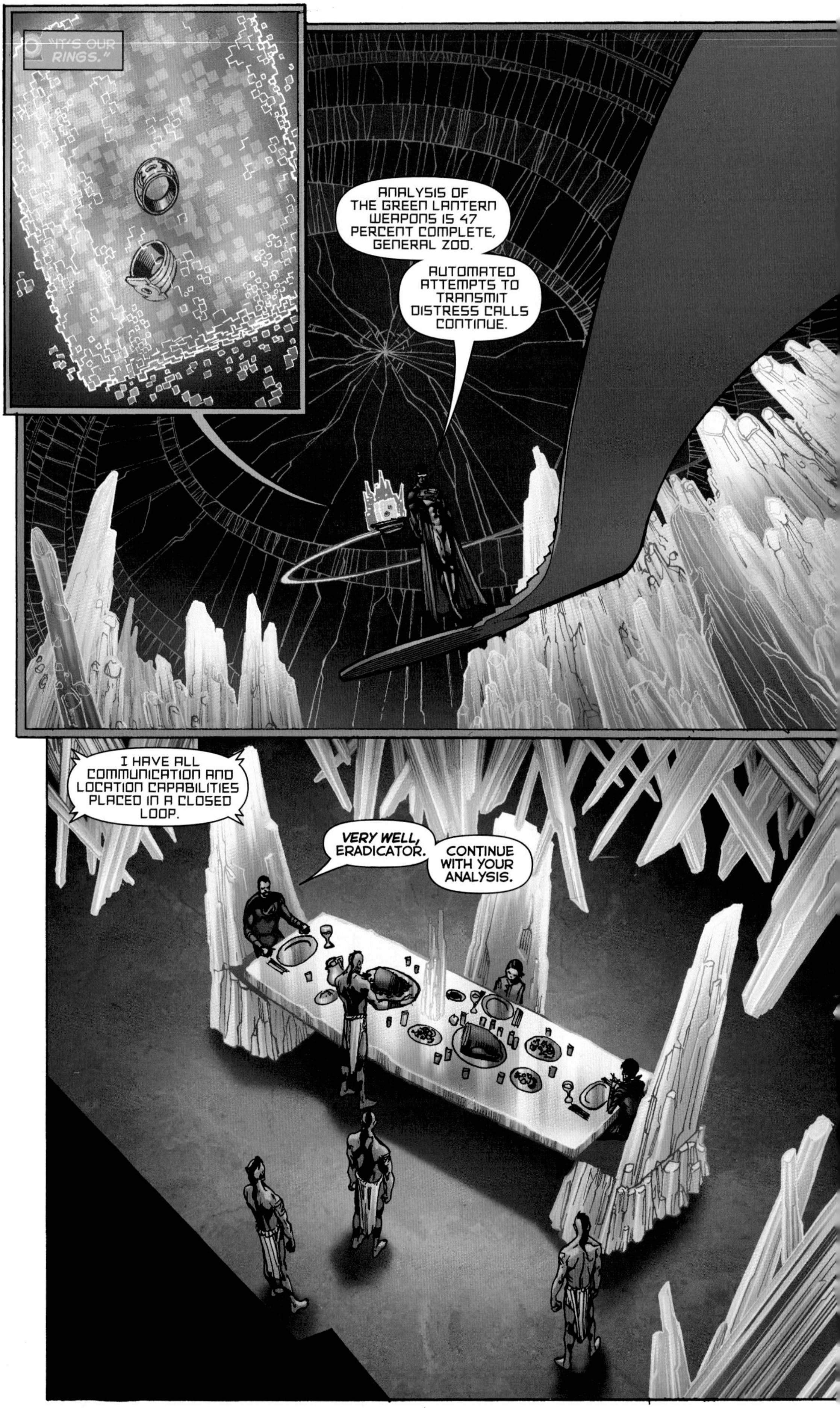

"IT'S OUR RINGS."
ANALYSIS OF THE GREEN LANTERN WEAPONS IS 47 PERCENT COMPLETE, GENERAL ZOD.
AUTOMATED ATTEMPTS TO TRANSMIT DISTRESS CALLS CONTINUE.
I HAVE ALL COMMUNICATION AND LOCATION CAPABILITIES PLACED IN A CLOSED LOOP.
VERY WELL, ERADICATOR.
CONTINUE WITH YOUR ANALYSIS.

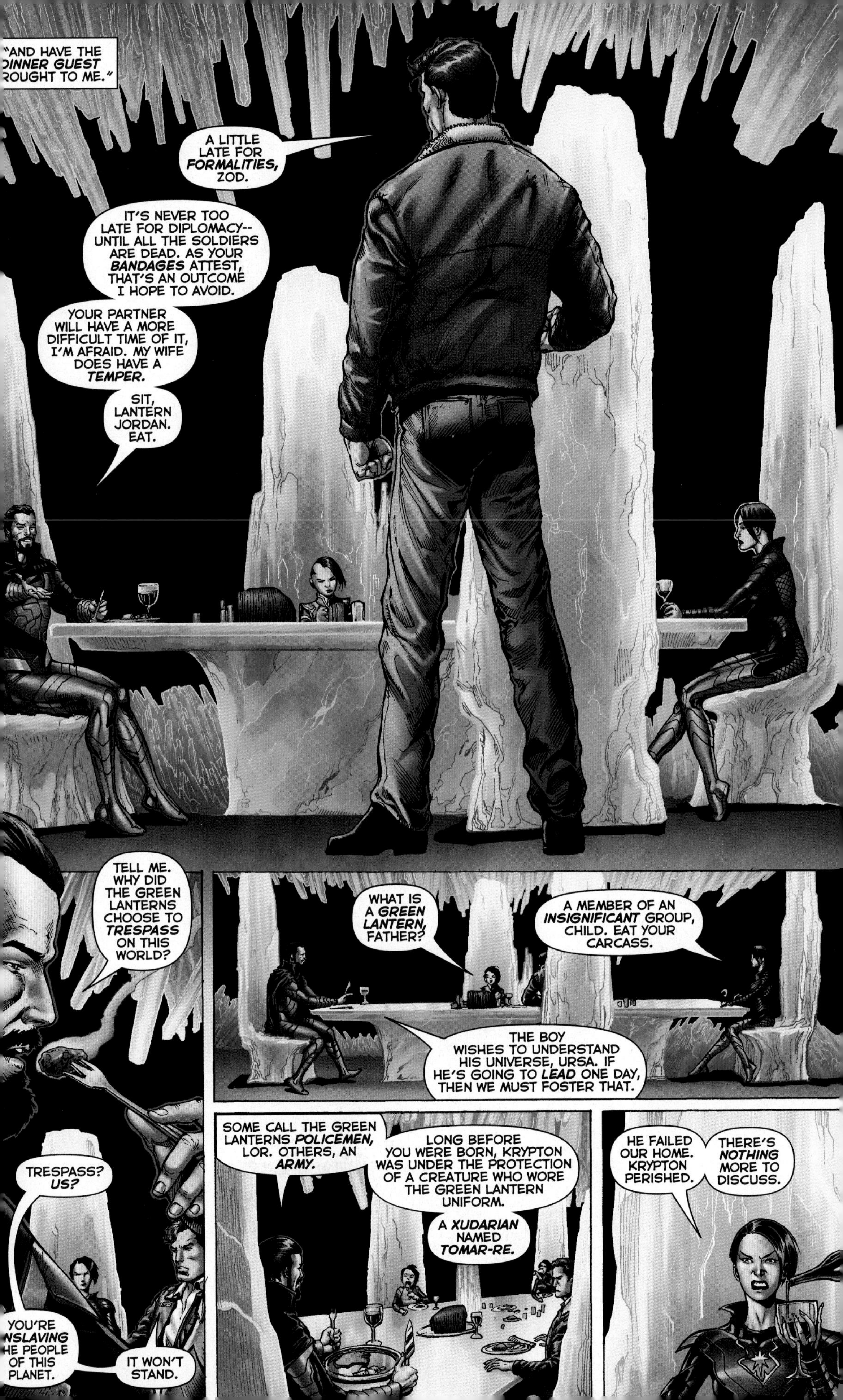

"AND HAVE THE DINNER GUEST BROUGHT TO ME."
A LITTLE LATE FOR FORMALITIES, ZOD.
IT'S NEVER TOO LATE FOR DIPLOMACY-- UNTIL ALL THE SOLDIERS ARE DEAD. AS YOUR BANDAGES ATTEST, THAT'S AN OUTCOME I HOPE TO AVOID.
YOUR PARTNER WILL HAVE A MORE DIFFICULT TIME OF IT, I'M AFRAID. MY WIFE DOES HAVE A TEMPER.
SIT, LANTERN JORDAN. EAT.
TELL ME. WHY DID THE GREEN LANTERNS CHOOSE TO TRESPASS ON THIS WORLD?
TRESPASS? US?
YOU'RE ENSLAVING THE PEOPLE OF THIS PLANET.
IT WON'T STAND.
WHAT IS A GREEN LANTERN, FATHER?
A MEMBER OF AN INSIGNIFICANT GROUP, CHILD. EAT YOUR CARCASS.
THE BOY WISHES TO UNDERSTAND HIS UNIVERSE, URSA. IF HE'S GOING TO LEAD ONE DAY, THEN WE MUST FOSTER THAT.
SOME CALL THE GREEN LANTERNS POLICEMEN, LOR. OTHERS, AN ARMY.
LONG BEFORE YOU WERE BORN, KRYPTON WAS UNDER THE PROTECTION OF A CREATURE WHO WORE THE GREEN LANTERN UNIFORM.
A XUDARIAN NAMED TOMAR-RE.
HE FAILED OUR HOME. KRYPTON PERISHED.
THERE'S NOTHING MORE TO DISCUSS.

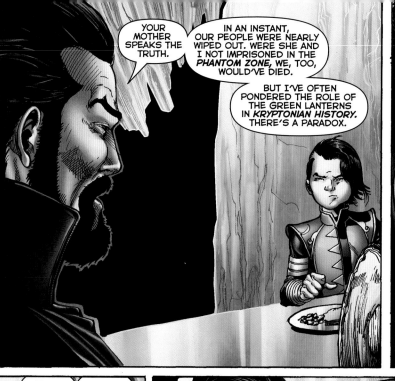

YOUR MOTHER SPEAKS THE TRUTH.

IN AN INSTANT, OUR PEOPLE WERE NEARLY WIPED OUT. WERE SHE AND I NOT IMPRISONED IN THE *PHANTOM ZONE,* WE, TOO, WOULD'VE DIED.

BUT I'VE OFTEN PONDERED THE ROLE OF THE GREEN LANTERNS IN *KRYPTONIAN HISTORY.* THERE'S A PARADOX.

WITHOUT THAT *TRAGEDY* AND THE CHAIN OF EVENTS IT SET IN MOTION, WE NEVER WOULD HAVE VENTURED TO *EARTH* AND LIVED BENEATH ITS *YELLOW SUN.* WE NEVER WOULD HAVE REACHED OUR FULLEST *KRYPTONIAN* POTENTIAL.

NOW WE CAN BRING OUR RACE TO *NEW HEIGHTS.*

I SUPPOSE, IN THAT WAY, WE OW THE GREEN LANTER A DEBT.

HERE'S AN *EASIER* ANSWER, KID.

I KNEW TOMAR-RE. HE WAS MY *FRIEND.*

THE GREEN LANTERNS ARE THE *GOOD GUYS.*

YOU INSOLENT, *WEAK--*

PERHAPS THIS WAS A MISTAKE, LANTERN.

I'D HOPED WE COULD TALK AS CIVILIZED MEN-- *MILITARY* MEN. CLEARLY, THE WOUNDS ARE YET TOO FRESH.

ERADICATOR WILL RETURN Y TO YOUR CELL. WILL TALK AGA IN DUE TIME.

UNTIL THEN, I LEAVE YOU WITH THIS.

JUST AS TOMAR-RE UNWITTINGLY CREATED A *TURNING POINT* FOR THE KRYPTONIAN RACE--

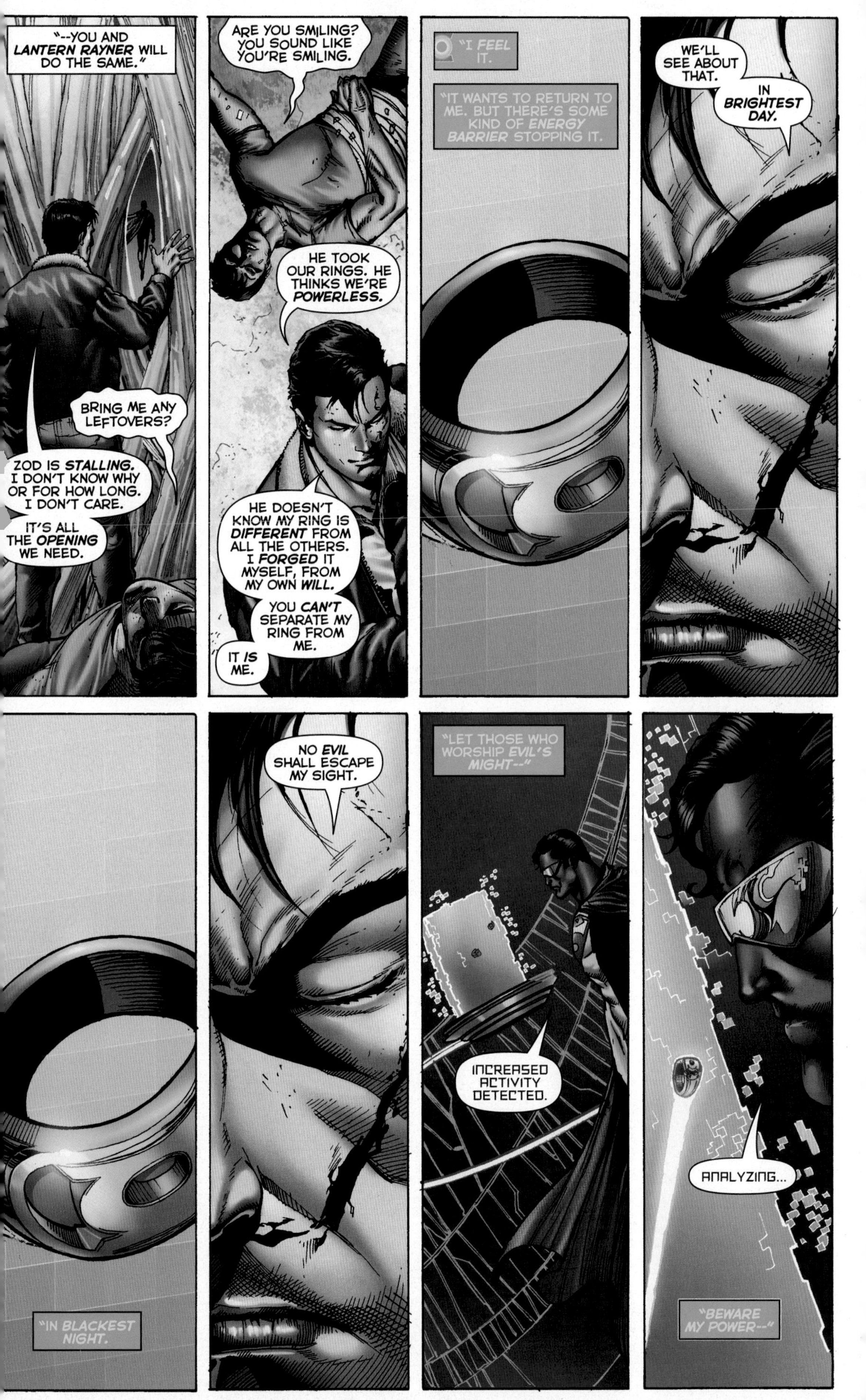

"--YOU AND LANTERN RAYNER WILL DO THE SAME."
BRING ME ANY LEFTOVERS?
ZOD IS STALLING. I DON'T KNOW WHY OR FOR HOW LONG. I DON'T CARE.
IT'S ALL THE OPENING WE NEED.
ARE YOU SMILING? YOU SOUND LIKE YOU'RE SMILING.
HE TOOK OUR RINGS. HE THINKS WE'RE POWERLESS.
HE DOESN'T KNOW MY RING IS DIFFERENT FROM ALL THE OTHERS. I FORGED IT MYSELF, FROM MY OWN WILL.
YOU CAN'T SEPARATE MY RING FROM ME.
IT IS ME.
"I FEEL IT.
"IT WANTS TO RETURN TO ME. BUT THERE'S SOME KIND OF ENERGY BARRIER STOPPING IT.
WE'LL SEE ABOUT THAT.
IN BRIGHTEST DAY.
"IN BLACKEST NIGHT.
NO EVIL SHALL ESCAPE MY SIGHT.
"LET THOSE WHO WORSHIP EVIL'S MIGHT--"
INCREASED ACTIVITY DETECTED.
ANALYZING...
"BEWARE MY POWER--"

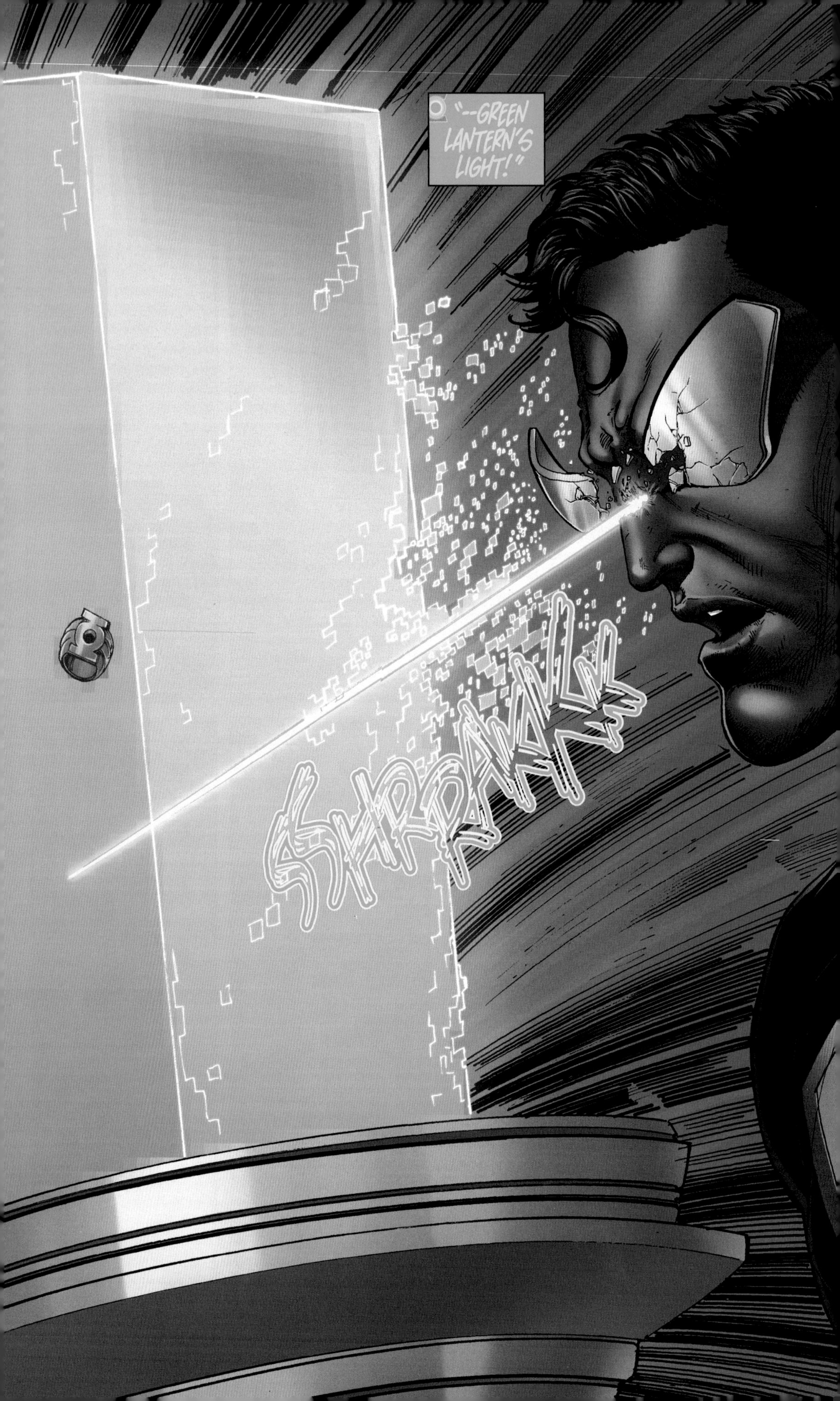
"--GREEN LANTERN'S LIGHT!"

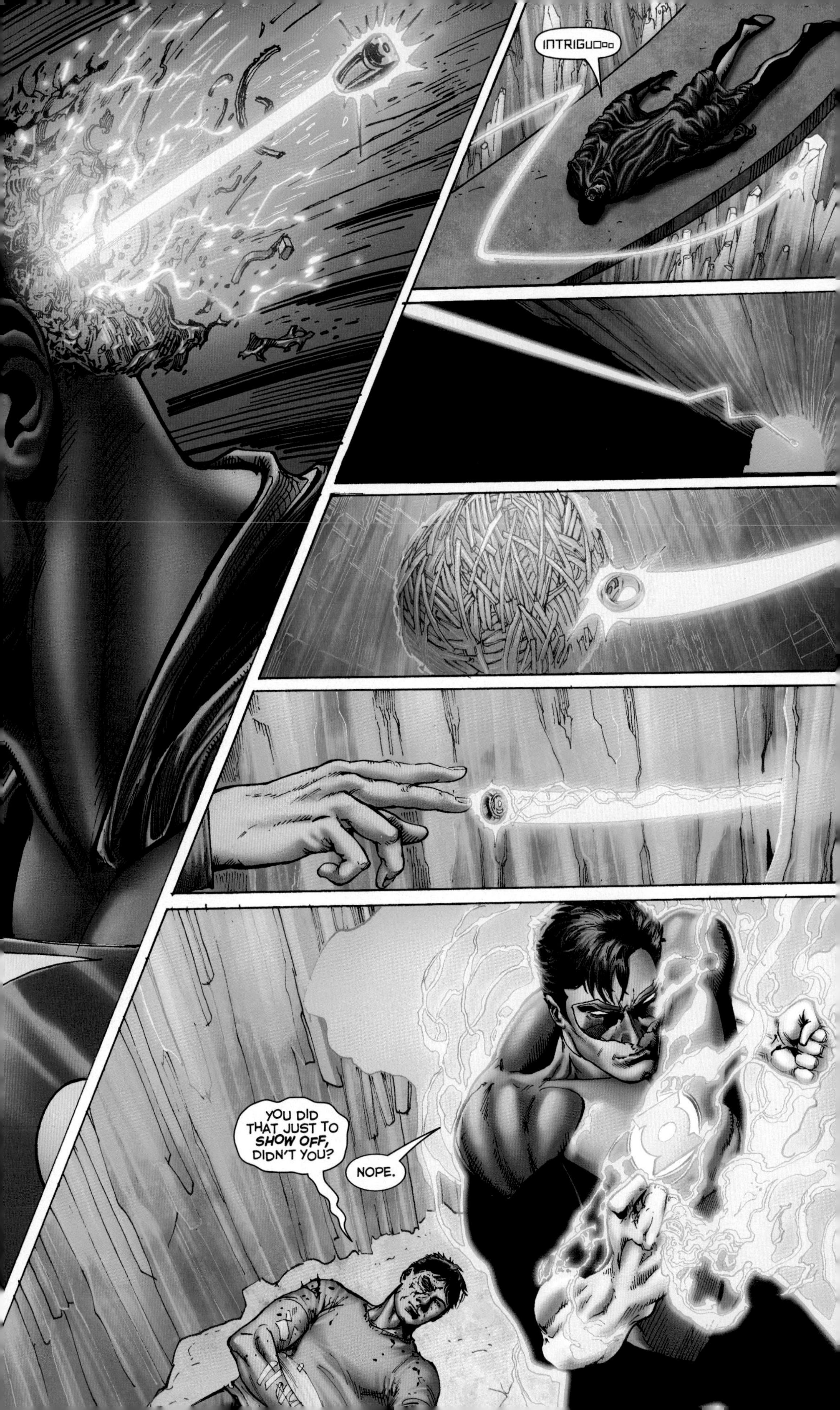
INTRIGUooo
YOU DID THAT JUST TO SHOW OFF, DIDN'T YOU?
NOPE.

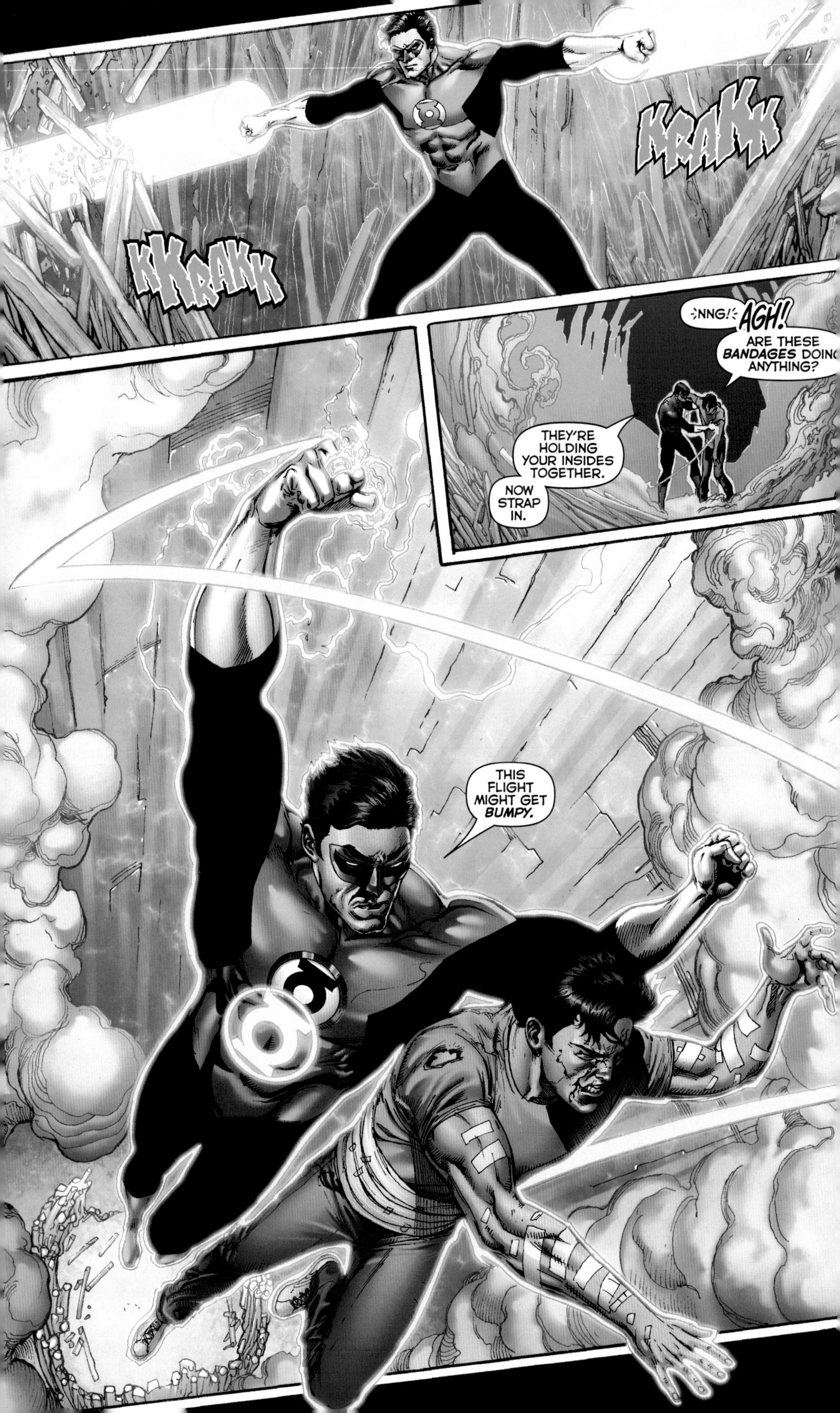
KRAKK
KKRAKK
NNG! AGH!
ARE THESE BANDAGES DOING ANYTHING?
THEY'RE HOLDING YOUR INSIDES TOGETHER.
NOW STRAP IN.
THIS FLIGHT MIGHT GET BUMPY.

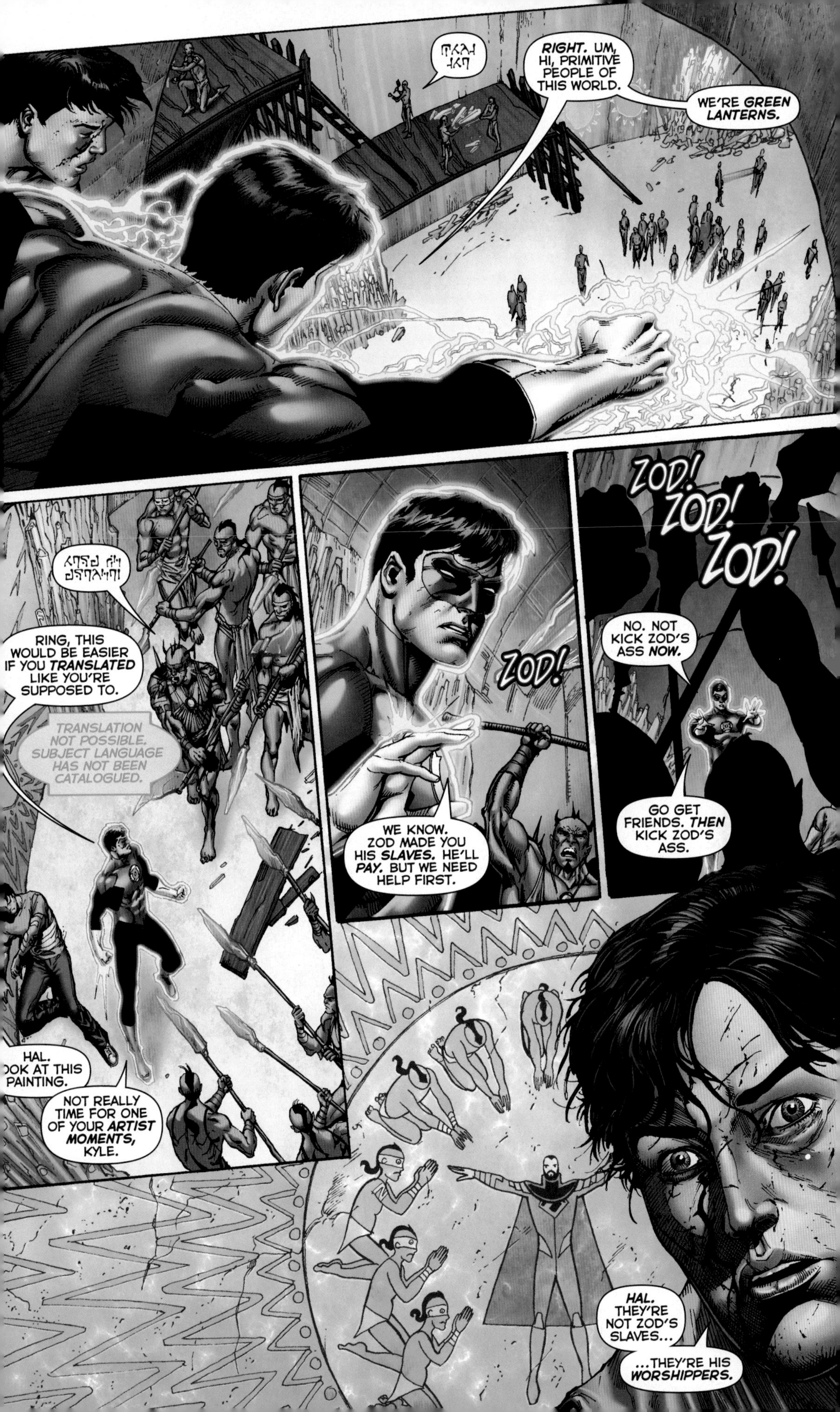

RIGHT. UM, HI, PRIMITIVE PEOPLE OF THIS WORLD.
WE'RE GREEN LANTERNS.
RING, THIS WOULD BE EASIER IF YOU TRANSLATED LIKE YOU'RE SUPPOSED TO.
TRANSLATION NOT POSSIBLE. SUBJECT LANGUAGE HAS NOT BEEN CATALOGUED.
ZOD!
WE KNOW. ZOD MADE YOU HIS SLAVES. HE'LL PAY. BUT WE NEED HELP FIRST.
ZOD! ZOD! ZOD!
NO. NOT KICK ZOD'S ASS NOW.
GO GET FRIENDS. THEN KICK ZOD'S ASS.
HAL. OOK AT THIS PAINTING.
NOT REALLY TIME FOR ONE OF YOUR ARTIST MOMENTS, KYLE.
HAL. THEY'RE NOT ZOD'S SLAVES...
...THEY'RE HIS WORSHIPPERS.

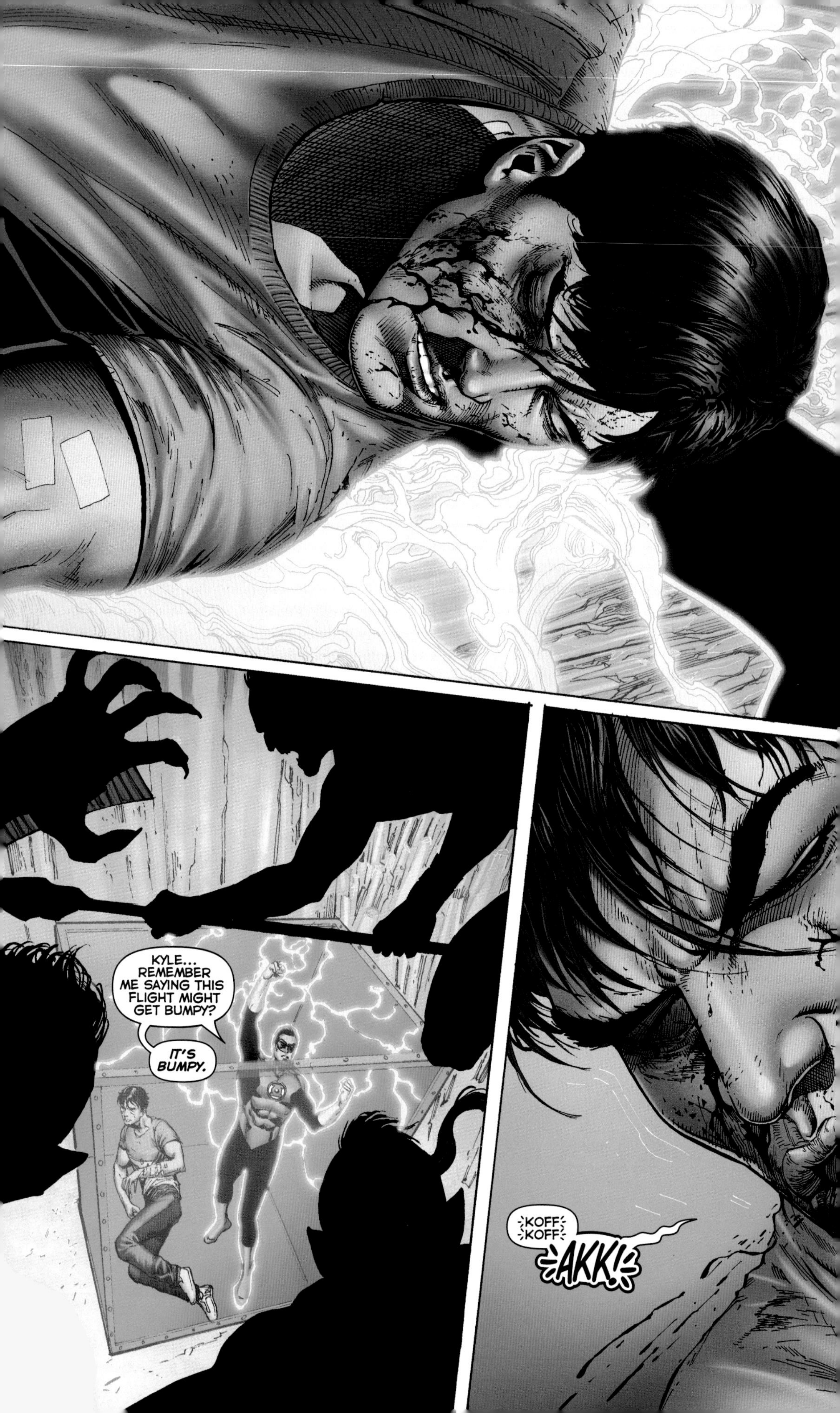

KYLE... REMEMBER ME SAYING THIS FLIGHT MIGHT GET BUMPY?
IT'S BUMPY.
KOFF KOFF
AKK!

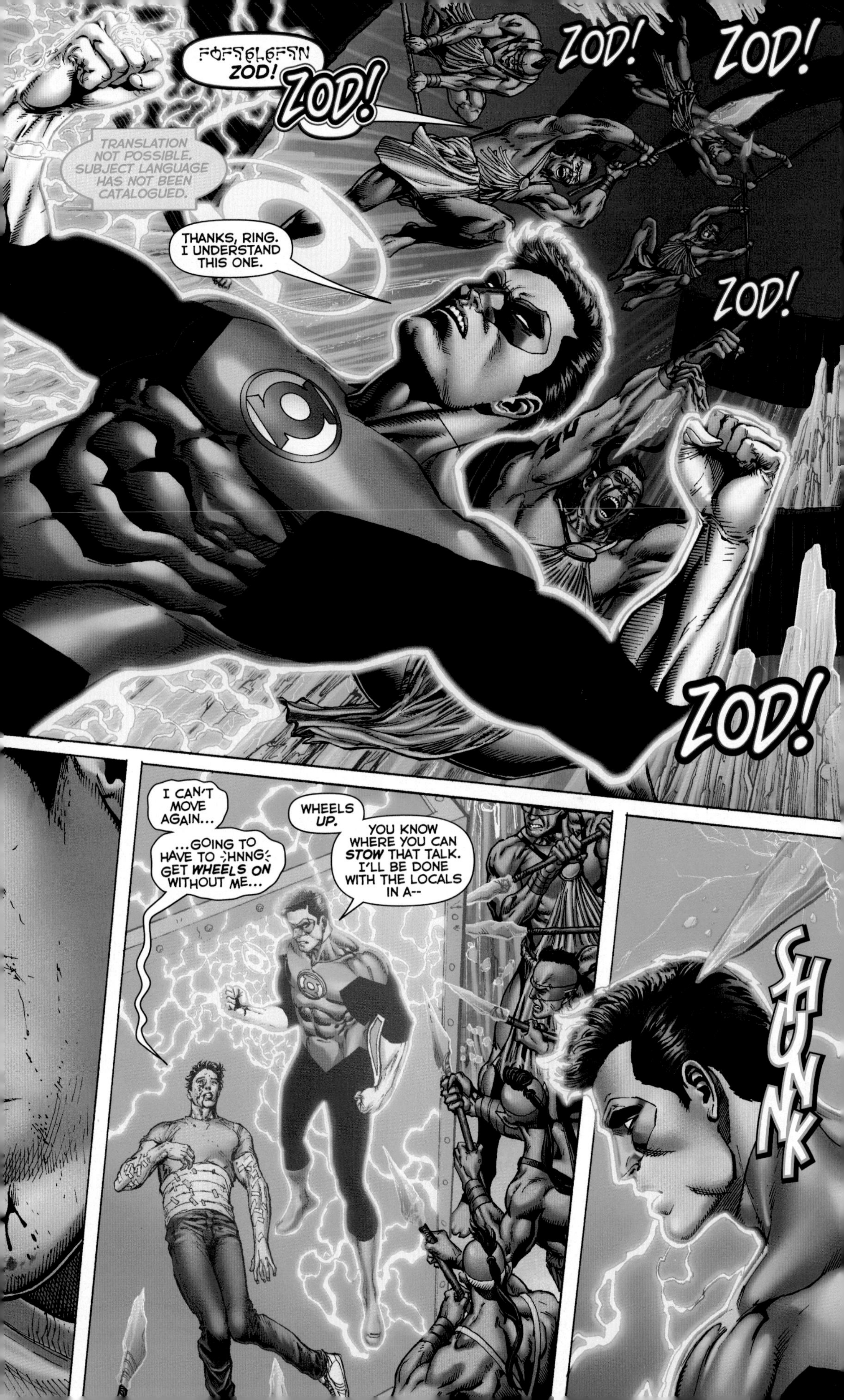
ZOD!
ZOD!
ZOD!
ZOD!
TRANSLATION NOT POSSIBLE. SUBJECT LANGUAGE HAS NOT BEEN CATALOGUED.
THANKS, RING. I UNDERSTAND THIS ONE.
ZOD!
ZOD!
I CAN'T MOVE AGAIN...
...GOING TO HAVE TO -HNNG- GET *WHEELS ON* WITHOUT ME...
WHEELS *UP.*
YOU KNOW WHERE YOU CAN *STOW* THAT TALK. I'LL BE DONE WITH THE LOCALS IN A--
SHUNK

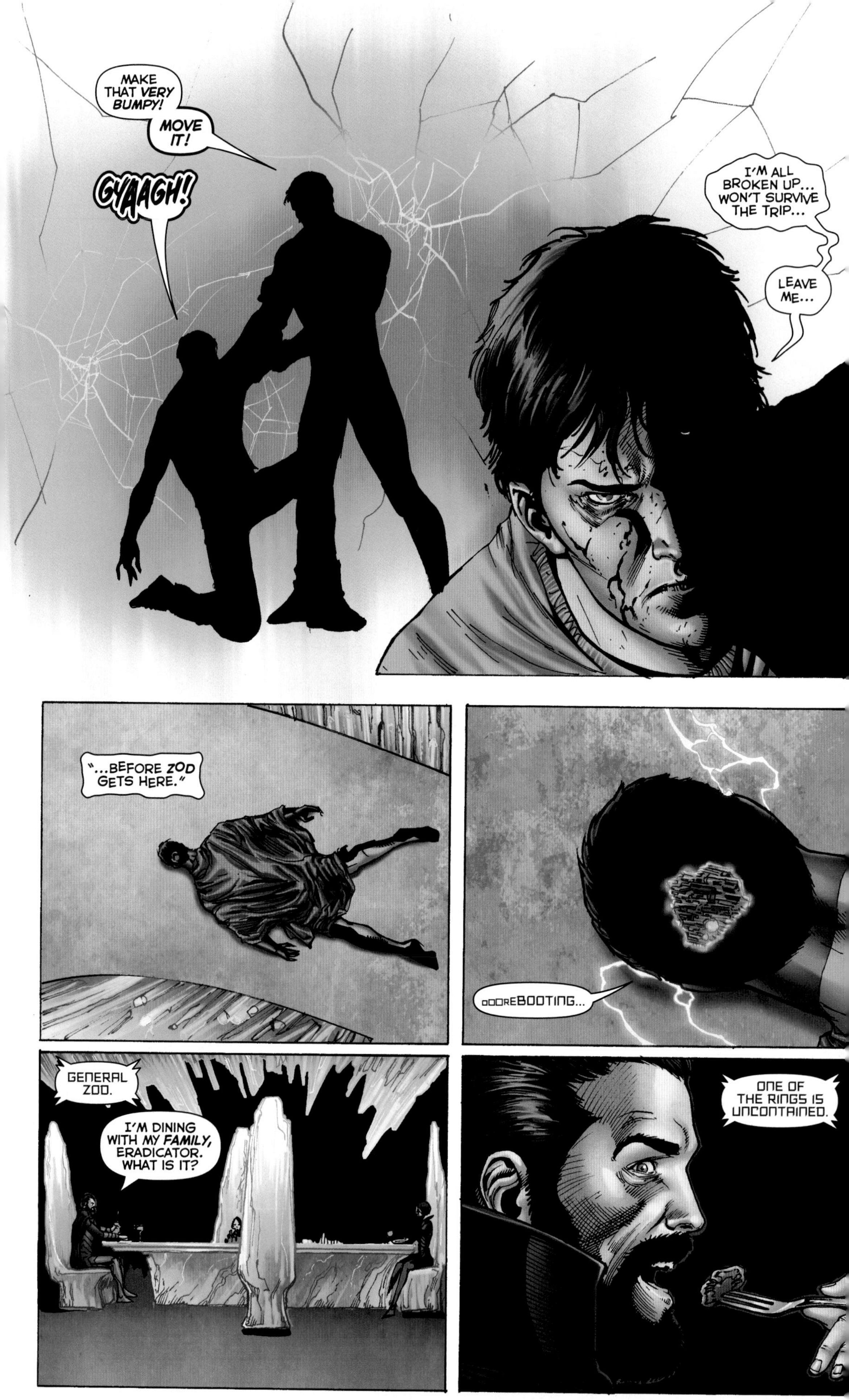
MAKE THAT VERY BUMPY!
MOVE IT!
GYAAGH!
I'M ALL BROKEN UP... WON'T SURVIVE THE TRIP...
LEAVE ME...
"...BEFORE ZOD GETS HERE."
REBOOTING...
GENERAL ZOD.
I'M DINING WITH MY FAMILY, ERADICATOR. WHAT IS IT?
ONE OF THE RINGS IS UNCONTAINED.

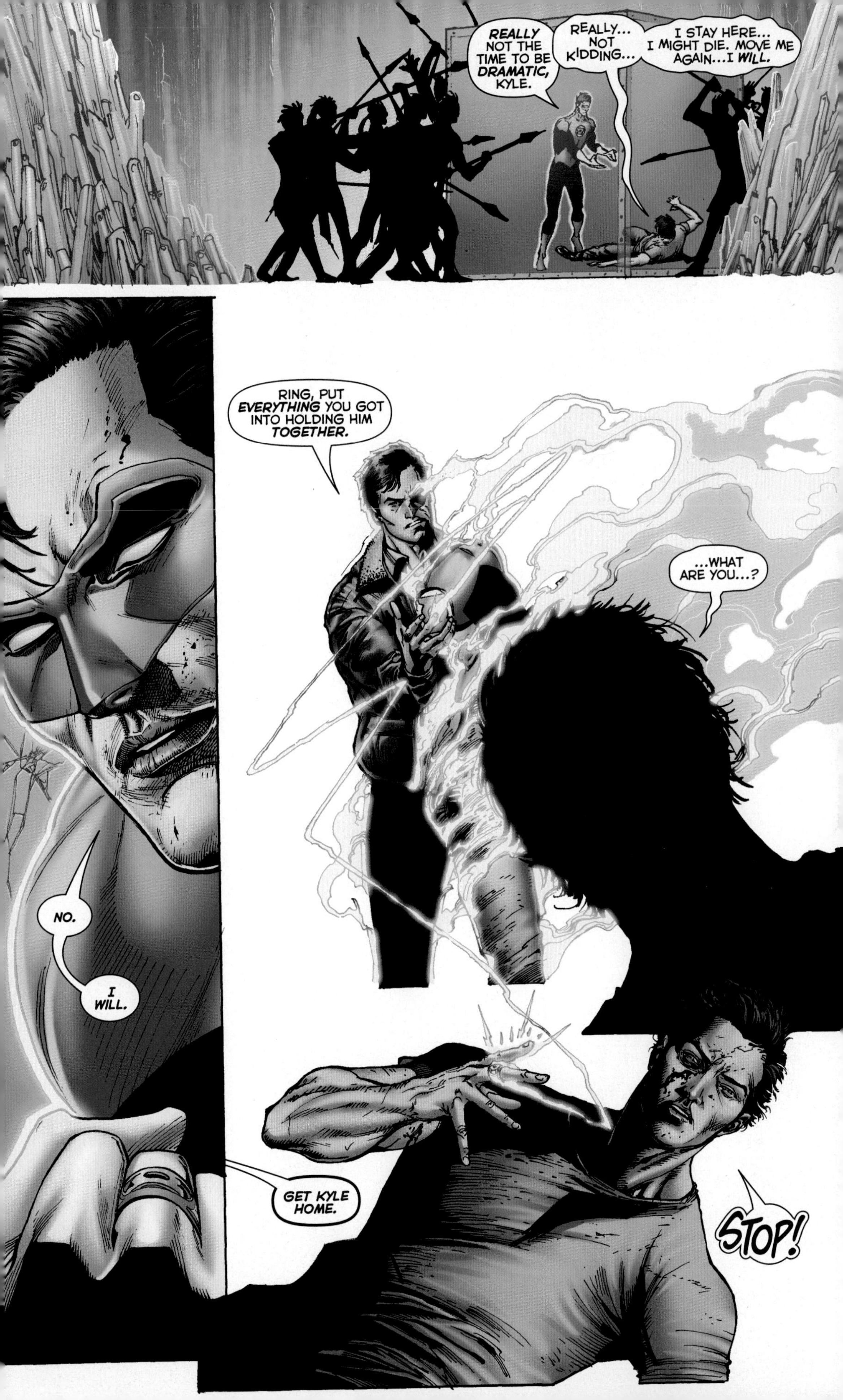
REALLY NOT THE TIME TO BE DRAMATIC, KYLE.
REALLY... NOT KIDDING...
I STAY HERE... I MIGHT DIE. MOVE ME AGAIN... I WILL.
NO.
I WILL.
GET KYLE HOME.
RING, PUT EVERYTHING YOU GOT INTO HOLDING HIM TOGETHER.
...WHAT ARE YOU...?
STOP!

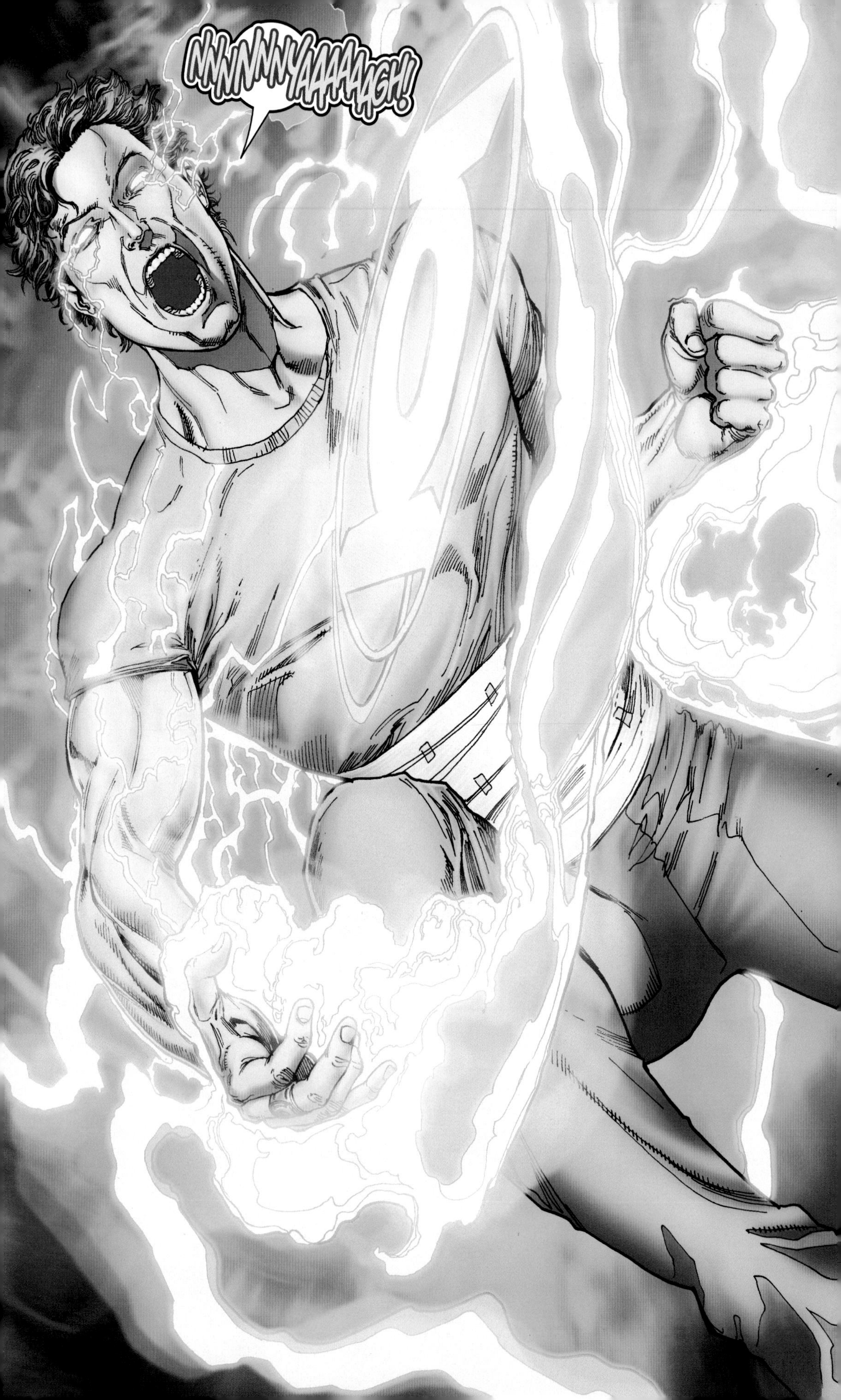
NNNNNNYAAAAAAGH!

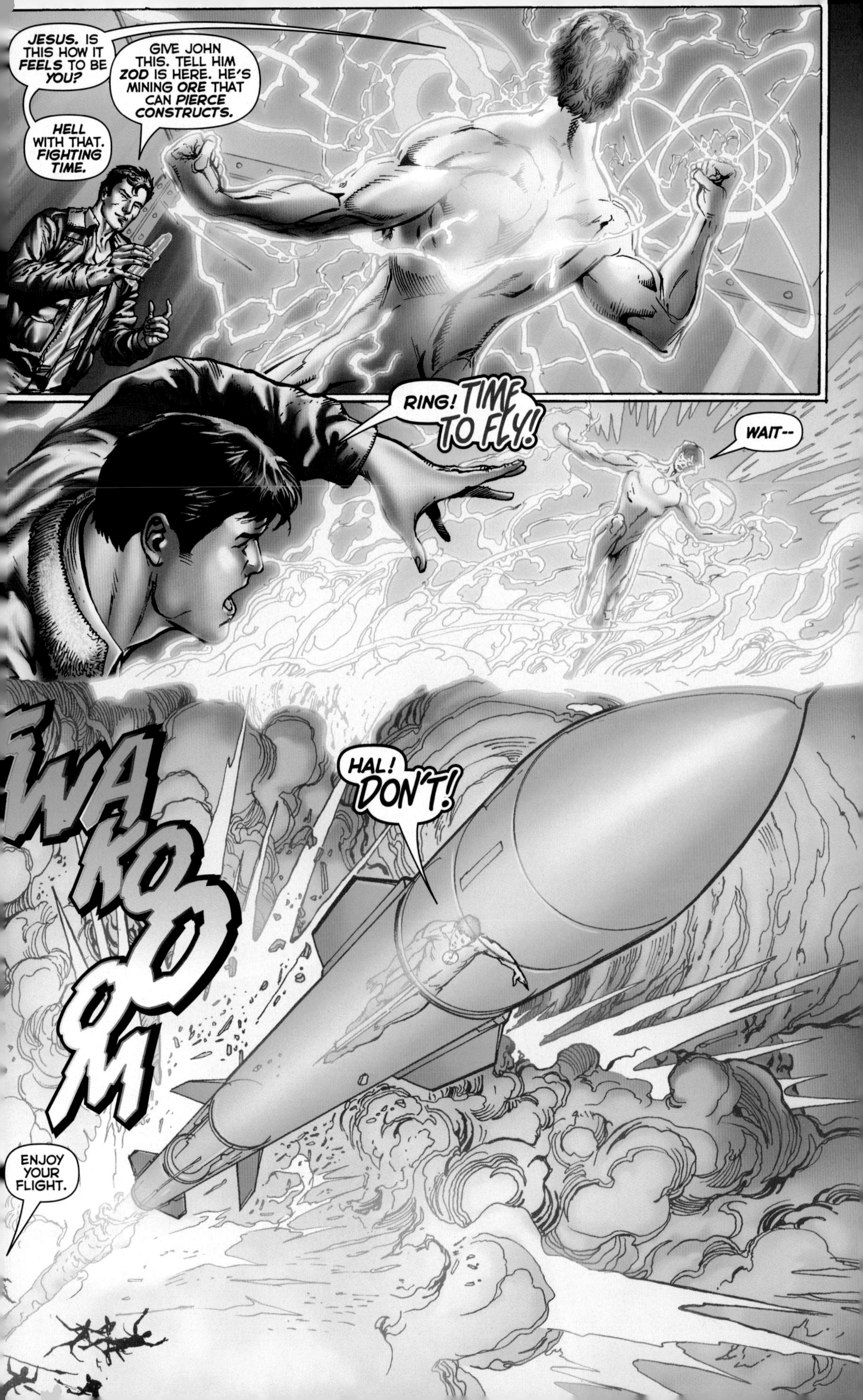
JESUS. IS THIS HOW IT FEELS TO BE YOU?
HELL WITH THAT. FIGHTING TIME.
GIVE JOHN THIS. TELL HIM ZOD IS HERE. HE'S MINING ORE THAT CAN PIERCE CONSTRUCTS.
RING! TIME TO FLY!
WAIT--
WAKOOOM
HAL! DON'T!
ENJOY YOUR FLIGHT.

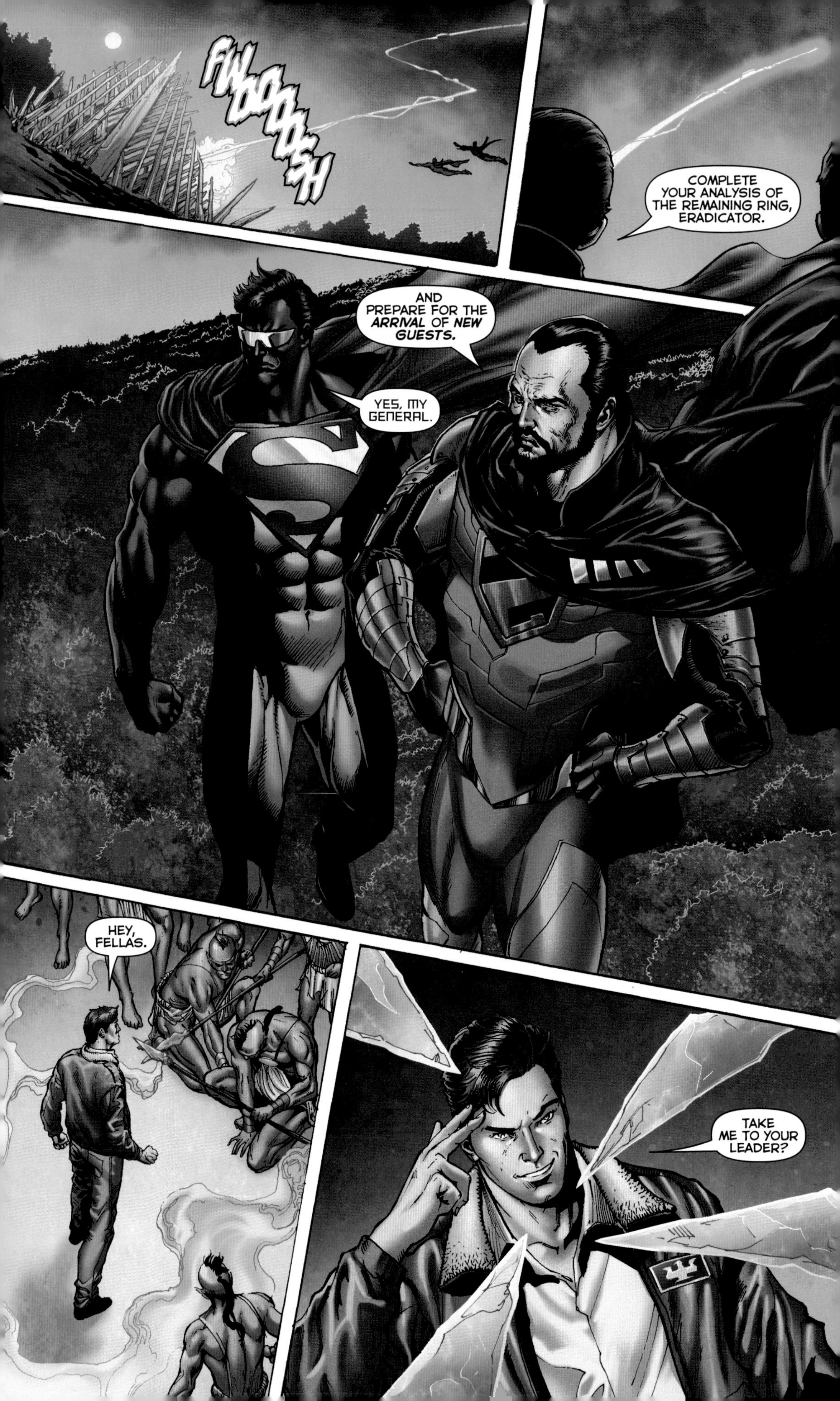
FWOOOOSH
COMPLETE YOUR ANALYSIS OF THE REMAINING RING, ERADICATOR.
AND PREPARE FOR THE *ARRIVAL* OF *NEW GUESTS.*
YES, MY GENERAL.
HEY, FELLAS.
TAKE ME TO YOUR LEADER?

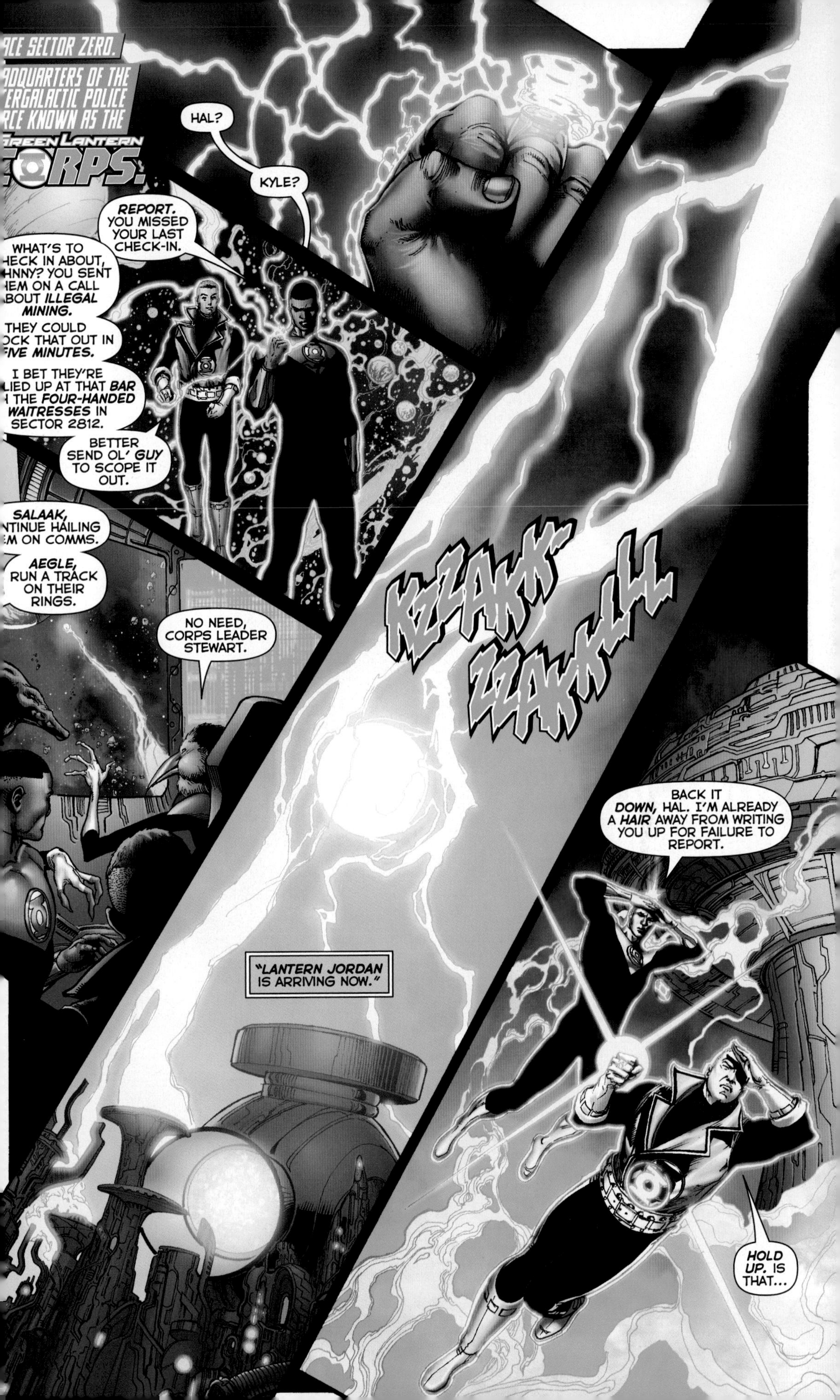

ACE SECTOR ZERO.
ADQUARTERS OF THE ERGALACTIC POLICE RCE KNOWN AS THE GREEN LANTERN CORPS.
HAL?
KYLE?
REPORT. YOU MISSED YOUR LAST CHECK-IN.
WHAT'S TO HECK IN ABOUT, HNNY? YOU SENT HEM ON A CALL BOUT ILLEGAL MINING.
THEY COULD OCK THAT OUT IN FIVE MINUTES.
I BET THEY'RE LIED UP AT THAT BAR H THE FOUR-HANDED WAITRESSES IN SECTOR 2812.
BETTER SEND OL' GUY TO SCOPE IT OUT.
SALAAK, NTINUE HAILING EM ON COMMS.
AEGLE, RUN A TRACK ON THEIR RINGS.
NO NEED, CORPS LEADER STEWART.
KZZAKK-ZZAKKLLL
"LANTERN JORDAN IS ARRIVING NOW."
BACK IT DOWN, HAL. I'M ALREADY A HAIR AWAY FROM WRITING YOU UP FOR FAILURE TO REPORT.
HOLD UP. IS THAT...

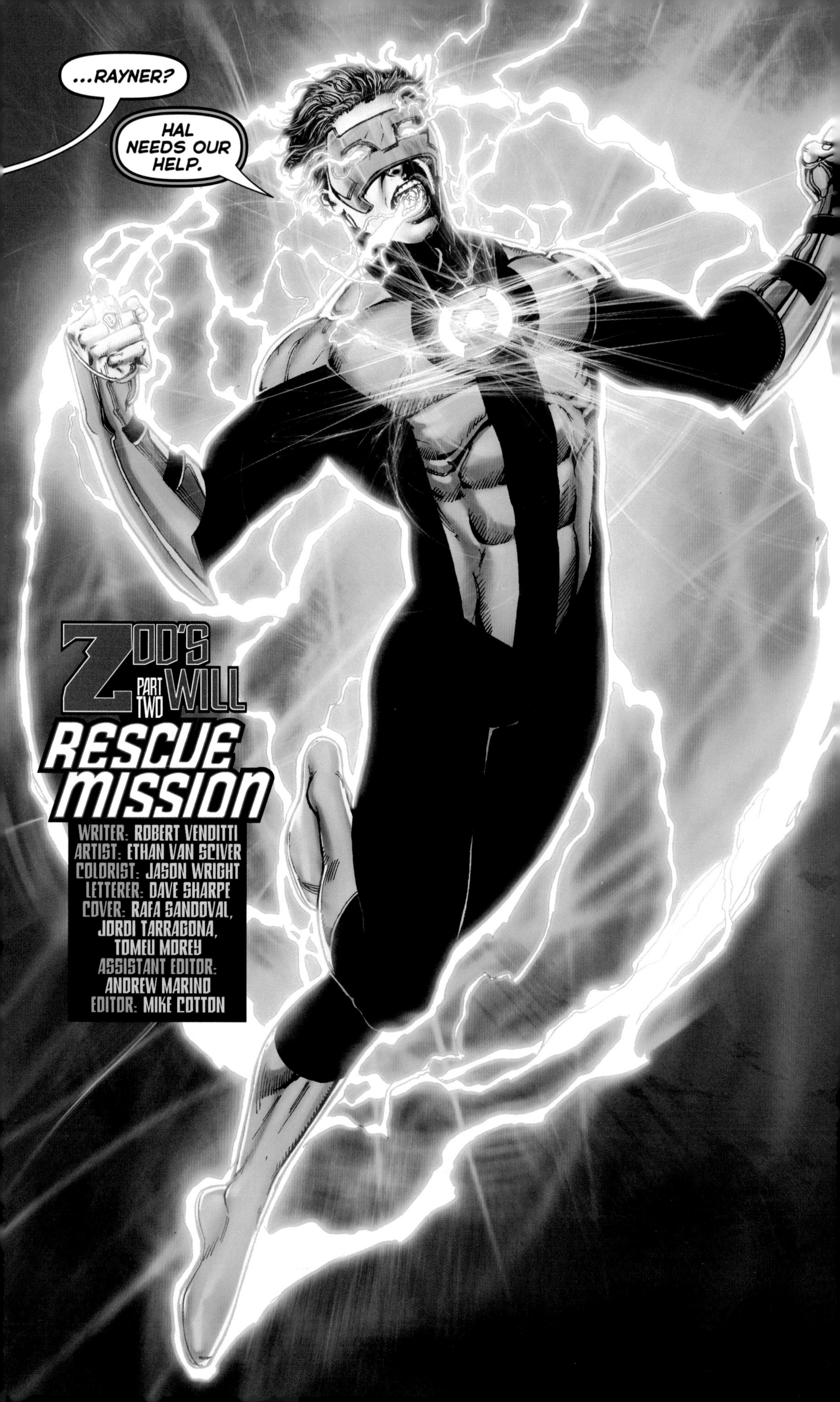

...RAYNER?
HAL NEEDS OUR HELP.
ZOD'S WILL PART TWO
RESCUE MISSION
WRITER: ROBERT VENDITTI
ARTIST: ETHAN VAN SCIVER
COLORIST: JASON WRIGHT
LETTERER: DAVE SHARPE
COVER: RAFA SANDOVAL, JORDI TARRAGONA, TOMEU MOREY
ASSISTANT EDITOR: ANDREW MARINO
EDITOR: MIKE COTTON

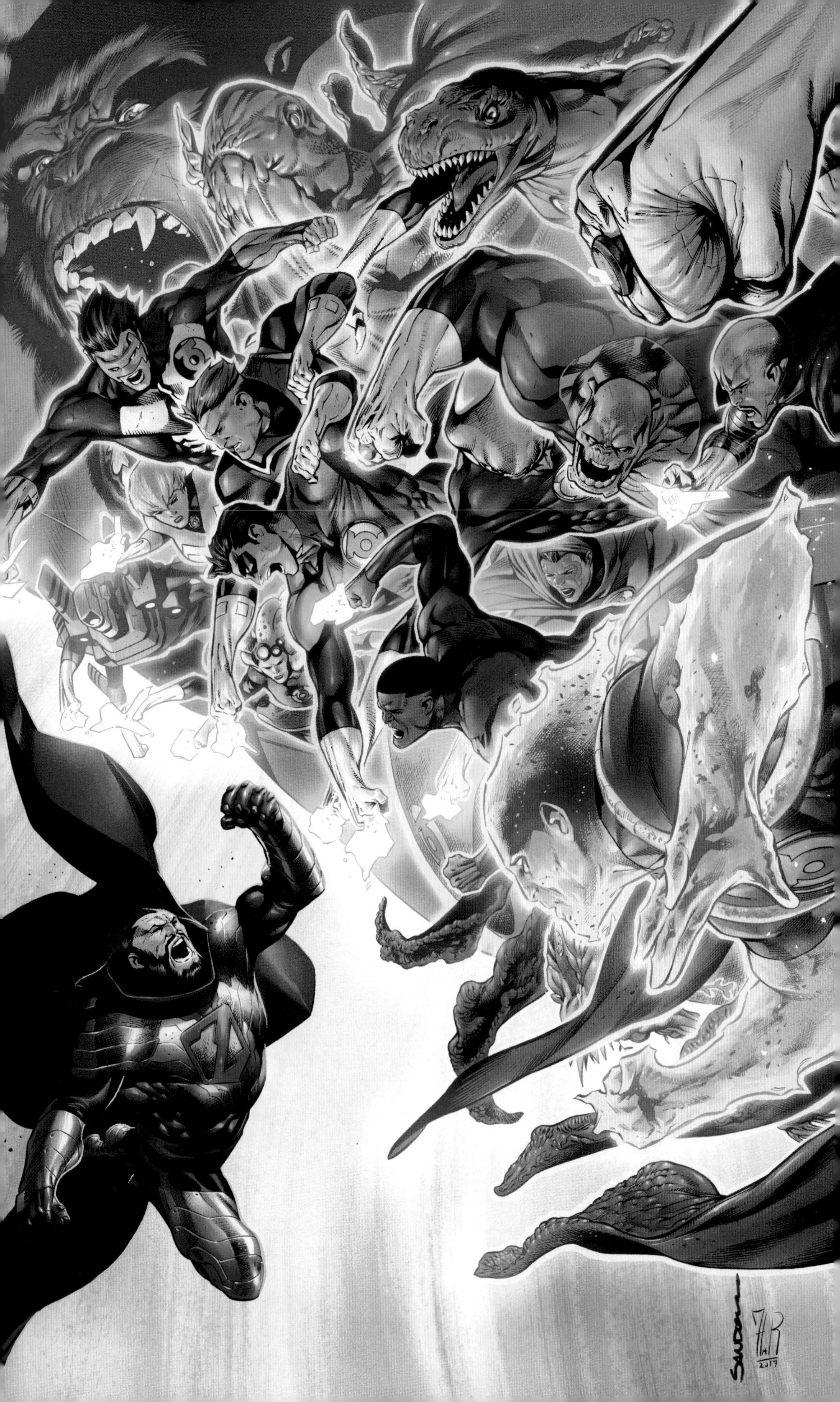

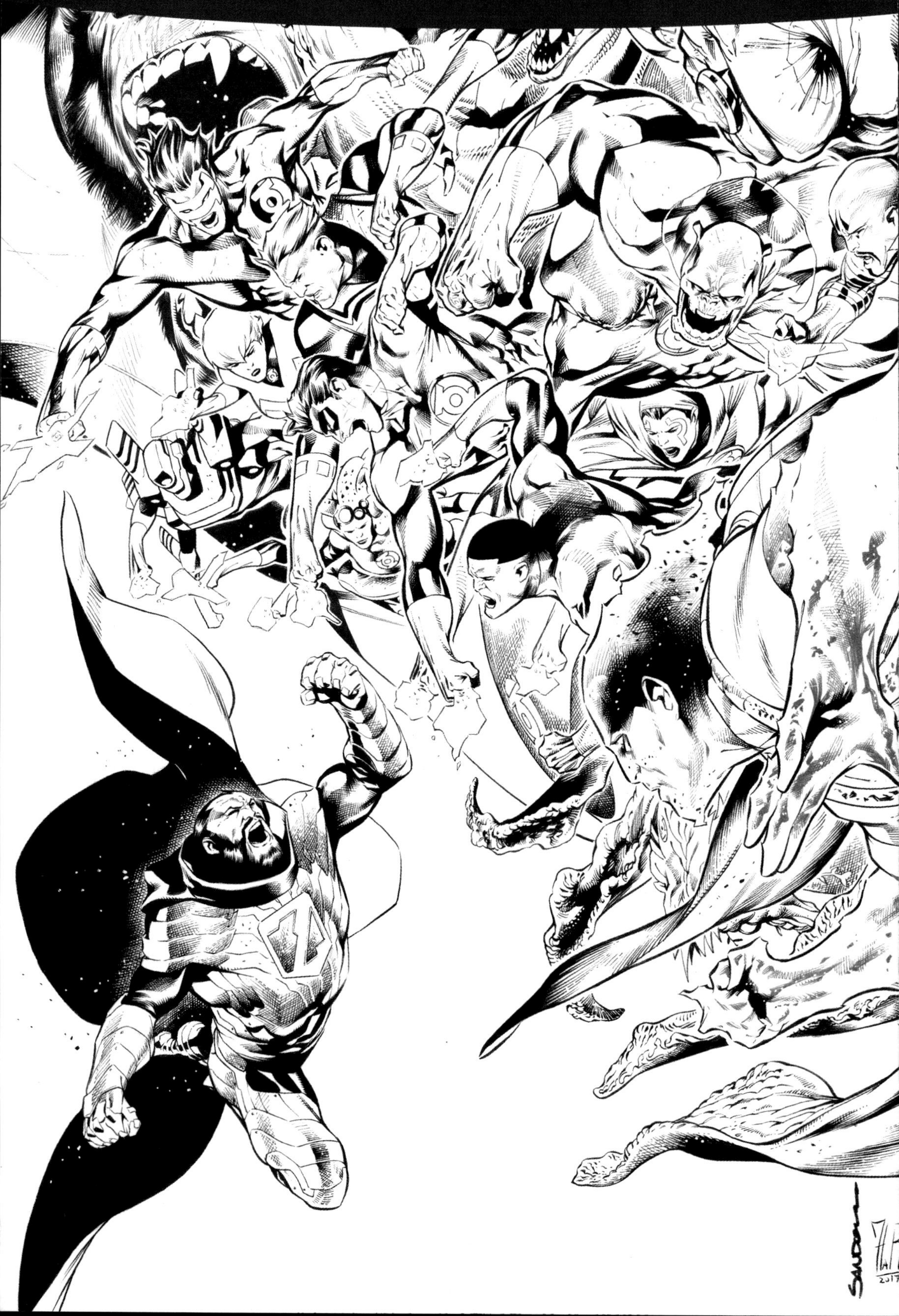

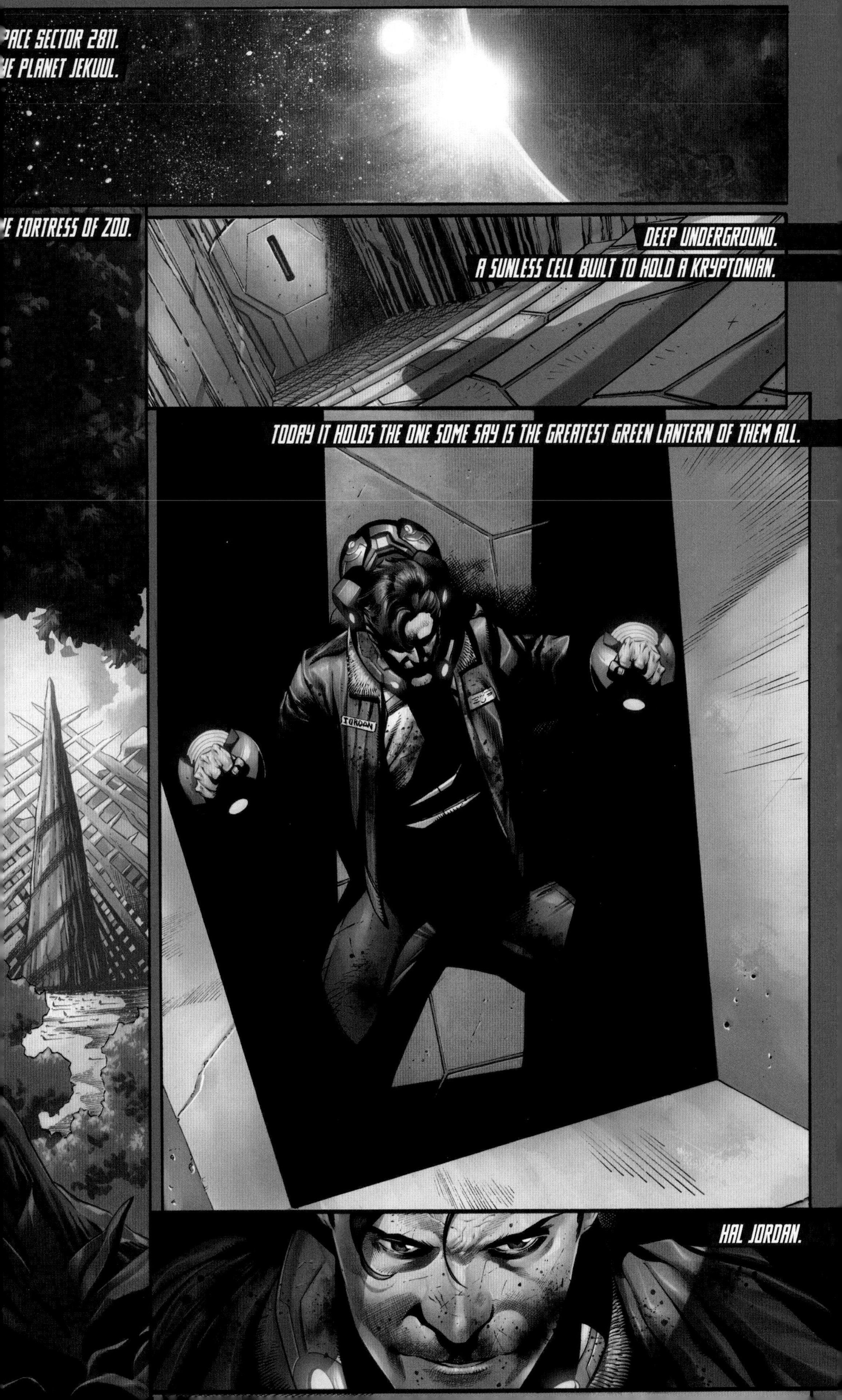

PACE SECTOR 2811.
E PLANET JEKUUL.
E FORTRESS OF ZOD.
DEEP UNDERGROUND.
A SUNLESS CELL BUILT TO HOLD A KRYPTONIAN.
TODAY IT HOLDS THE ONE SOME SAY IS THE GREATEST GREEN LANTERN OF THEM ALL.
JORDAN
HAL JORDAN.

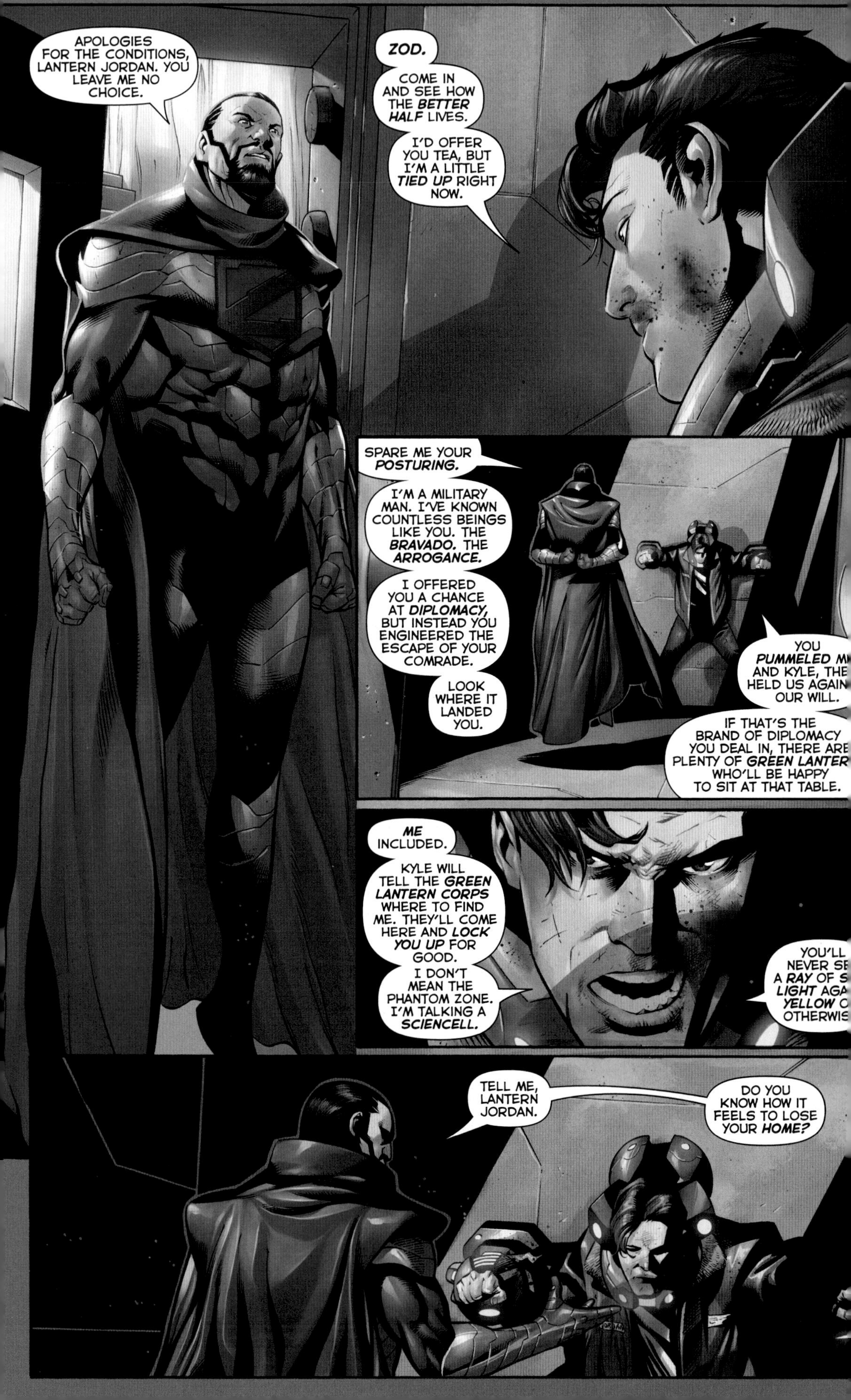
APOLOGIES FOR THE CONDITIONS, LANTERN JORDAN. YOU LEAVE ME NO CHOICE.
ZOD.
COME IN AND SEE HOW THE BETTER HALF LIVES.
I'D OFFER YOU TEA, BUT I'M A LITTLE TIED UP RIGHT NOW.
SPARE ME YOUR POSTURING.
I'M A MILITARY MAN. I'VE KNOWN COUNTLESS BEINGS LIKE YOU. THE BRAVADO. THE ARROGANCE.
I OFFERED YOU A CHANCE AT DIPLOMACY, BUT INSTEAD YOU ENGINEERED THE ESCAPE OF YOUR COMRADE.
LOOK WHERE IT LANDED YOU.
YOU PUMMELED M AND KYLE, THE HELD US AGAIN OUR WILL.
IF THAT'S THE BRAND OF DIPLOMACY YOU DEAL IN, THERE ARE PLENTY OF GREEN LANTER WHO'LL BE HAPPY TO SIT AT THAT TABLE.
ME INCLUDED.
KYLE WILL TELL THE GREEN LANTERN CORPS WHERE TO FIND ME. THEY'LL COME HERE AND LOCK YOU UP FOR GOOD.
I DON'T MEAN THE PHANTOM ZONE. I'M TALKING A SCIENCELL.
YOU'LL NEVER SE A RAY OF S LIGHT AGA YELLOW O OTHERWIS
TELL ME, LANTERN JORDAN.
DO YOU KNOW HOW IT FEELS TO LOSE YOUR HOME?

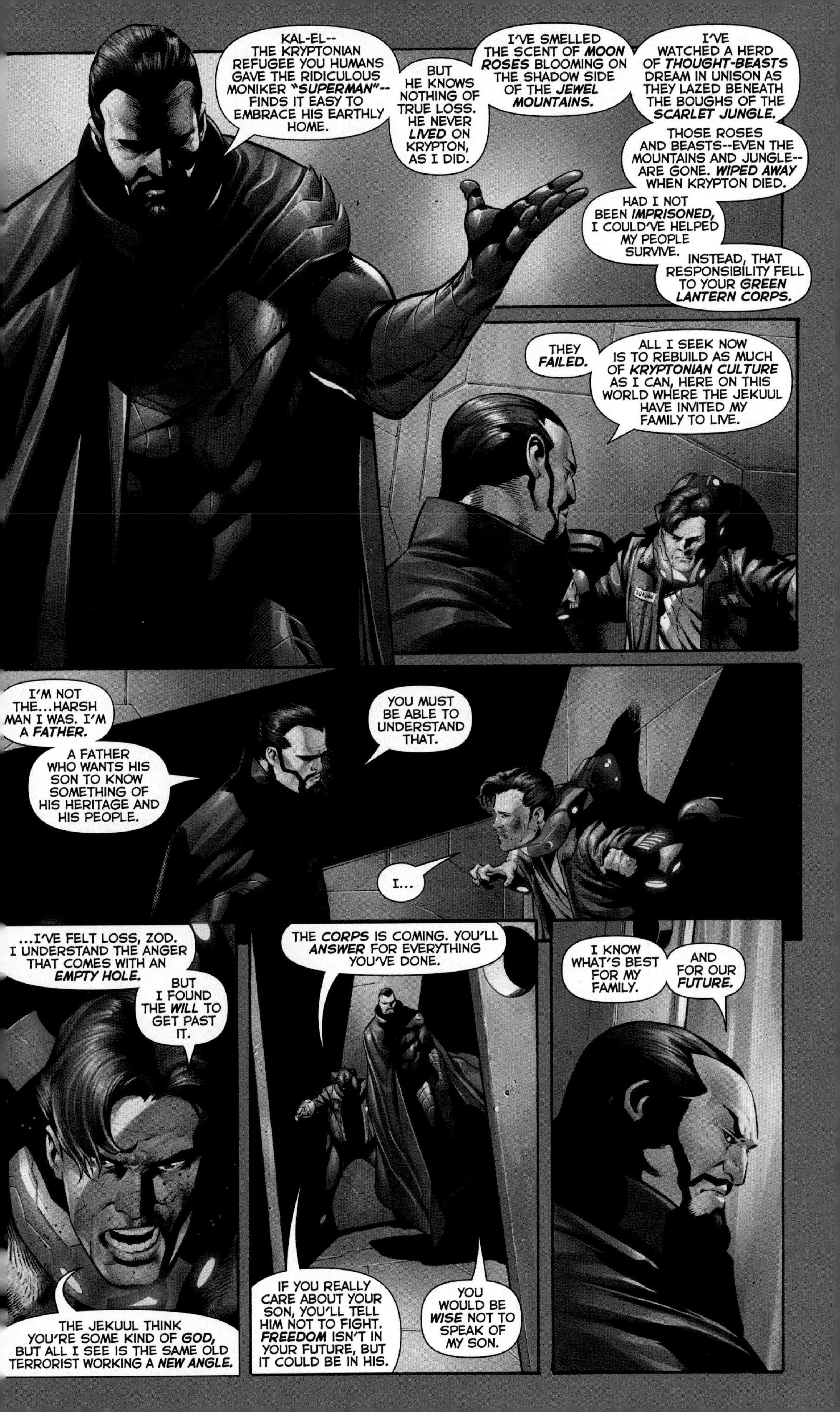
KAL-EL-- THE KRYPTONIAN REFUGEE YOU HUMANS GAVE THE RIDICULOUS MONIKER "SUPERMAN"-- FINDS IT EASY TO EMBRACE HIS EARTHLY HOME.
BUT HE KNOWS NOTHING OF TRUE LOSS. HE NEVER LIVED ON KRYPTON, AS I DID.
I'VE SMELLED THE SCENT OF MOON ROSES BLOOMING ON THE SHADOW SIDE OF THE JEWEL MOUNTAINS.
I'VE WATCHED A HERD OF THOUGHT-BEASTS DREAM IN UNISON AS THEY LAZED BENEATH THE BOUGHS OF THE SCARLET JUNGLE.
THOSE ROSES AND BEASTS--EVEN THE MOUNTAINS AND JUNGLE-- ARE GONE. WIPED AWAY WHEN KRYPTON DIED.
HAD I NOT BEEN IMPRISONED, I COULD'VE HELPED MY PEOPLE SURVIVE.
INSTEAD, THAT RESPONSIBILITY FELL TO YOUR GREEN LANTERN CORPS.
THEY FAILED.
ALL I SEEK NOW IS TO REBUILD AS MUCH OF KRYPTONIAN CULTURE AS I CAN, HERE ON THIS WORLD WHERE THE JEKUUL HAVE INVITED MY FAMILY TO LIVE.
I'M NOT THE...HARSH MAN I WAS. I'M A FATHER.
A FATHER WHO WANTS HIS SON TO KNOW SOMETHING OF HIS HERITAGE AND HIS PEOPLE.
YOU MUST BE ABLE TO UNDERSTAND THAT.
I...
...I'VE FELT LOSS, ZOD. I UNDERSTAND THE ANGER THAT COMES WITH AN EMPTY HOLE.
BUT I FOUND THE WILL TO GET PAST IT.
THE JEKUUL THINK YOU'RE SOME KIND OF GOD, BUT ALL I SEE IS THE SAME OLD TERRORIST WORKING A NEW ANGLE.
THE CORPS IS COMING. YOU'LL ANSWER FOR EVERYTHING YOU'VE DONE.
IF YOU REALLY CARE ABOUT YOUR SON, YOU'LL TELL HIM NOT TO FIGHT. FREEDOM ISN'T IN YOUR FUTURE, BUT IT COULD BE IN HIS.
YOU WOULD BE WISE NOT TO SPEAK OF MY SON.
I KNOW WHAT'S BEST FOR MY FAMILY.
AND FOR OUR FUTURE.

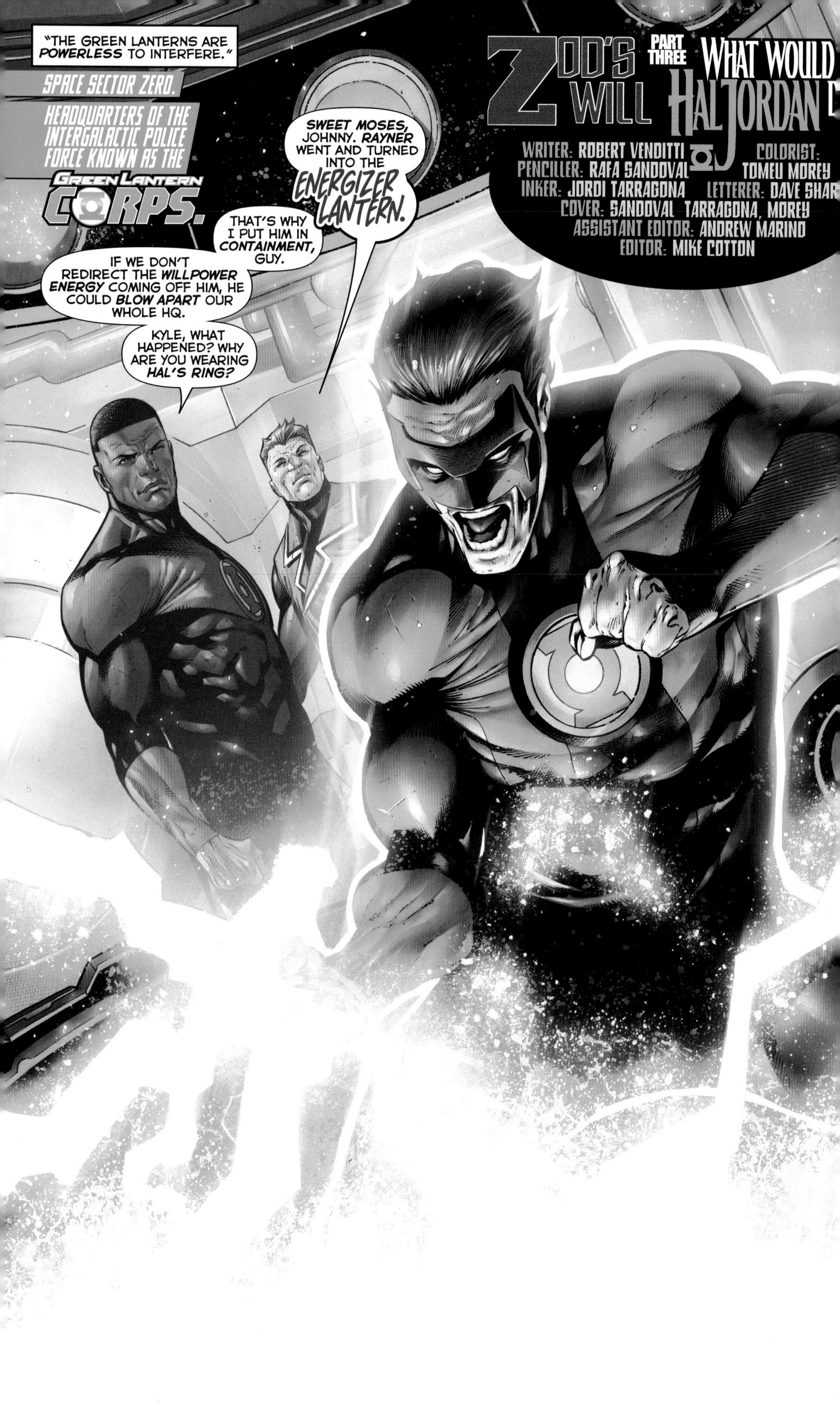

"THE GREEN LANTERNS ARE POWERLESS TO INTERFERE."
SPACE SECTOR ZERO.
HEADQUARTERS OF THE INTERGALACTIC POLICE FORCE KNOWN AS THE
GREEN LANTERN CORPS.
ZOD'S WILL PART THREE WHAT WOULD HAL JORDAN D
WRITER: ROBERT VENDITTI
PENCILLER: RAFA SANDOVAL
INKER: JORDI TARRAGONA
COLORIST: TOMEU MOREY
LETTERER: DAVE SHAR
COVER: SANDOVAL TARRAGONA, MOREY
ASSISTANT EDITOR: ANDREW MARINO
EDITOR: MIKE COTTON
SWEET MOSES, JOHNNY. RAYNER WENT AND TURNED INTO THE ENERGIZER LANTERN.
THAT'S WHY I PUT HIM IN CONTAINMENT, GUY.
IF WE DON'T REDIRECT THE WILLPOWER ENERGY COMING OFF HIM, HE COULD BLOW APART OUR WHOLE HQ.
KYLE, WHAT HAPPENED? WHY ARE YOU WEARING HAL'S RING?

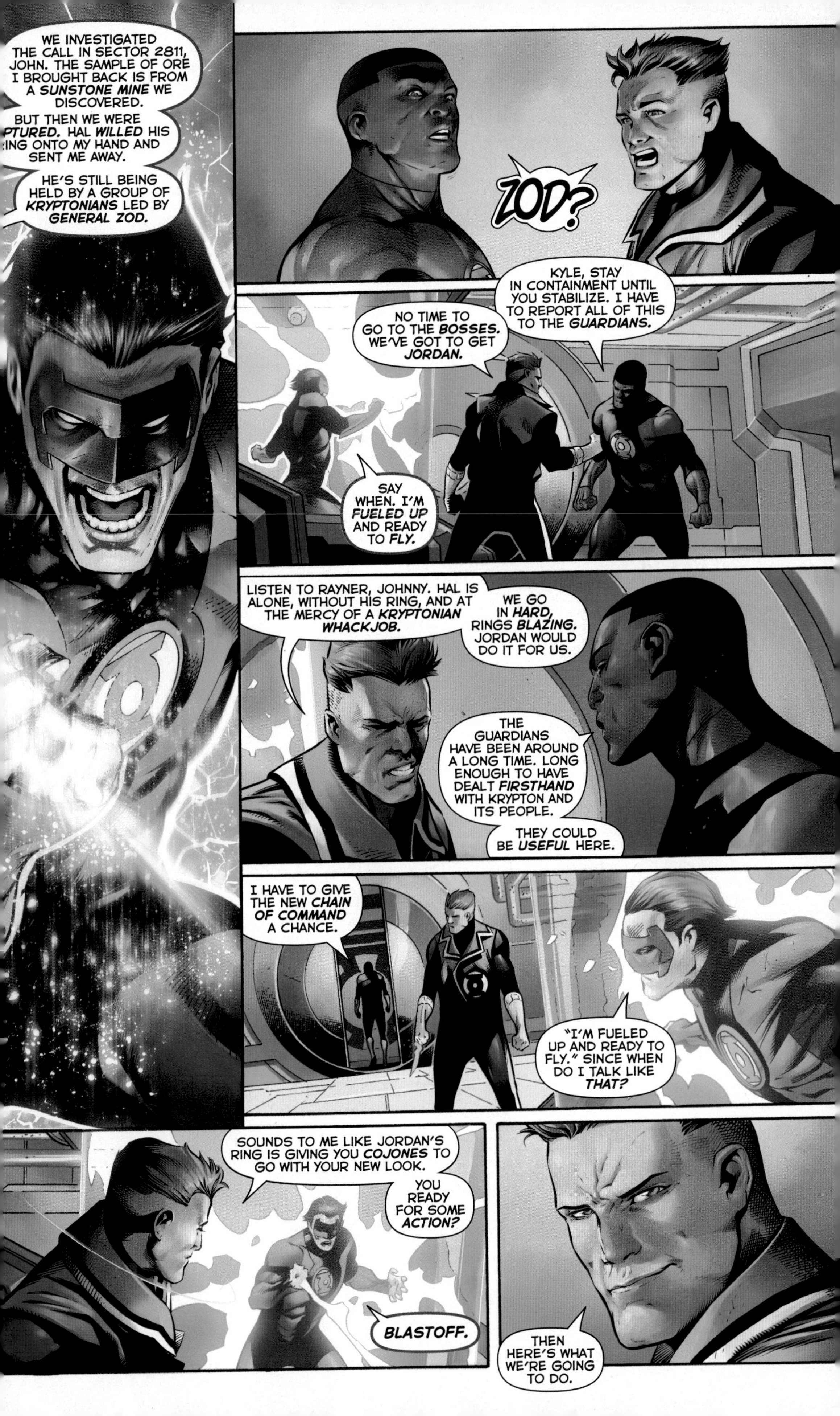

WE INVESTIGATED THE CALL IN SECTOR 2811, JOHN. THE SAMPLE OF ORE I BROUGHT BACK IS FROM A SUNSTONE MINE WE DISCOVERED.
BUT THEN WE WERE PTURED. HAL WILLED HIS ING ONTO MY HAND AND SENT ME AWAY.
HE'S STILL BEING HELD BY A GROUP OF KRYPTONIANS LED BY GENERAL ZOD.
ZOD?
KYLE, STAY IN CONTAINMENT UNTIL YOU STABILIZE. I HAVE TO REPORT ALL OF THIS TO THE GUARDIANS.
NO TIME TO GO TO THE BOSSES. WE'VE GOT TO GET JORDAN.
SAY WHEN. I'M FUELED UP AND READY TO FLY.
LISTEN TO RAYNER, JOHNNY. HAL IS ALONE, WITHOUT HIS RING, AND AT THE MERCY OF A KRYPTONIAN WHACKJOB.
WE GO IN HARD, RINGS BLAZING. JORDAN WOULD DO IT FOR US.
THE GUARDIANS HAVE BEEN AROUND A LONG TIME. LONG ENOUGH TO HAVE DEALT FIRSTHAND WITH KRYPTON AND ITS PEOPLE.
THEY COULD BE USEFUL HERE.
I HAVE TO GIVE THE NEW CHAIN OF COMMAND A CHANCE.
"I'M FUELED UP AND READY TO FLY." SINCE WHEN DO I TALK LIKE THAT?
SOUNDS TO ME LIKE JORDAN'S RING IS GIVING YOU COJONES TO GO WITH YOUR NEW LOOK.
YOU READY FOR SOME ACTION?
BLASTOFF.
THEN HERE'S WHAT WE'RE GOING TO DO.

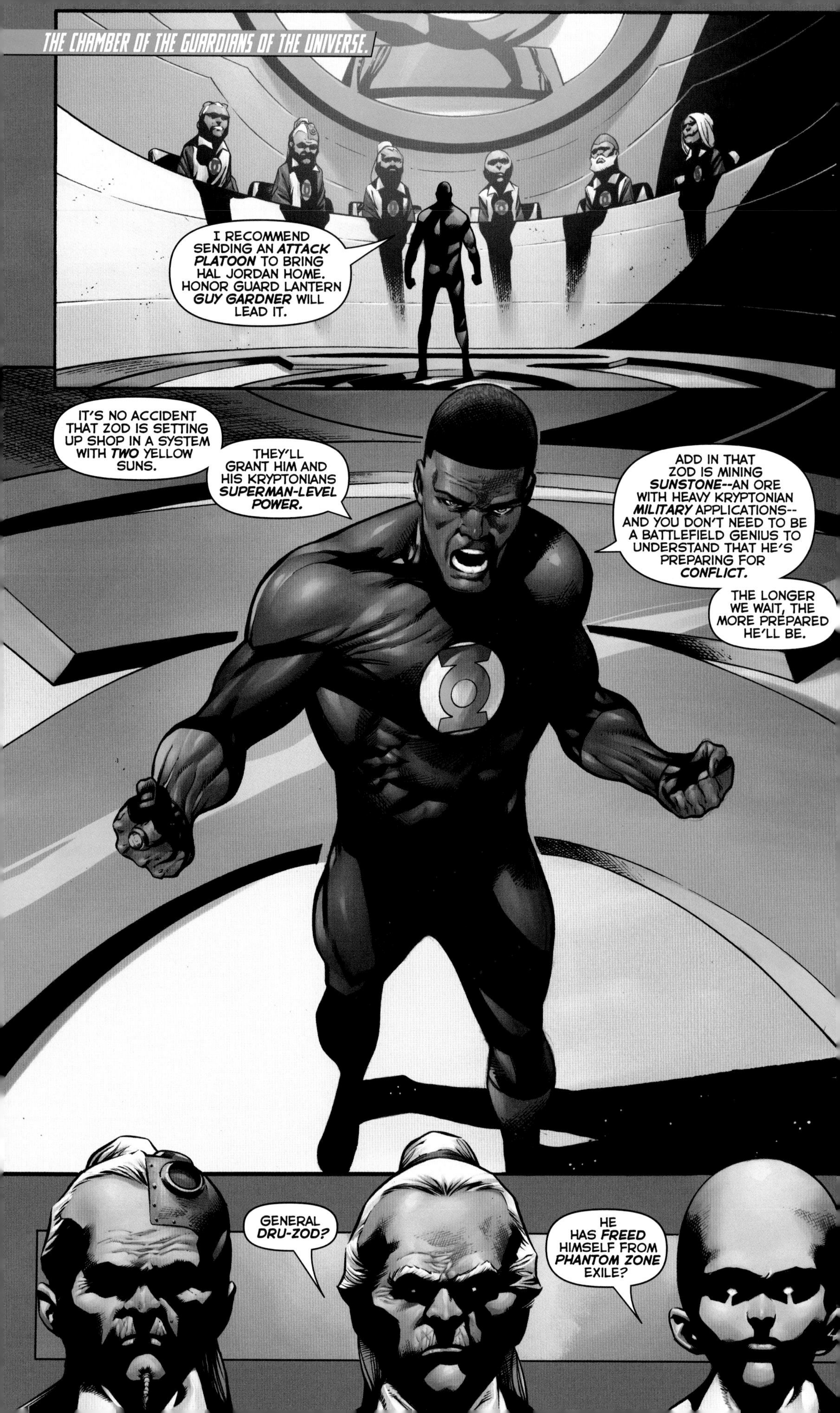
THE CHAMBER OF THE GUARDIANS OF THE UNIVERSE.
I RECOMMEND SENDING AN ATTACK PLATOON TO BRING HAL JORDAN HOME. HONOR GUARD LANTERN GUY GARDNER WILL LEAD IT.
IT'S NO ACCIDENT THAT ZOD IS SETTING UP SHOP IN A SYSTEM WITH TWO YELLOW SUNS.
THEY'LL GRANT HIM AND HIS KRYPTONIANS SUPERMAN-LEVEL POWER.
ADD IN THAT ZOD IS MINING SUNSTONE--AN ORE WITH HEAVY KRYPTONIAN MILITARY APPLICATIONS--AND YOU DON'T NEED TO BE A BATTLEFIELD GENIUS TO UNDERSTAND THAT HE'S PREPARING FOR CONFLICT.
THE LONGER WE WAIT, THE MORE PREPARED HE'LL BE.
GENERAL DRU-ZOD?
HE HAS FREED HIMSELF FROM PHANTOM ZONE EXILE?

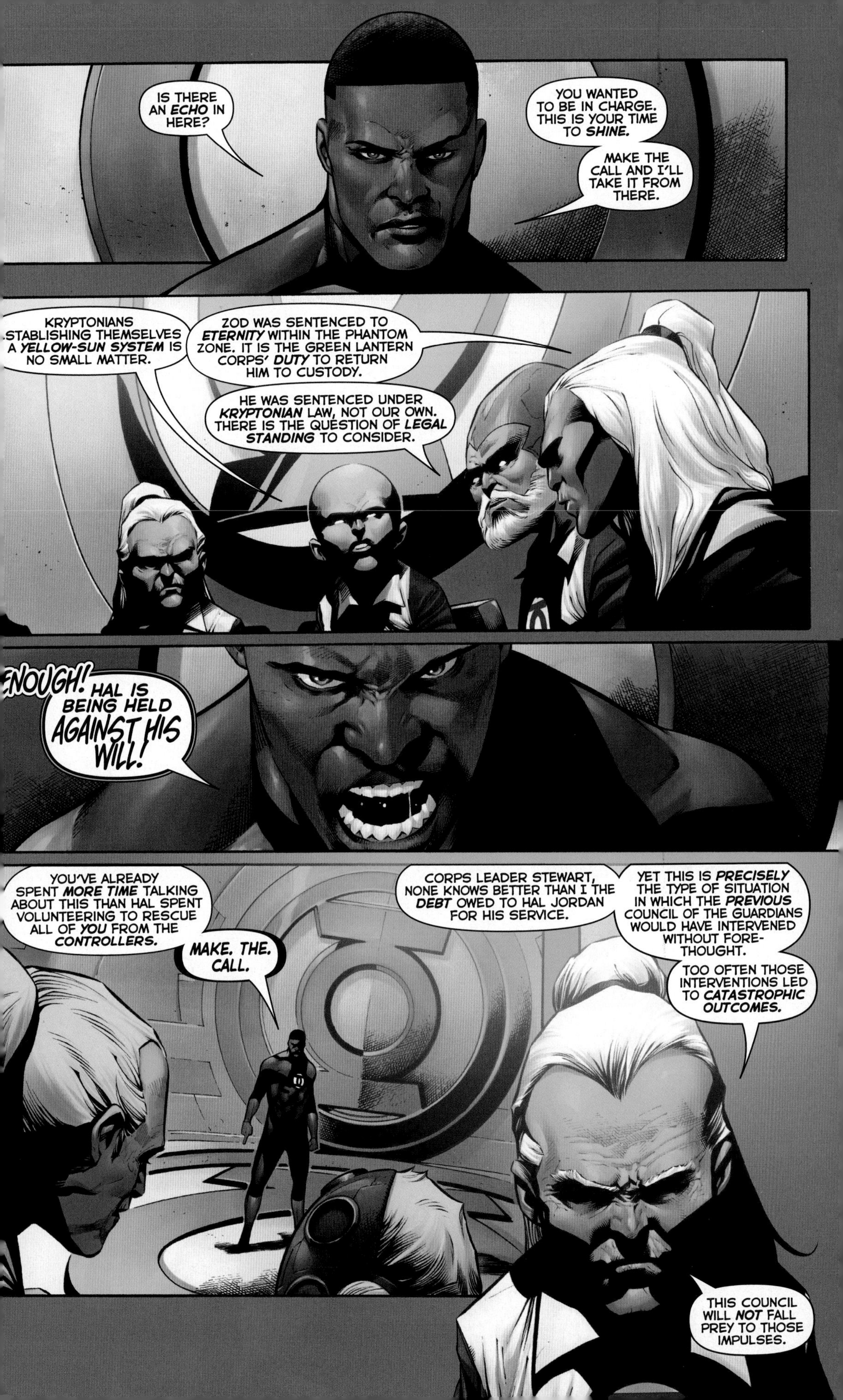
IS THERE AN ECHO IN HERE?
YOU WANTED TO BE IN CHARGE. THIS IS YOUR TIME TO SHINE.
MAKE THE CALL AND I'LL TAKE IT FROM THERE.
KRYPTONIANS STABLISHING THEMSELVES A YELLOW-SUN SYSTEM IS NO SMALL MATTER.
ZOD WAS SENTENCED TO ETERNITY WITHIN THE PHANTOM ZONE. IT IS THE GREEN LANTERN CORPS' DUTY TO RETURN HIM TO CUSTODY.
HE WAS SENTENCED UNDER KRYPTONIAN LAW, NOT OUR OWN. THERE IS THE QUESTION OF LEGAL STANDING TO CONSIDER.
ENOUGH! HAL IS BEING HELD AGAINST HIS WILL!
YOU'VE ALREADY SPENT MORE TIME TALKING ABOUT THIS THAN HAL SPENT VOLUNTEERING TO RESCUE ALL OF YOU FROM THE CONTROLLERS.
MAKE. THE. CALL.
CORPS LEADER STEWART, NONE KNOWS BETTER THAN I THE DEBT OWED TO HAL JORDAN FOR HIS SERVICE.
YET THIS IS PRECISELY THE TYPE OF SITUATION IN WHICH THE PREVIOUS COUNCIL OF THE GUARDIANS WOULD HAVE INTERVENED WITHOUT FORE-THOUGHT.
TOO OFTEN THOSE INTERVENTIONS LED TO CATASTROPHIC OUTCOMES.
THIS COUNCIL WILL NOT FALL PREY TO THOSE IMPULSES.

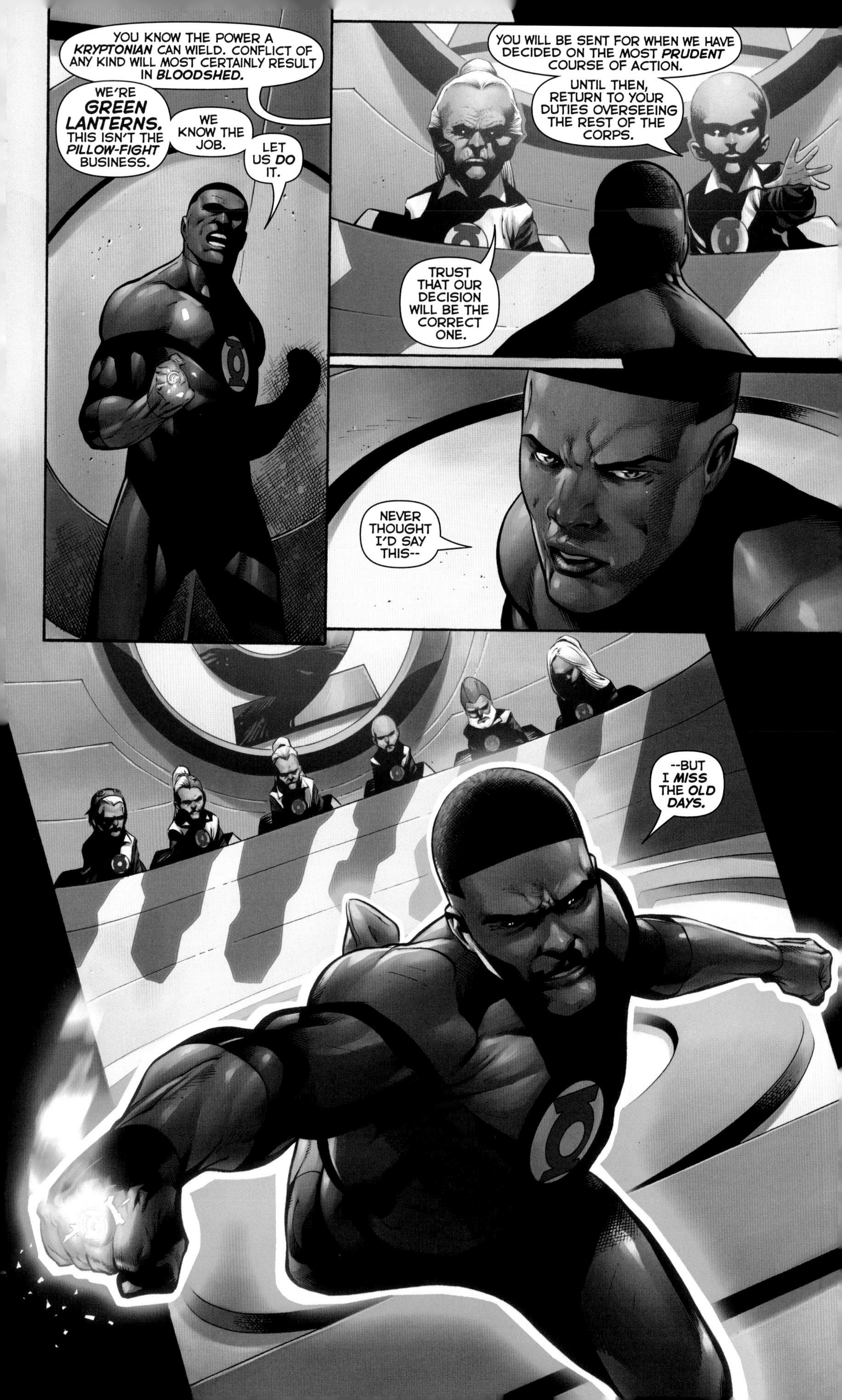

YOU KNOW THE POWER A *KRYPTONIAN* CAN WIELD. CONFLICT OF ANY KIND WILL MOST CERTAINLY RESULT IN *BLOODSHED.*
WE'RE **GREEN LANTERNS.** THIS ISN'T THE *PILLOW-FIGHT* BUSINESS.
WE KNOW THE JOB.
LET US *DO* IT.
YOU WILL BE SENT FOR WHEN WE HAVE DECIDED ON THE MOST *PRUDENT* COURSE OF ACTION.
UNTIL THEN, RETURN TO YOUR DUTIES OVERSEEING THE REST OF THE CORPS.
TRUST THAT OUR DECISION WILL BE THE CORRECT ONE.
NEVER THOUGHT I'D SAY THIS--
--BUT I *MISS* THE *OLD DAYS.*

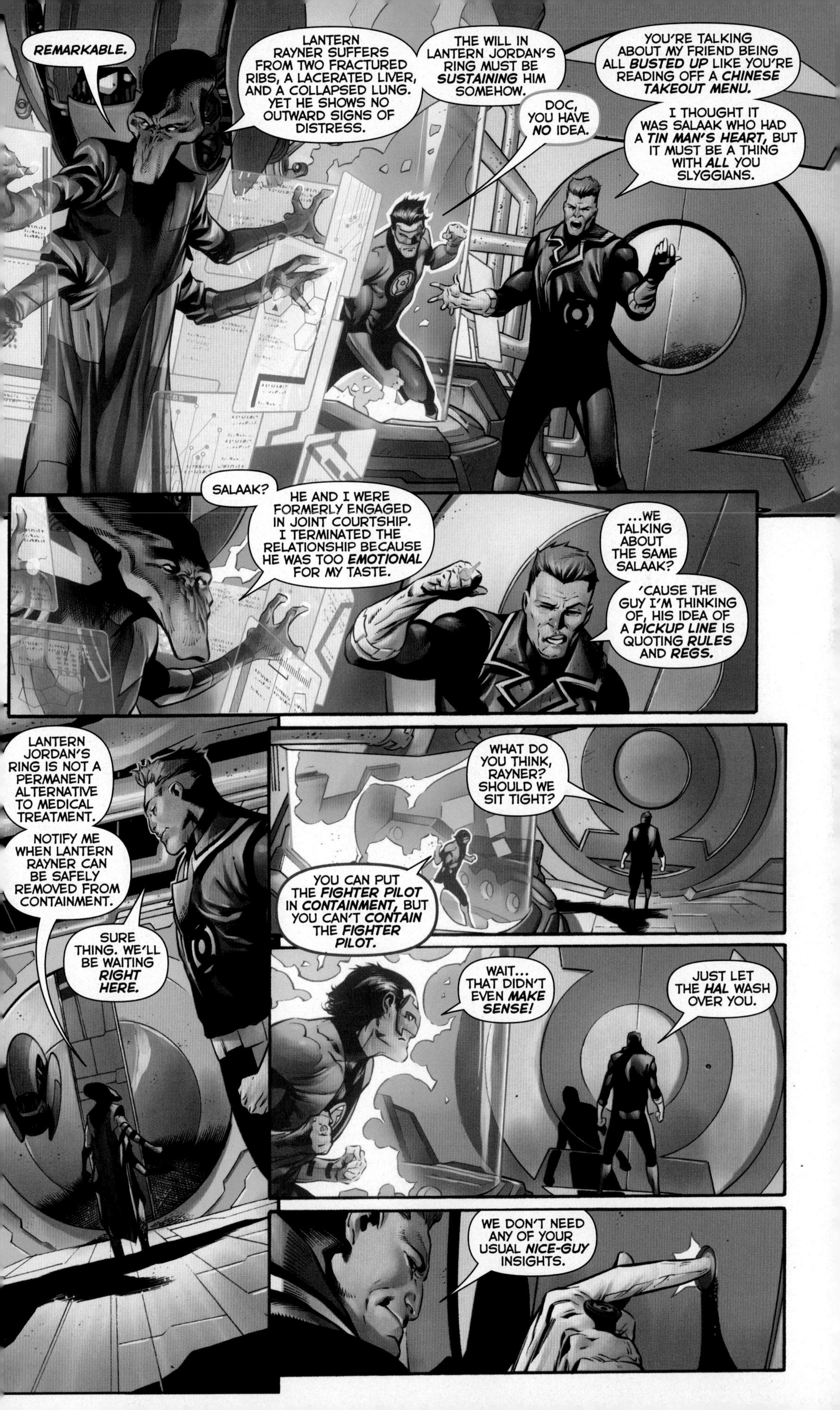

REMARKABLE.
LANTERN RAYNER SUFFERS FROM TWO FRACTURED RIBS, A LACERATED LIVER, AND A COLLAPSED LUNG. YET HE SHOWS NO OUTWARD SIGNS OF DISTRESS.
THE WILL IN LANTERN JORDAN'S RING MUST BE SUSTAINING HIM SOMEHOW.
DOC, YOU HAVE NO IDEA.
YOU'RE TALKING ABOUT MY FRIEND BEING ALL BUSTED UP LIKE YOU'RE READING OFF A CHINESE TAKEOUT MENU.
I THOUGHT IT WAS SALAAK WHO HAD A TIN MAN'S HEART, BUT IT MUST BE A THING WITH ALL YOU SLYGGIANS.
SALAAK?
HE AND I WERE FORMERLY ENGAGED IN JOINT COURTSHIP. I TERMINATED THE RELATIONSHIP BECAUSE HE WAS TOO EMOTIONAL FOR MY TASTE.
...WE TALKING ABOUT THE SAME SALAAK?
'CAUSE THE GUY I'M THINKING OF, HIS IDEA OF A PICKUP LINE IS QUOTING RULES AND REGS.
LANTERN JORDAN'S RING IS NOT A PERMANENT ALTERNATIVE TO MEDICAL TREATMENT.
NOTIFY ME WHEN LANTERN RAYNER CAN BE SAFELY REMOVED FROM CONTAINMENT.
SURE THING. WE'LL BE WAITING RIGHT HERE.
WHAT DO YOU THINK, RAYNER? SHOULD WE SIT TIGHT?
YOU CAN PUT THE FIGHTER PILOT IN CONTAINMENT, BUT YOU CAN'T CONTAIN THE FIGHTER PILOT.
WAIT... THAT DIDN'T EVEN MAKE SENSE!
JUST LET THE HAL WASH OVER YOU.
WE DON'T NEED ANY OF YOUR USUAL NICE-GUY INSIGHTS.

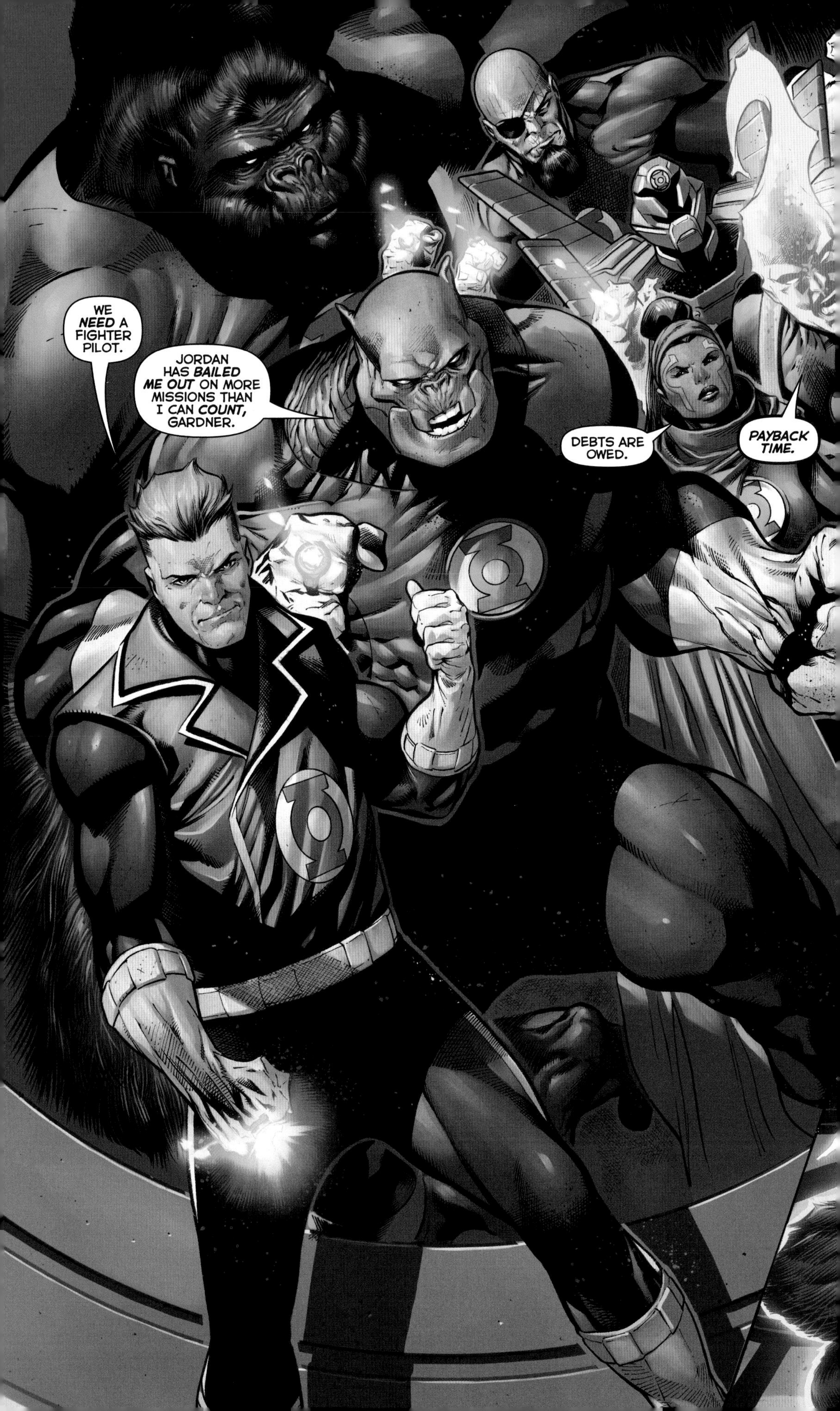
WE NEED A FIGHTER PILOT.
JORDAN HAS BAILED ME OUT ON MORE MISSIONS THAN I CAN COUNT, GARDNER.
DEBTS ARE OWED.
PAYBACK TIME.

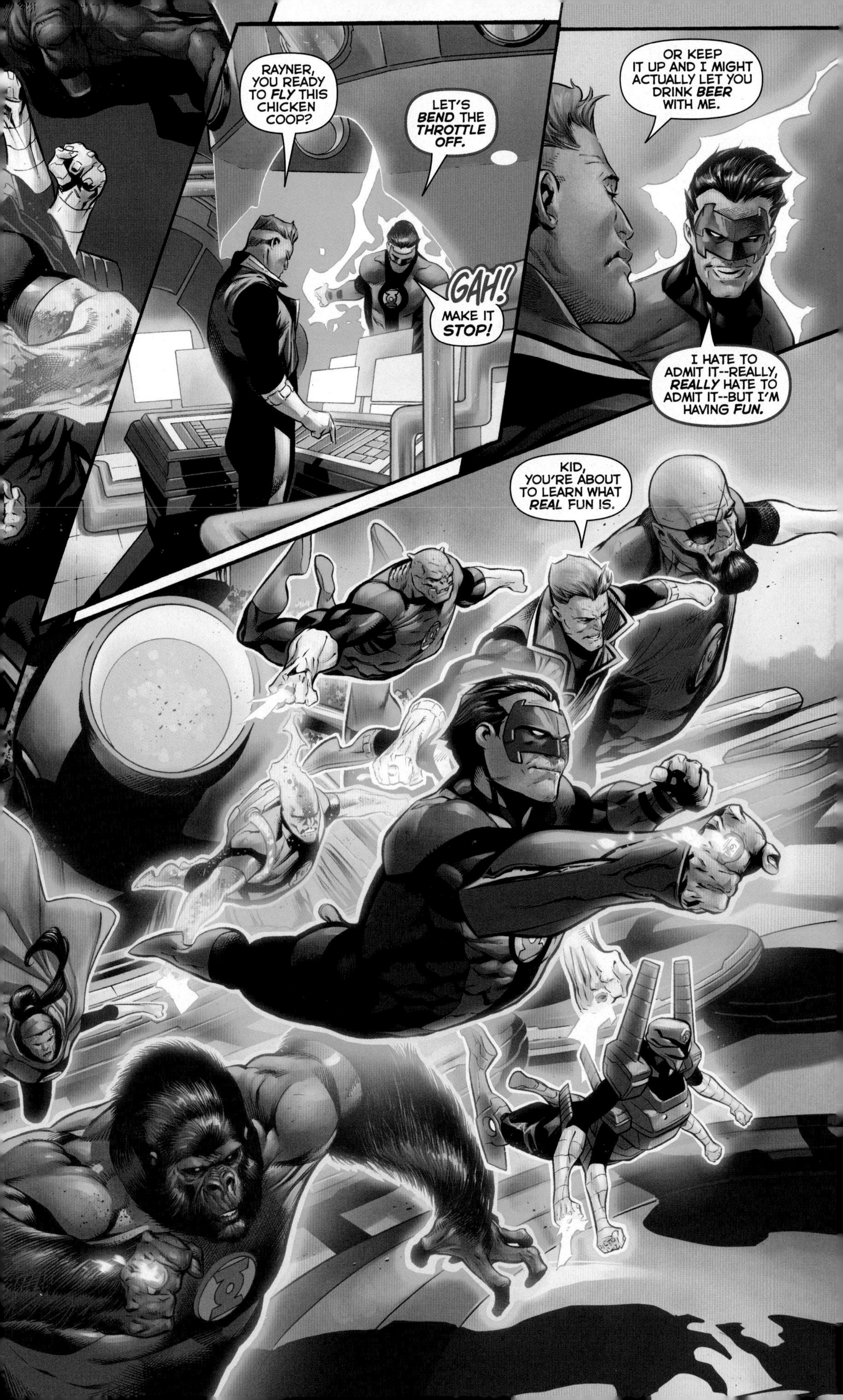

RAYNER, YOU READY TO FLY THIS CHICKEN COOP?
LET'S BEND THE THROTTLE OFF.
GAH!
MAKE IT STOP!
OR KEEP IT UP AND I MIGHT ACTUALLY LET YOU DRINK BEER WITH ME.
I HATE TO ADMIT IT--REALLY, REALLY HATE TO ADMIT IT--BUT I'M HAVING FUN.
KID, YOU'RE ABOUT TO LEARN WHAT REAL FUN IS.

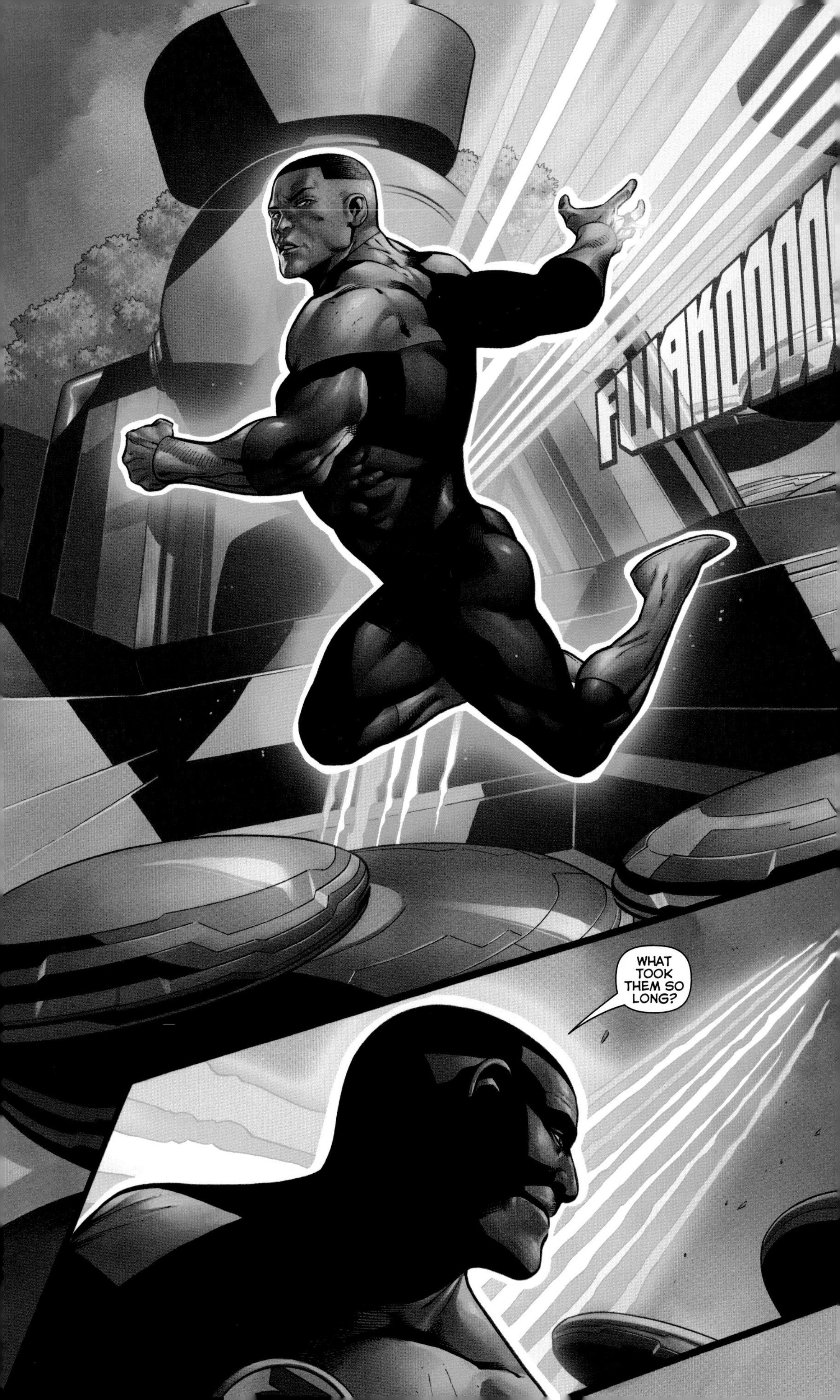
FWAKOOO
WHAT TOOK THEM SO LONG?

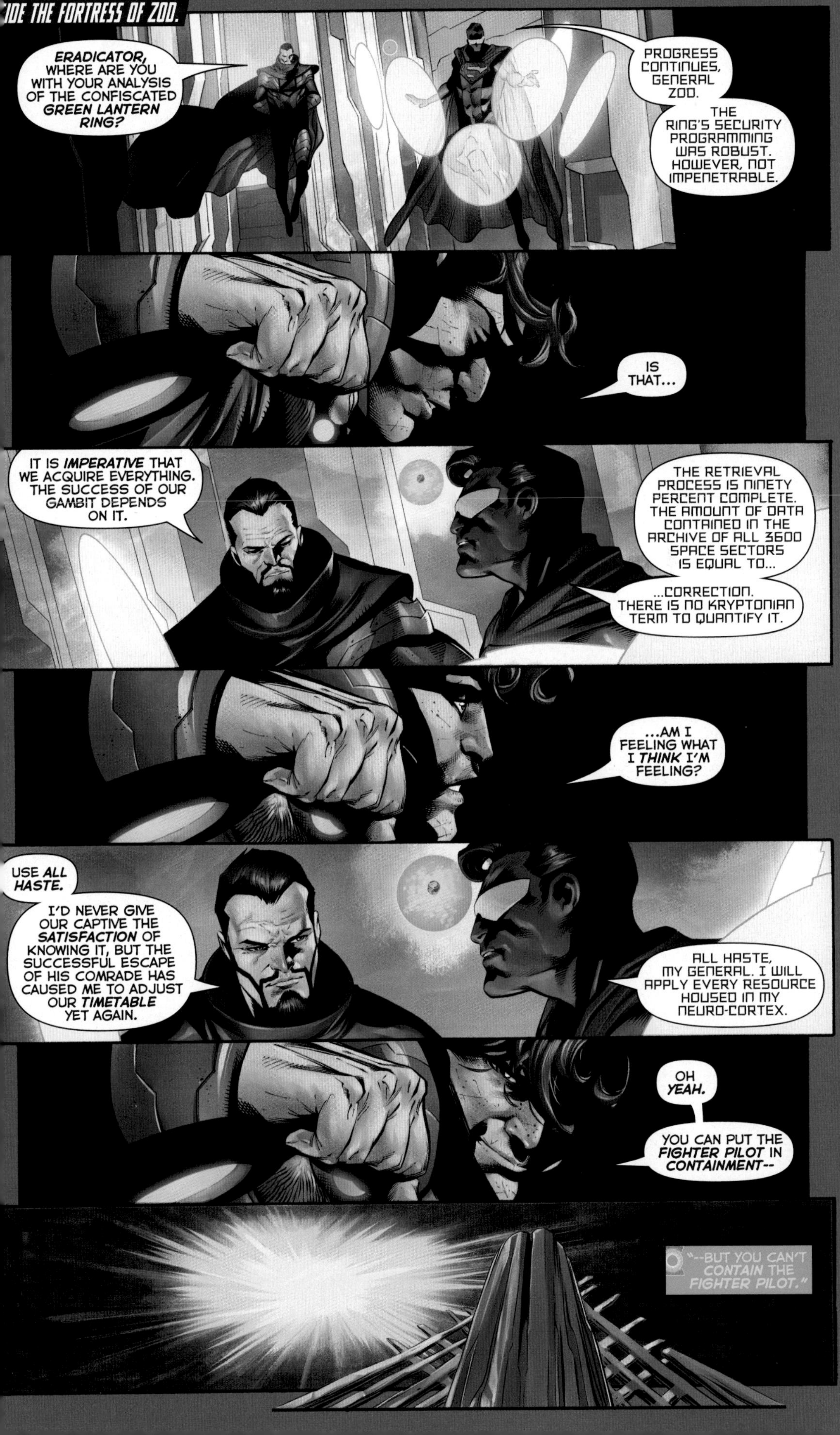
IDE THE FORTRESS OF ZOD.
ERADICATOR, WHERE ARE YOU WITH YOUR ANALYSIS OF THE CONFISCATED GREEN LANTERN RING?
PROGRESS CONTINUES, GENERAL ZOD.
THE RING'S SECURITY PROGRAMMING WAS ROBUST. HOWEVER, NOT IMPENETRABLE.
IS THAT...
IT IS IMPERATIVE THAT WE ACQUIRE EVERYTHING. THE SUCCESS OF OUR GAMBIT DEPENDS ON IT.
THE RETRIEVAL PROCESS IS NINETY PERCENT COMPLETE. THE AMOUNT OF DATA CONTAINED IN THE ARCHIVE OF ALL 3600 SPACE SECTORS IS EQUAL TO...
...CORRECTION. THERE IS NO KRYPTONIAN TERM TO QUANTIFY IT.
...AM I FEELING WHAT I THINK I'M FEELING?
USE ALL HASTE.
I'D NEVER GIVE OUR CAPTIVE THE SATISFACTION OF KNOWING IT, BUT THE SUCCESSFUL ESCAPE OF HIS COMRADE HAS CAUSED ME TO ADJUST OUR TIMETABLE YET AGAIN.
ALL HASTE, MY GENERAL. I WILL APPLY EVERY RESOURCE HOUSED IN MY NEURO-CORTEX.
OH YEAH.
YOU CAN PUT THE FIGHTER PILOT IN CONTAINMENT--
"--BUT YOU CAN'T CONTAIN THE FIGHTER PILOT."

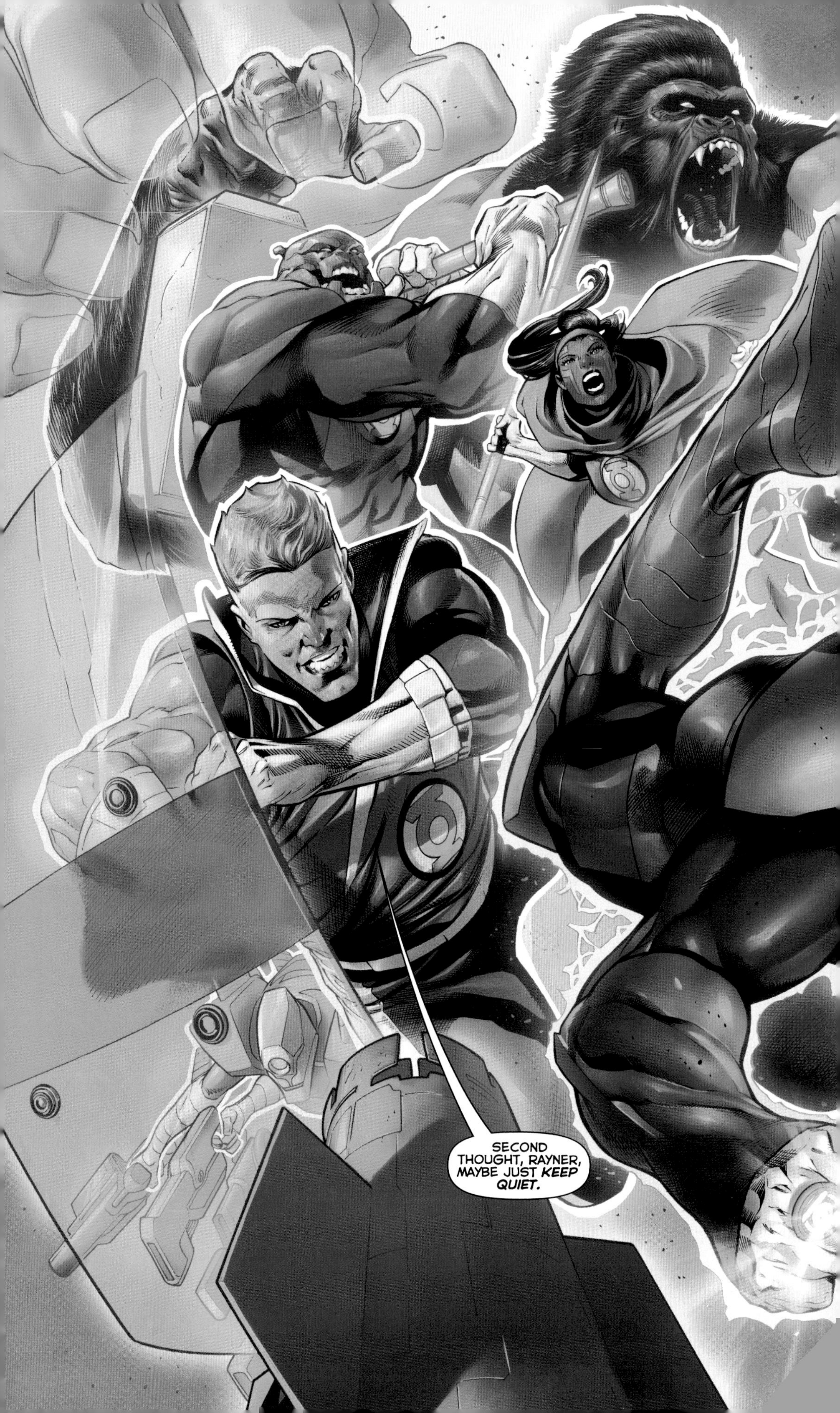
SECOND THOUGHT, RAYNER, MAYBE JUST *KEEP QUIET*.

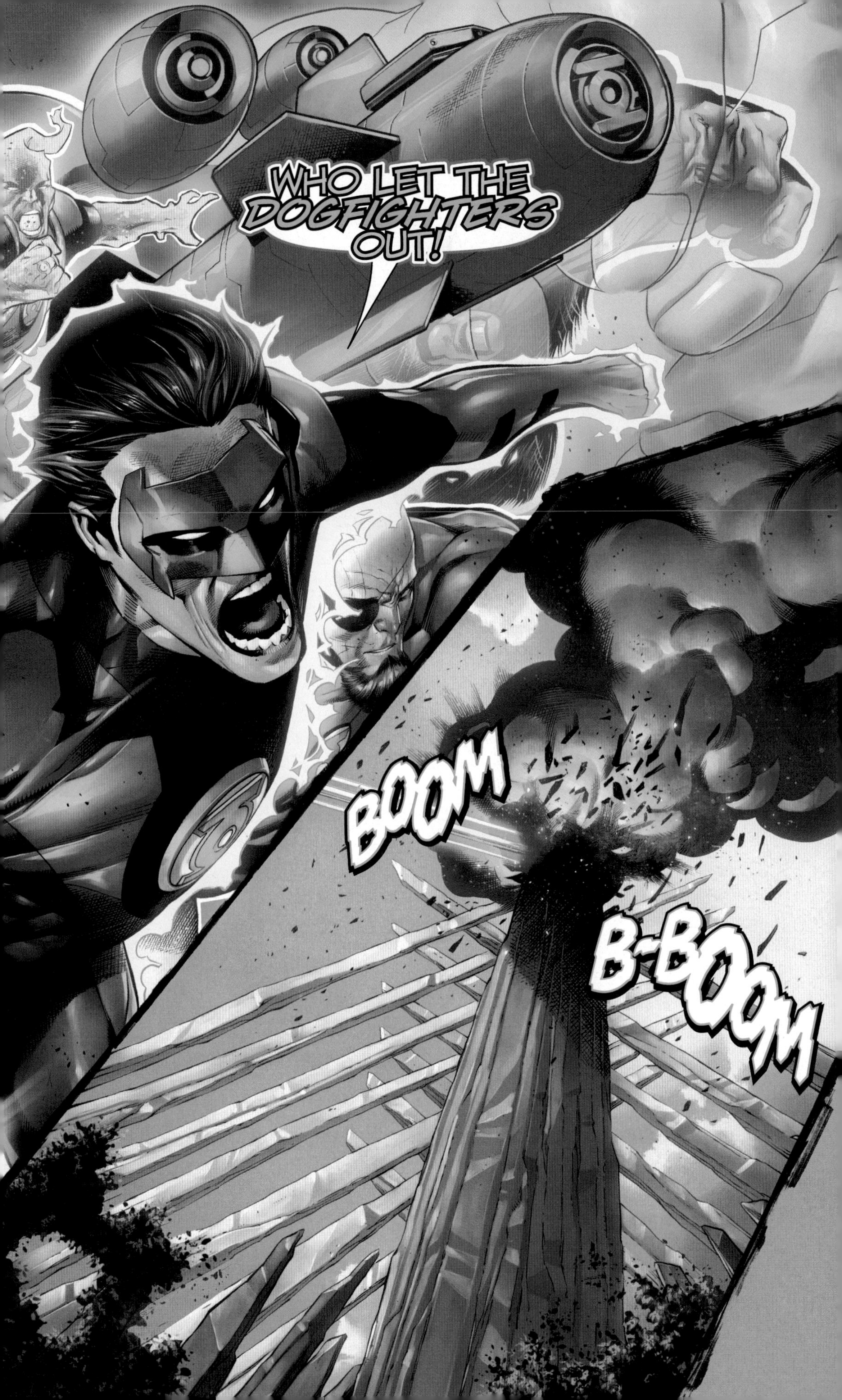
WHO LET THE DOGFIGHTERS OUT!
BOOM
B-BOOM

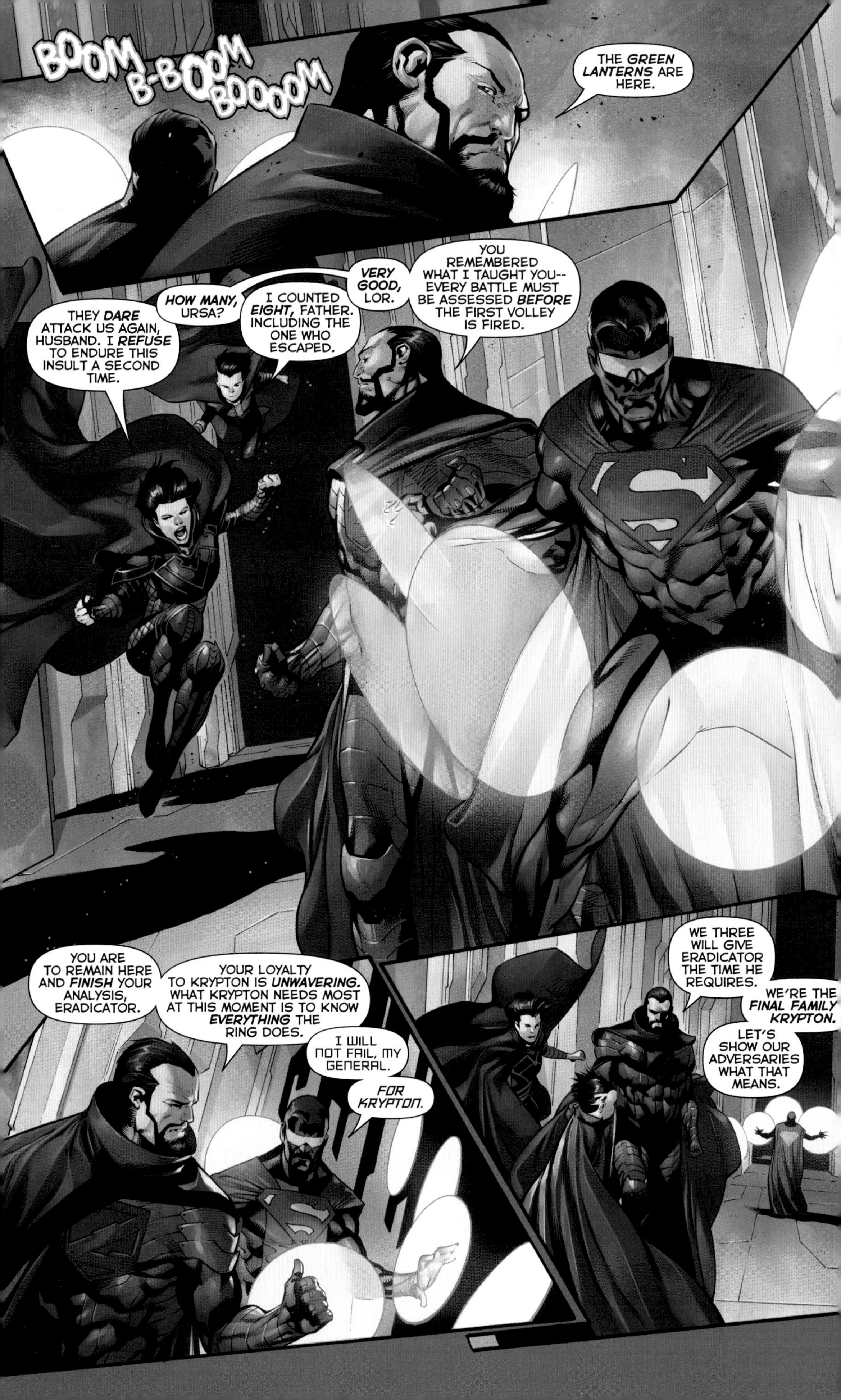
BOOM B-BOOM BOOOOM
THE GREEN LANTERNS ARE HERE.
THEY DARE ATTACK US AGAIN, HUSBAND. I REFUSE TO ENDURE THIS INSULT A SECOND TIME.
HOW MANY, URSA?
I COUNTED EIGHT, FATHER. INCLUDING THE ONE WHO ESCAPED.
VERY GOOD, LOR.
YOU REMEMBERED WHAT I TAUGHT YOU-- EVERY BATTLE MUST BE ASSESSED BEFORE THE FIRST VOLLEY IS FIRED.
YOU ARE TO REMAIN HERE AND FINISH YOUR ANALYSIS, ERADICATOR.
YOUR LOYALTY TO KRYPTON IS UNWAVERING. WHAT KRYPTON NEEDS MOST AT THIS MOMENT IS TO KNOW EVERYTHING THE RING DOES.
I WILL NOT FAIL, MY GENERAL.
FOR KRYPTON.
WE THREE WILL GIVE ERADICATOR THE TIME HE REQUIRES.
WE'RE THE FINAL FAMILY KRYPTON.
LET'S SHOW OUR ADVERSARIES WHAT THAT MEANS.

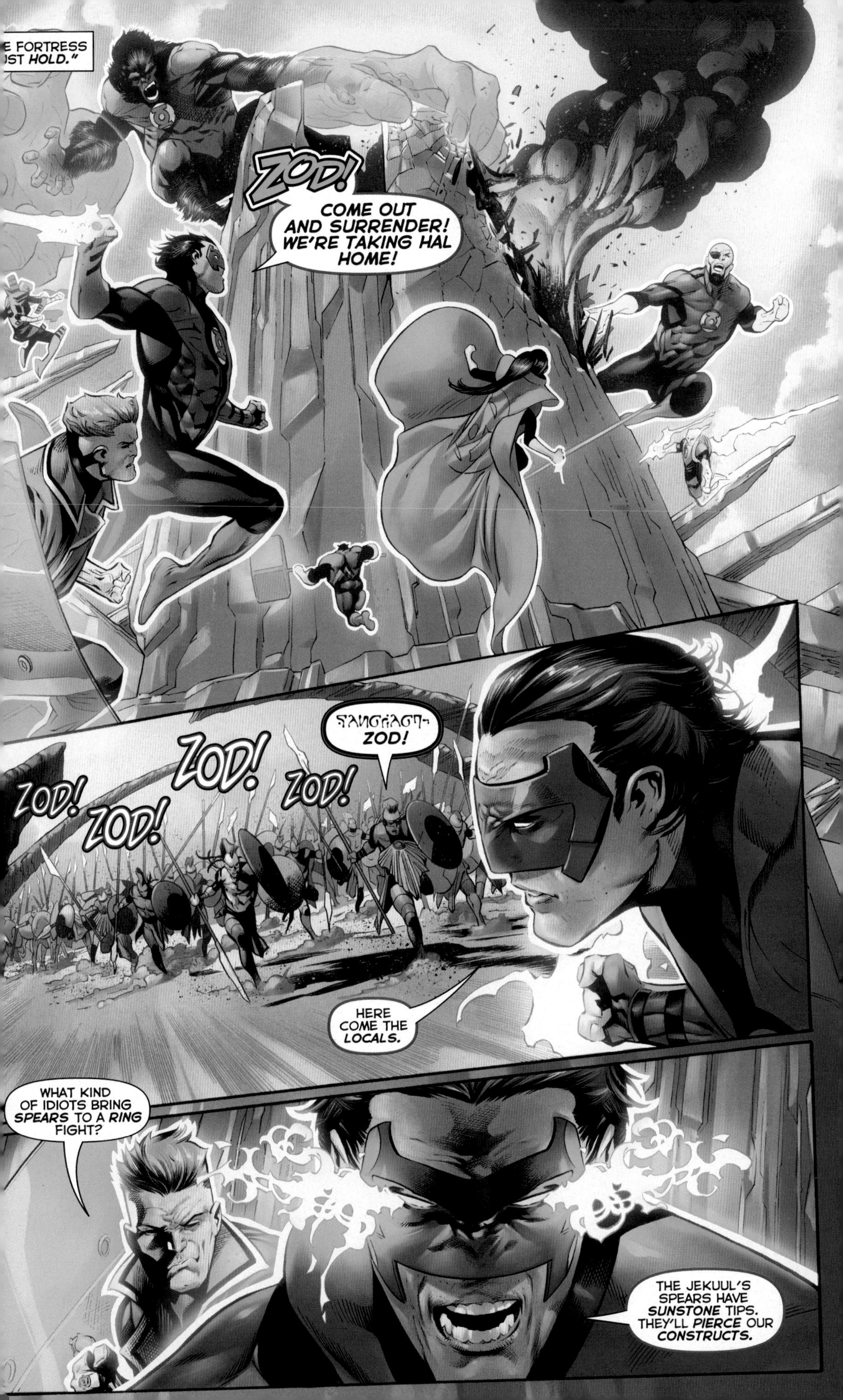

E FORTRESS
UST HOLD."
ZOD!
COME OUT AND SURRENDER! WE'RE TAKING HAL HOME!
ZOD!
ZOD!
ZOD!
ZOD!
ZOD!
HERE COME THE LOCALS.
WHAT KIND OF IDIOTS BRING SPEARS TO A RING FIGHT?
THE JEKUUL'S SPEARS HAVE SUNSTONE TIPS. THEY'LL PIERCE OUR CONSTRUCTS.

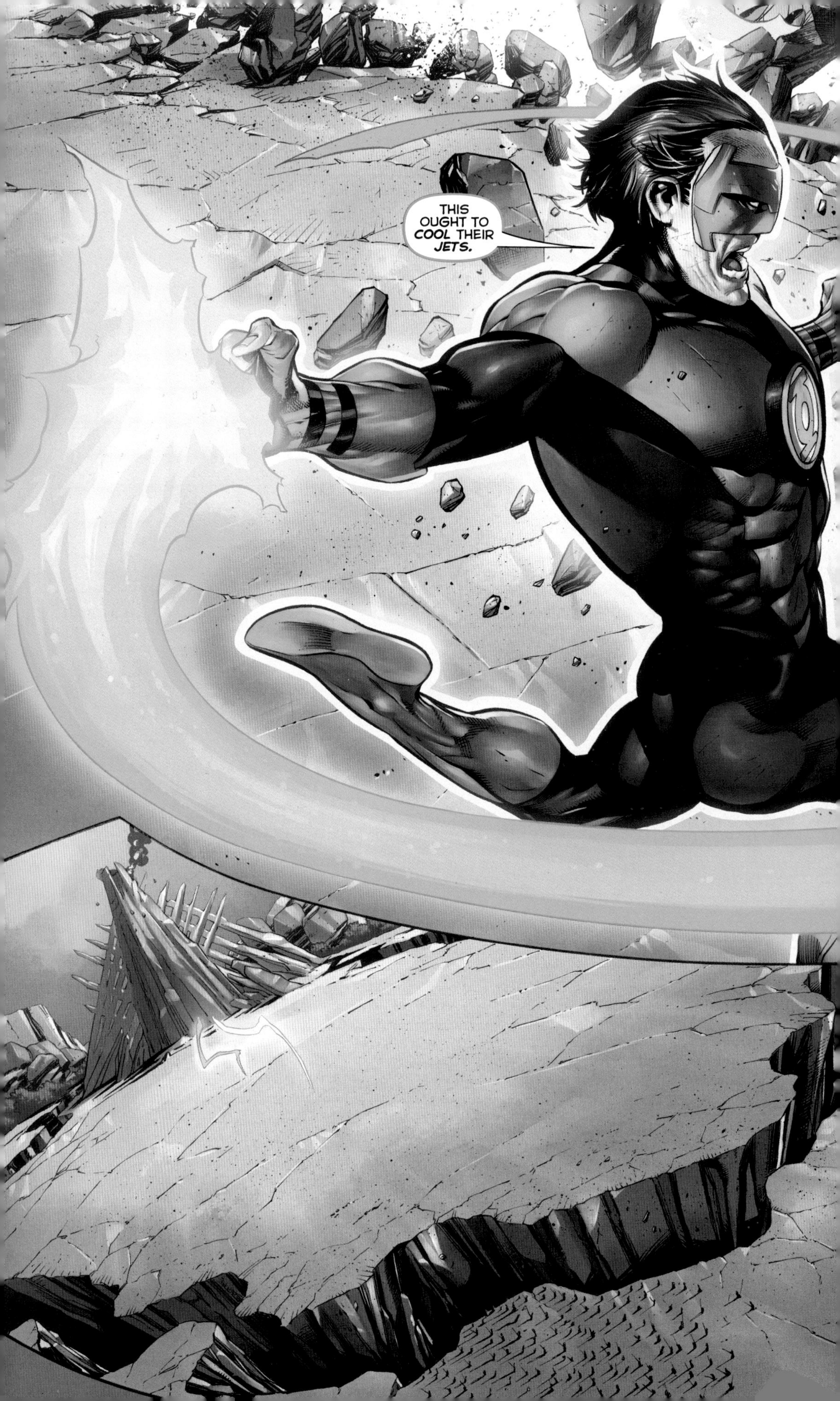
THIS OUGHT TO COOL THEIR JETS.

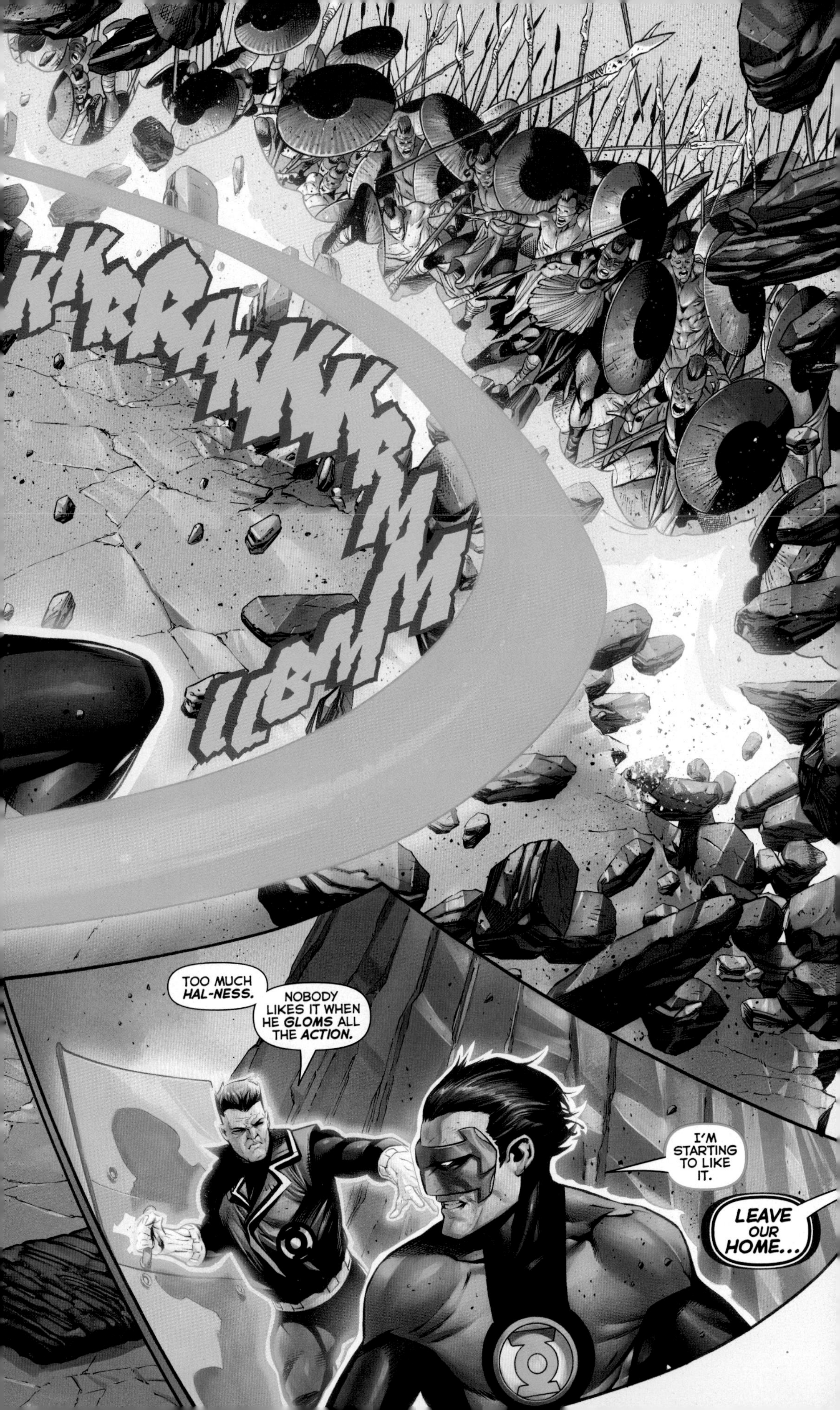

KKRRAKKKKRRRMMM
TOO MUCH HAL-NESS.
NOBODY LIKES IT WHEN HE GLOMS ALL THE ACTION.
I'M STARTING TO LIKE IT.
LEAVE OUR HOME...

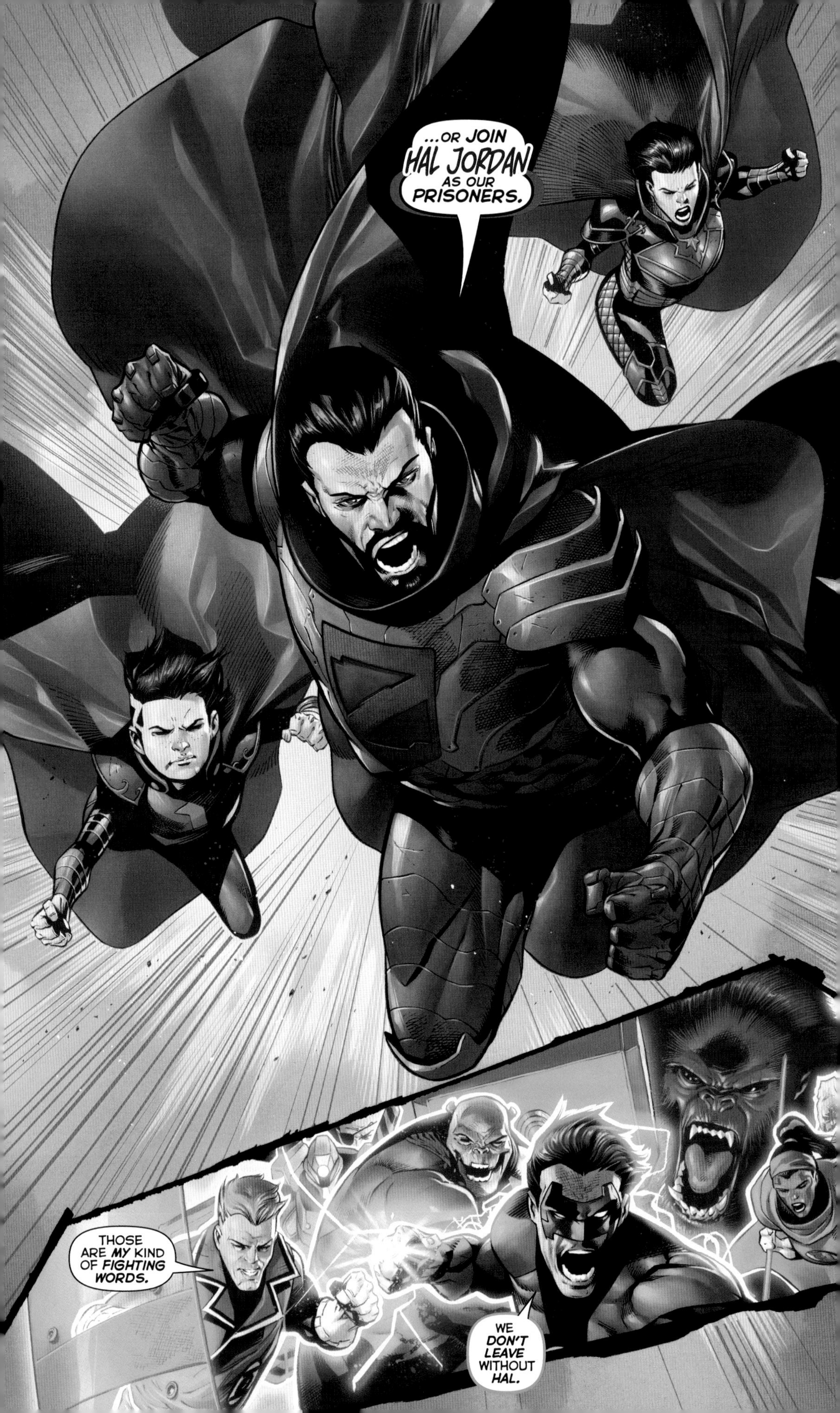
...OR JOIN HAL JORDAN AS OUR PRISONERS.
THOSE ARE MY KIND OF FIGHTING WORDS.
WE DON'T LEAVE WITHOUT HAL.

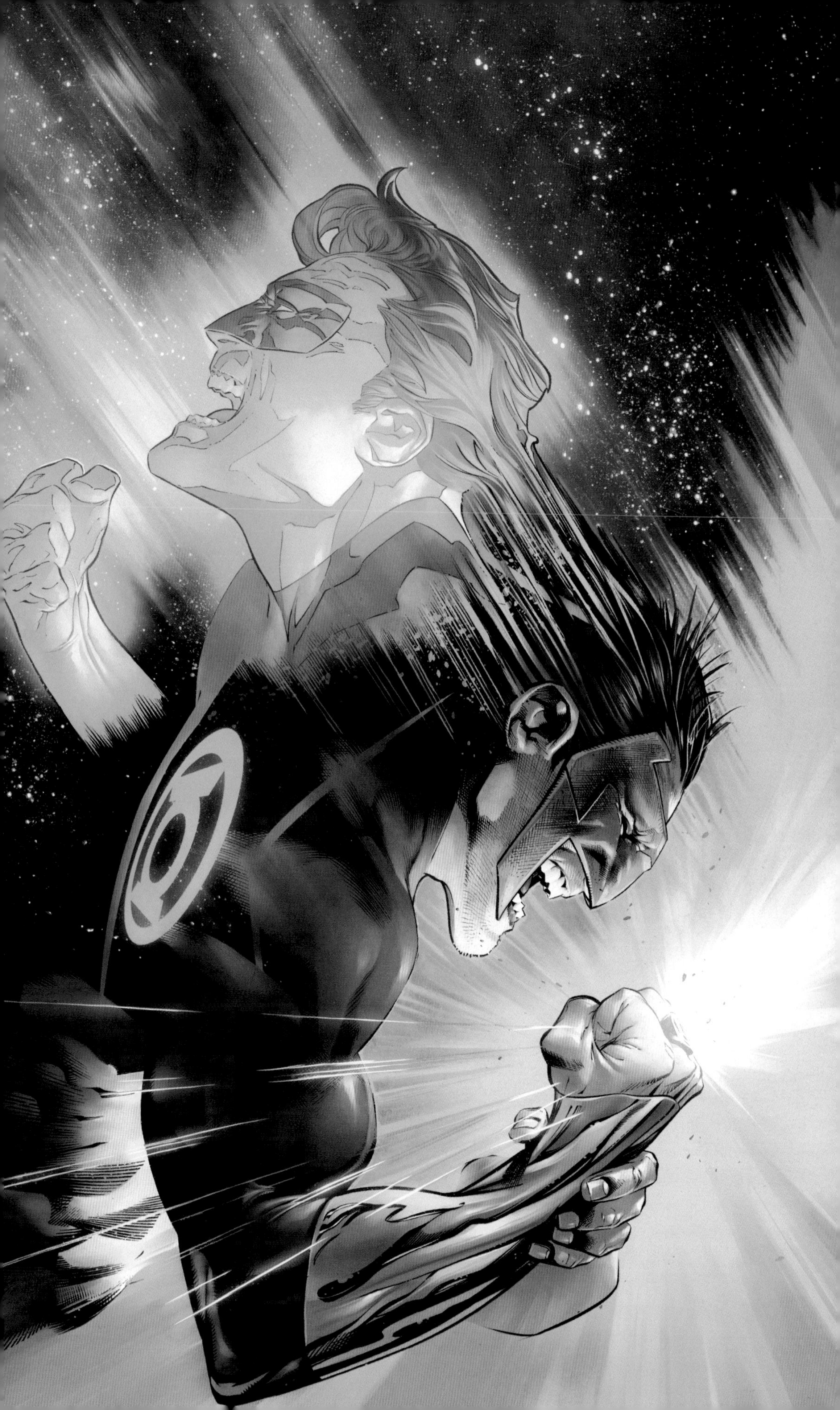

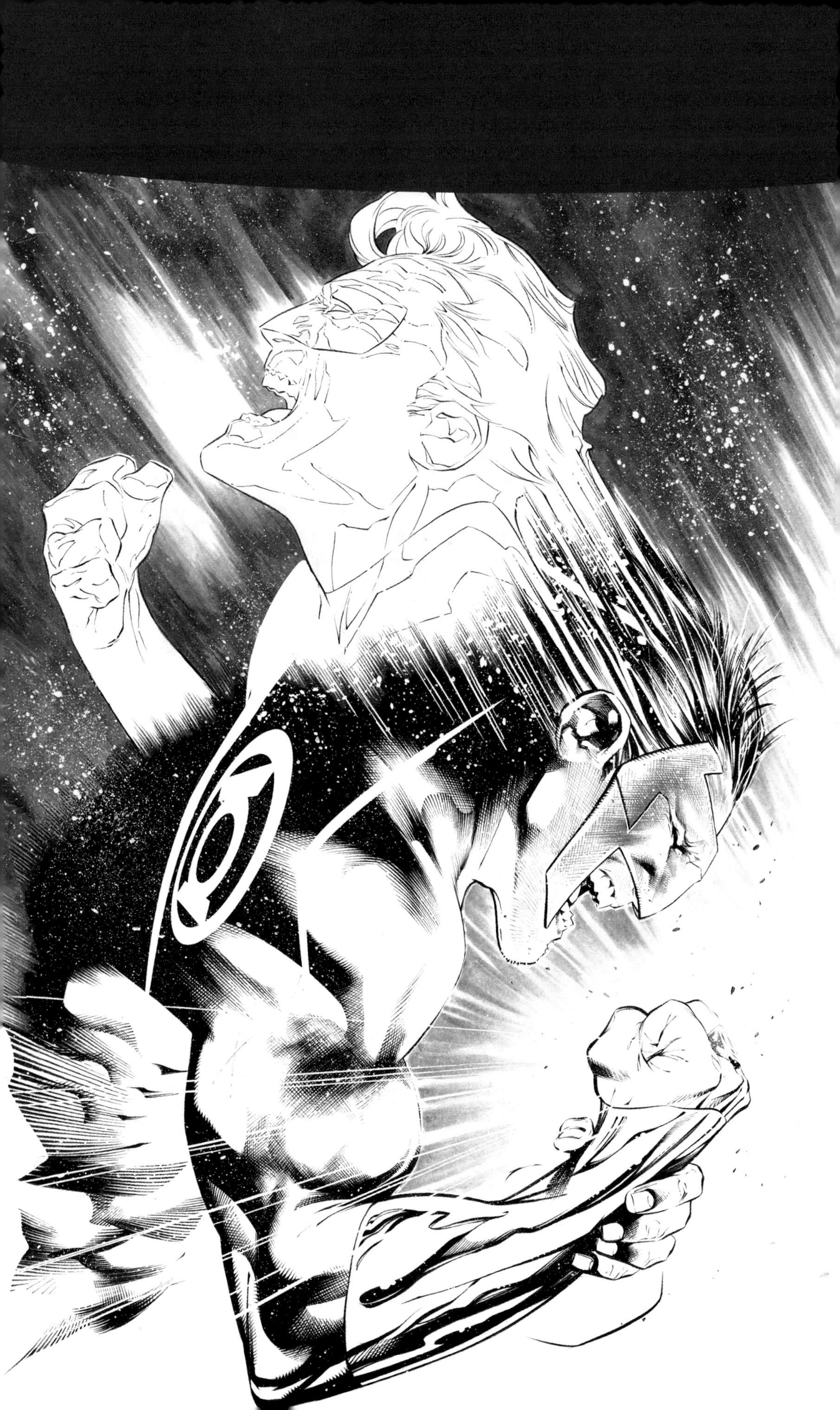

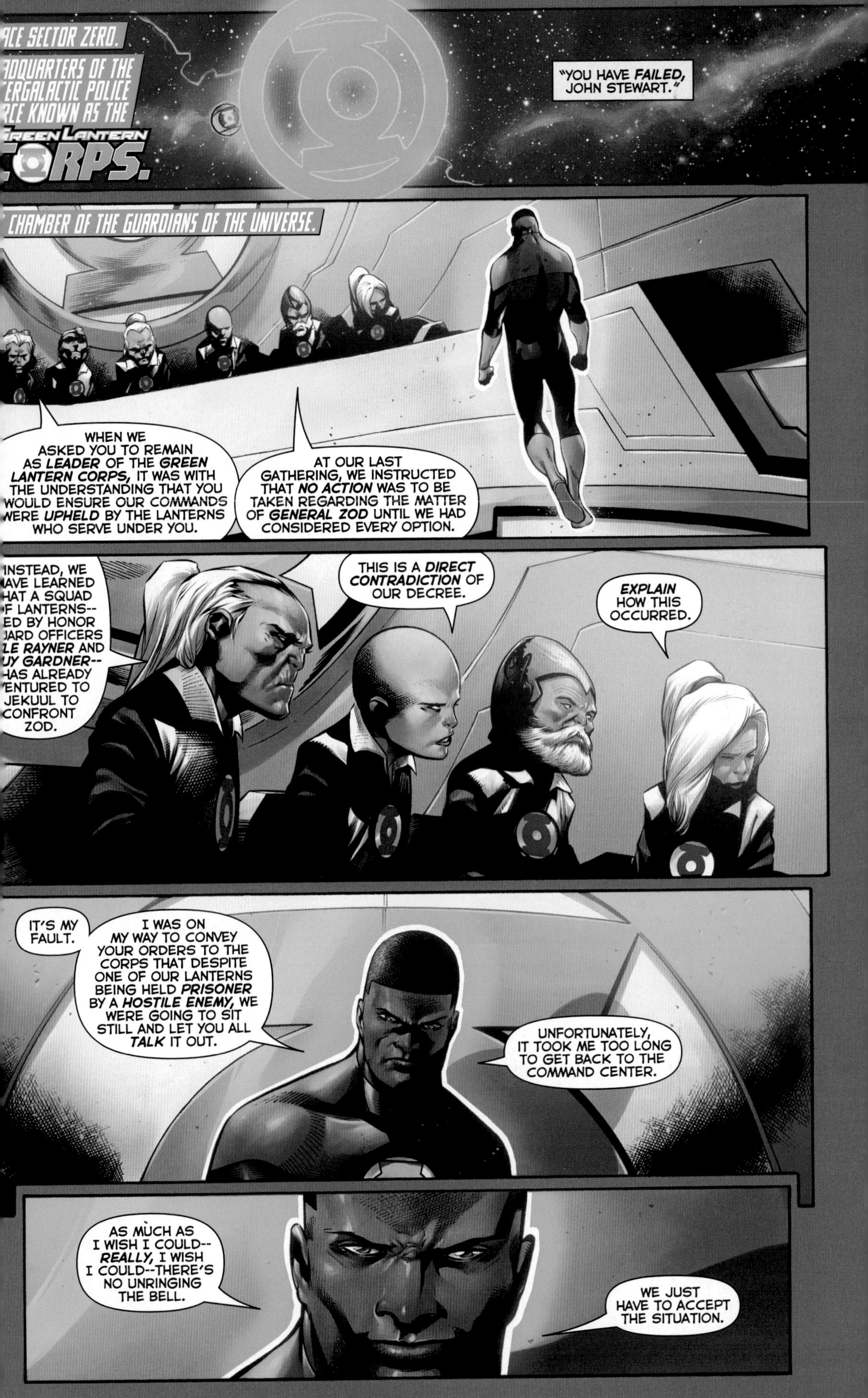
ACE SECTOR ZERO.
ADQUARTERS OF THE ERGALACTIC POLICE RCE KNOWN AS THE GREEN LANTERN CORPS.
"YOU HAVE FAILED, JOHN STEWART."
CHAMBER OF THE GUARDIANS OF THE UNIVERSE.
WHEN WE ASKED YOU TO REMAIN AS LEADER OF THE GREEN LANTERN CORPS, IT WAS WITH THE UNDERSTANDING THAT YOU WOULD ENSURE OUR COMMANDS WERE UPHELD BY THE LANTERNS WHO SERVE UNDER YOU.
AT OUR LAST GATHERING, WE INSTRUCTED THAT NO ACTION WAS TO BE TAKEN REGARDING THE MATTER OF GENERAL ZOD UNTIL WE HAD CONSIDERED EVERY OPTION.
INSTEAD, WE AVE LEARNED HAT A SQUAD F LANTERNS-- ED BY HONOR UARD OFFICERS LE RAYNER AND UY GARDNER-- HAS ALREADY VENTURED TO JEKUUL TO CONFRONT ZOD.
THIS IS A DIRECT CONTRADICTION OF OUR DECREE.
EXPLAIN HOW THIS OCCURRED.
IT'S MY FAULT.
I WAS ON MY WAY TO CONVEY YOUR ORDERS TO THE CORPS THAT DESPITE ONE OF OUR LANTERNS BEING HELD PRISONER BY A HOSTILE ENEMY, WE WERE GOING TO SIT STILL AND LET YOU ALL TALK IT OUT.
UNFORTUNATELY, IT TOOK ME TOO LONG TO GET BACK TO THE COMMAND CENTER.
AS MUCH AS I WISH I COULD-- REALLY, I WISH I COULD--THERE'S NO UNRINGING THE BELL.
WE JUST HAVE TO ACCEPT THE SITUATION.

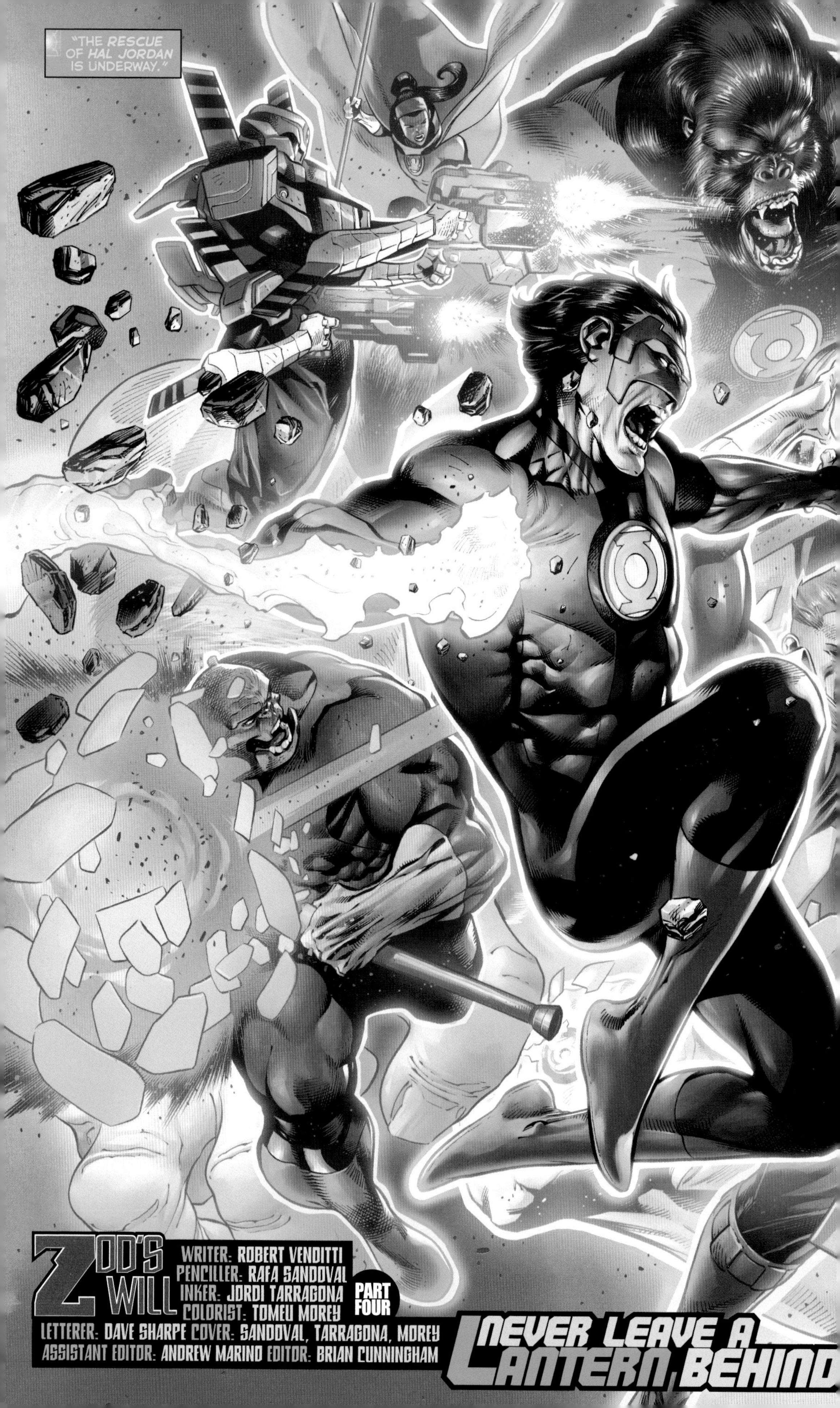
"THE RESCUE OF HAL JORDAN IS UNDERWAY."
ZOD'S WILL
WRITER: ROBERT VENDITTI
PENCILLER: RAFA SANDOVAL
INKER: JORDI TARRAGONA
COLORIST: TOMEU MOREY
PART FOUR
LETTERER: DAVE SHARPE COVER: SANDOVAL, TARRAGONA, MOREY
ASSISTANT EDITOR: ANDREW MARINO EDITOR: BRIAN CUNNINGHAM
NEVER LEAVE A LANTERN BEHIND

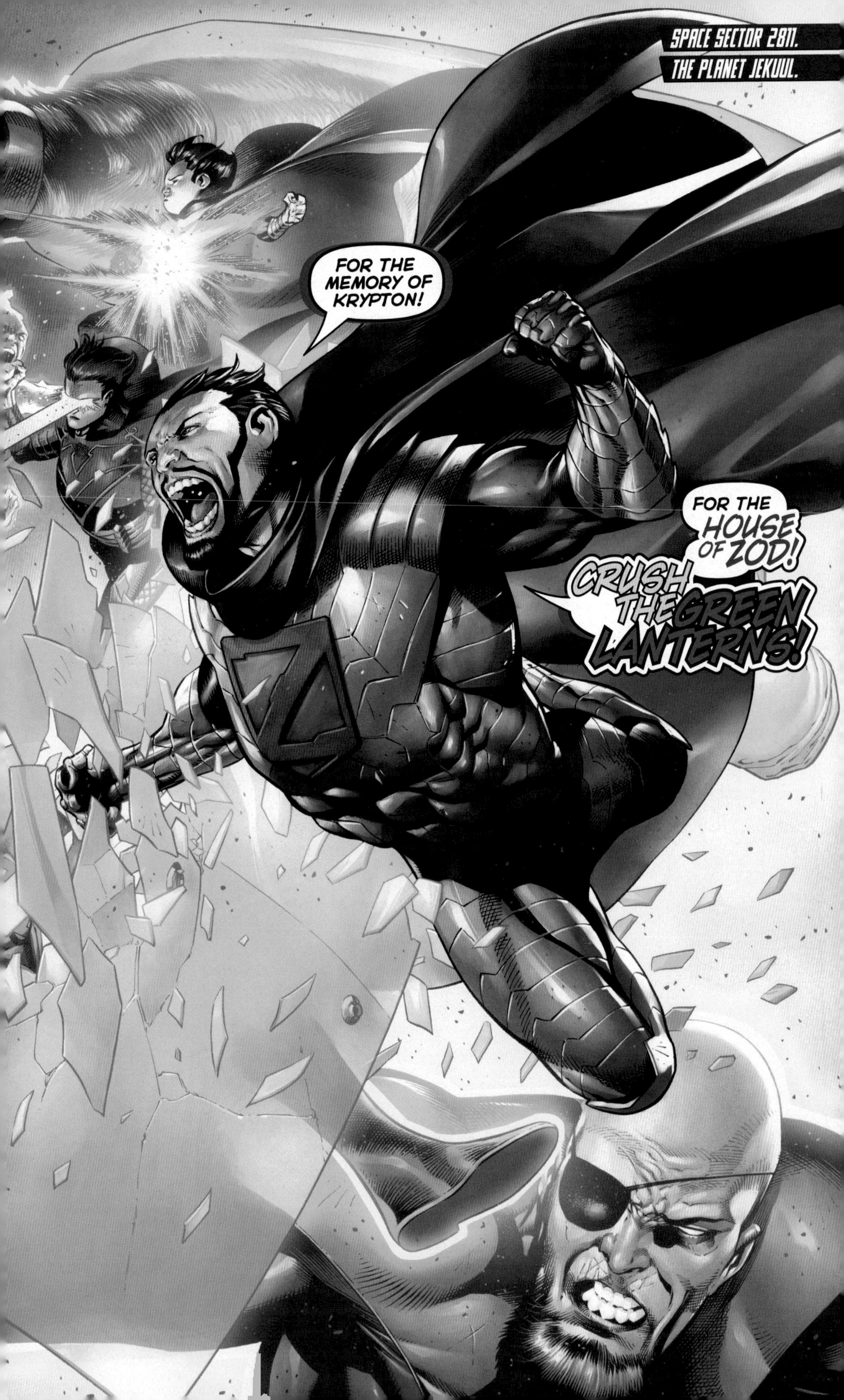
SPACE SECTOR 2811.
THE PLANET JEKUUL.
FOR THE MEMORY OF KRYPTON!
FOR THE HOUSE OF ZOD!
CRUSH THE GREEN LANTERNS!

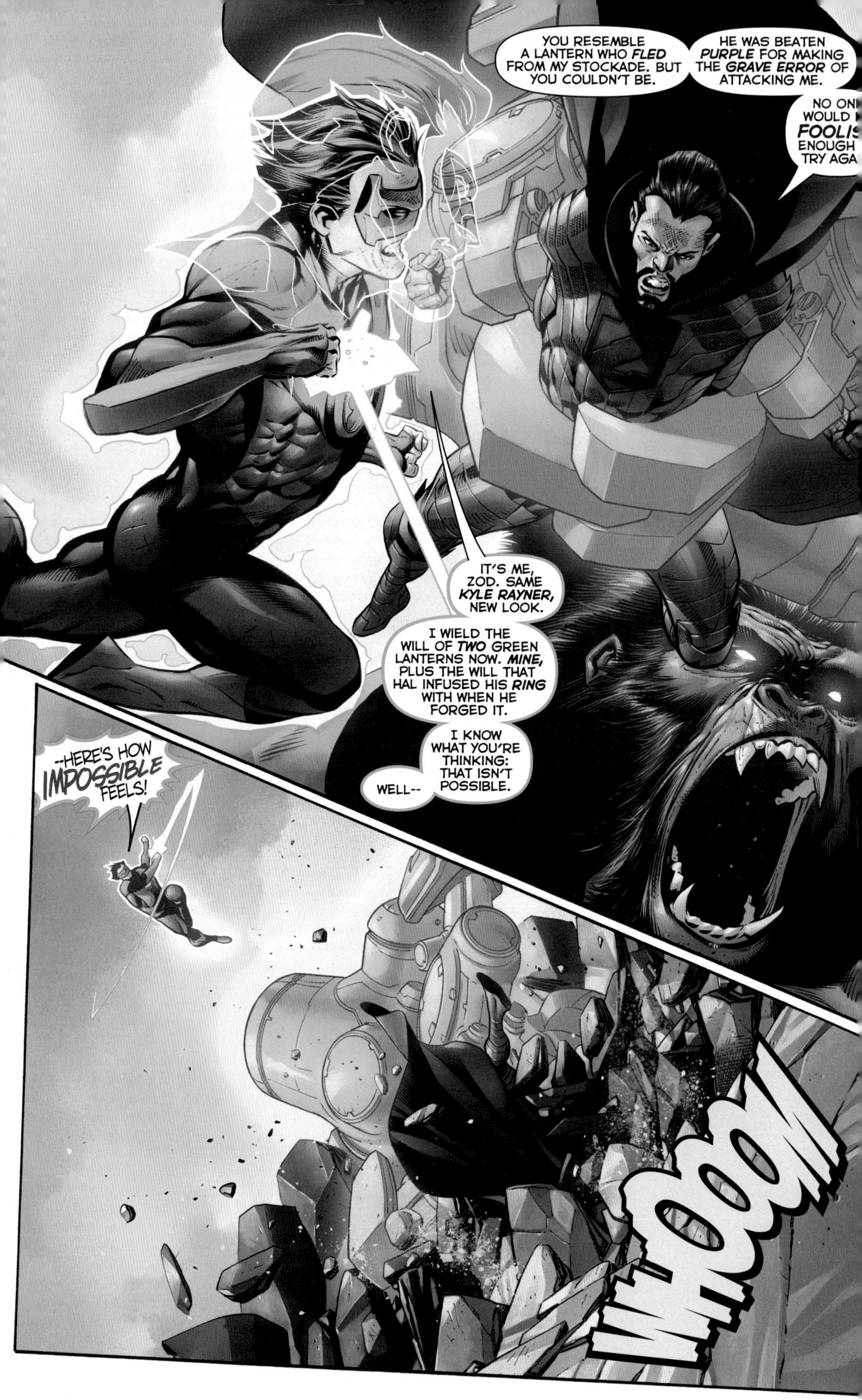

YOU RESEMBLE A LANTERN WHO FLED FROM MY STOCKADE. BUT YOU COULDN'T BE.
HE WAS BEATEN PURPLE FOR MAKING THE GRAVE ERROR OF ATTACKING ME.
IT'S ME, ZOD. SAME KYLE RAYNER, NEW LOOK.
I WIELD THE WILL OF TWO GREEN LANTERNS NOW. MINE, PLUS THE WILL THAT HAL INFUSED HIS RING WITH WHEN HE FORGED IT.
I KNOW WHAT YOU'RE THINKING: THAT ISN'T POSSIBLE.
WELL--
--HERE'S HOW IMPOSSIBLE FEELS!
WHOOOM

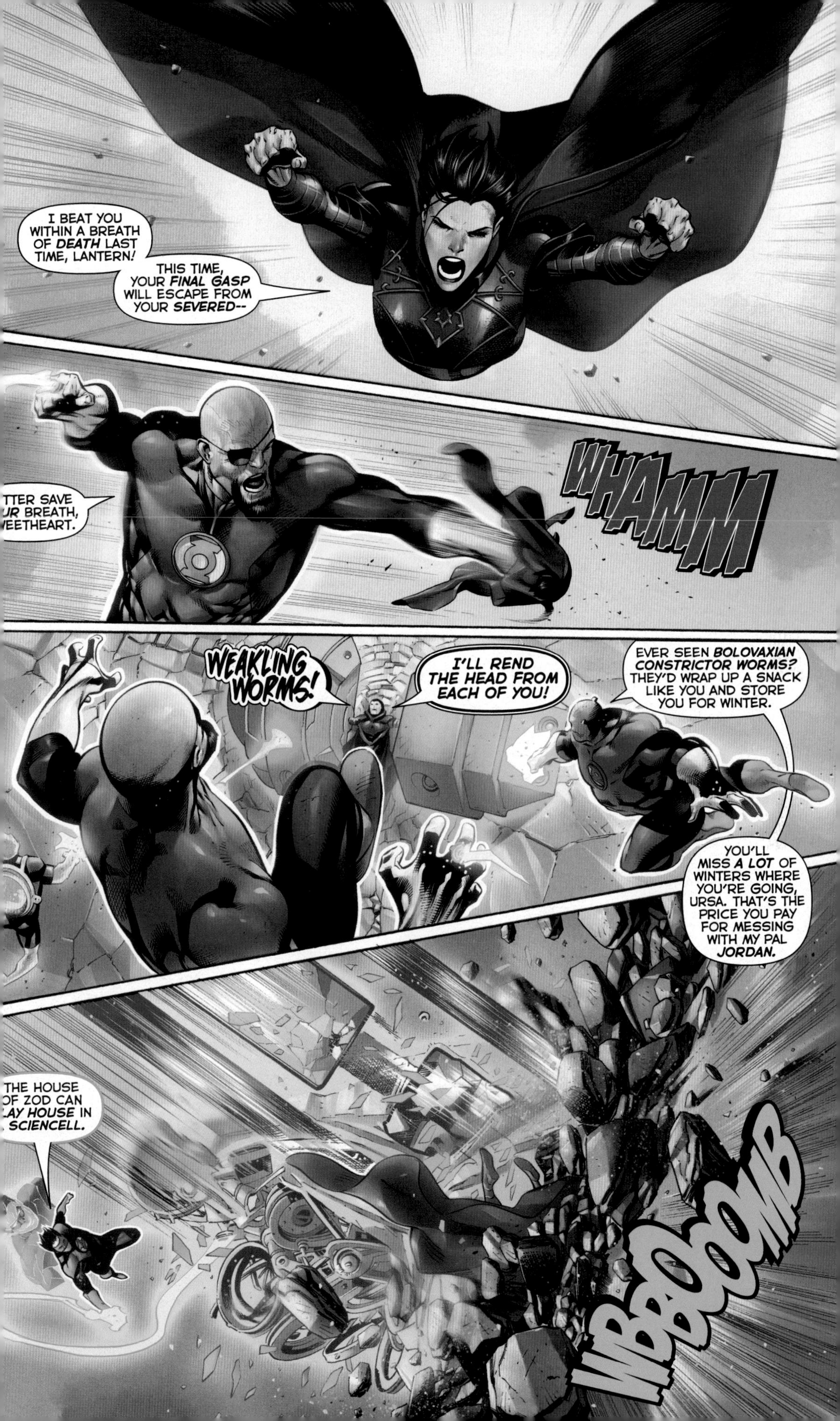

I BEAT YOU WITHIN A BREATH OF *DEATH* LAST TIME, LANTERN!
THIS TIME, YOUR *FINAL GASP* WILL ESCAPE FROM YOUR *SEVERED*--
TTER SAVE *UR* BREATH, EETHEART.
WHAMMM
WEAKLING WORMS!
I'LL REND THE HEAD FROM EACH OF YOU!
EVER SEEN *BOLOVAXIAN CONSTRICTOR WORMS?* THEY'D WRAP UP A SNACK LIKE YOU AND STORE YOU FOR WINTER.
YOU'LL MISS *A LOT* OF WINTERS WHERE YOU'RE GOING, URSA. THAT'S THE PRICE YOU PAY FOR MESSING WITH MY PAL *JORDAN.*
THE HOUSE F ZOD CAN *AY HOUSE* IN *SCIENCELL.*
WBBOOOMB

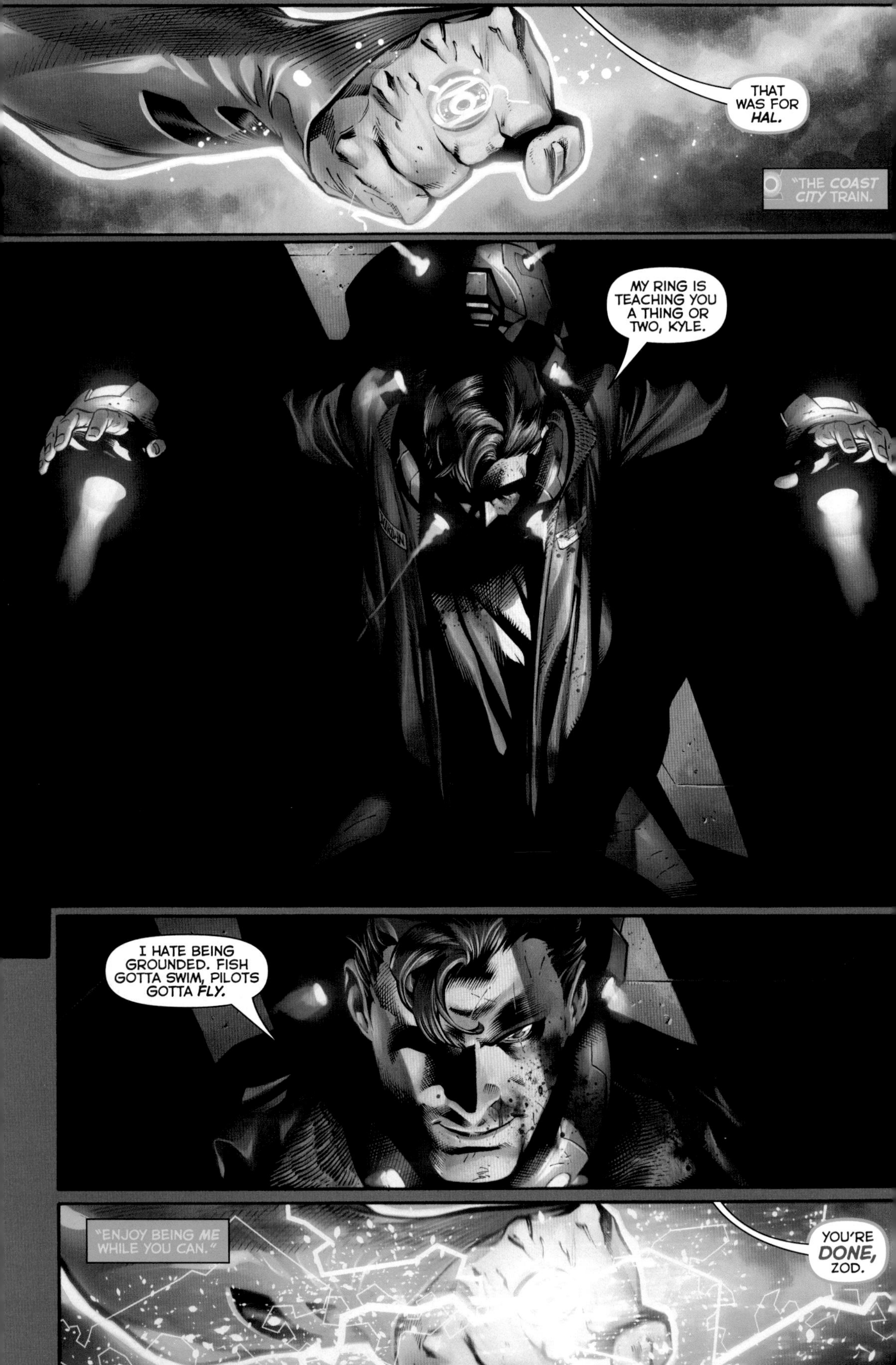
THAT WAS FOR HAL.
"THE COAST CITY TRAIN.
MY RING IS TEACHING YOU A THING OR TWO, KYLE.
I HATE BEING GROUNDED. FISH GOTTA SWIM, PILOTS GOTTA FLY.
"ENJOY BEING ME WHILE YOU CAN."
YOU'RE DONE, ZOD.

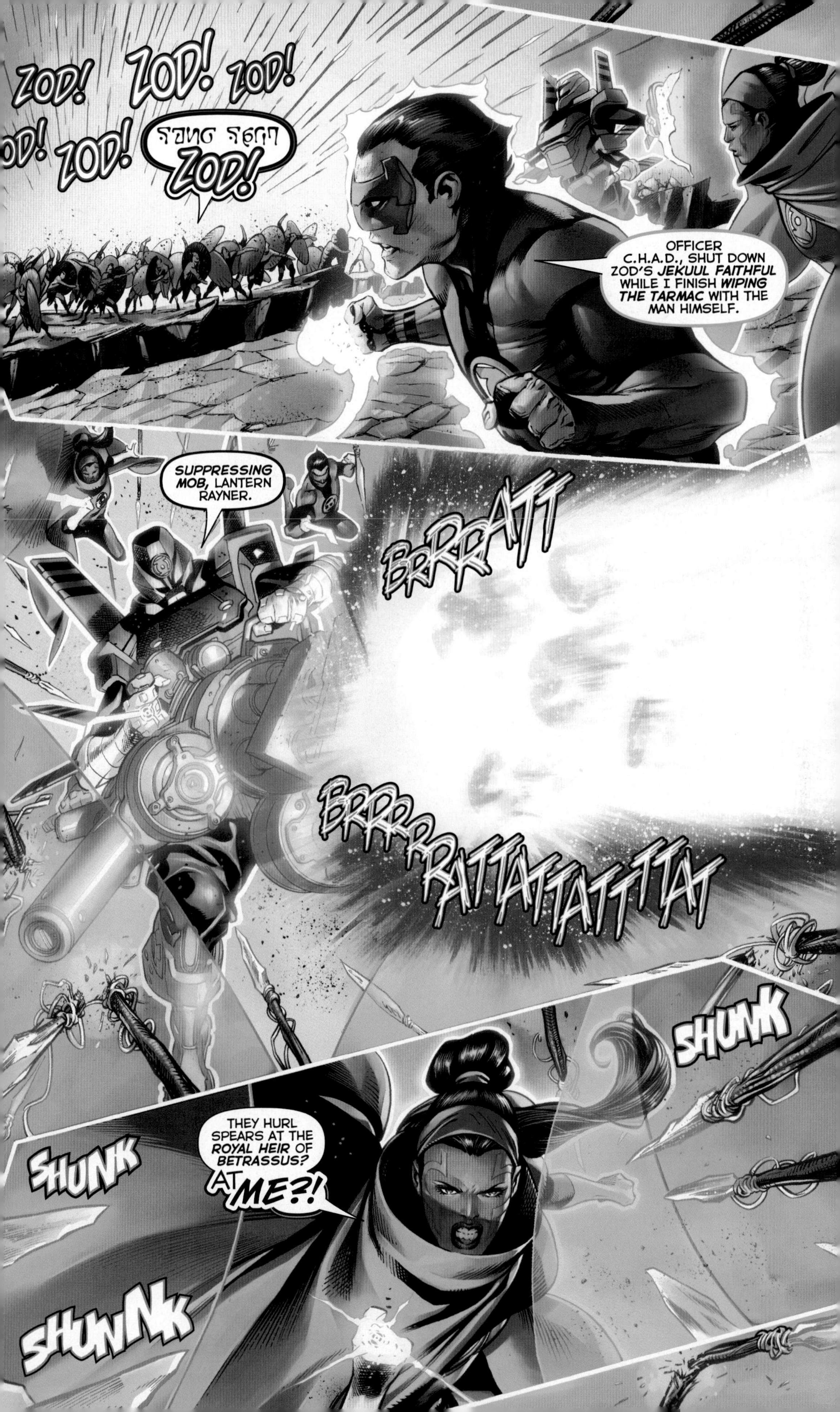
ZOD! ZOD! ZOD!
OD! ZOD!
ZOD!
OFFICER C.H.A.D., SHUT DOWN ZOD'S JEKUUL FAITHFUL WHILE I FINISH WIPING THE TARMAC WITH THE MAN HIMSELF.
SUPPRESSING MOB, LANTERN RAYNER.
BRRRATT
BRRRRRATTATTATTTTAT
SHUNK
SHUNK
THEY HURL SPEARS AT THE ROYAL HEIR OF BETRASSUS? AT ME?!
SHUNNK

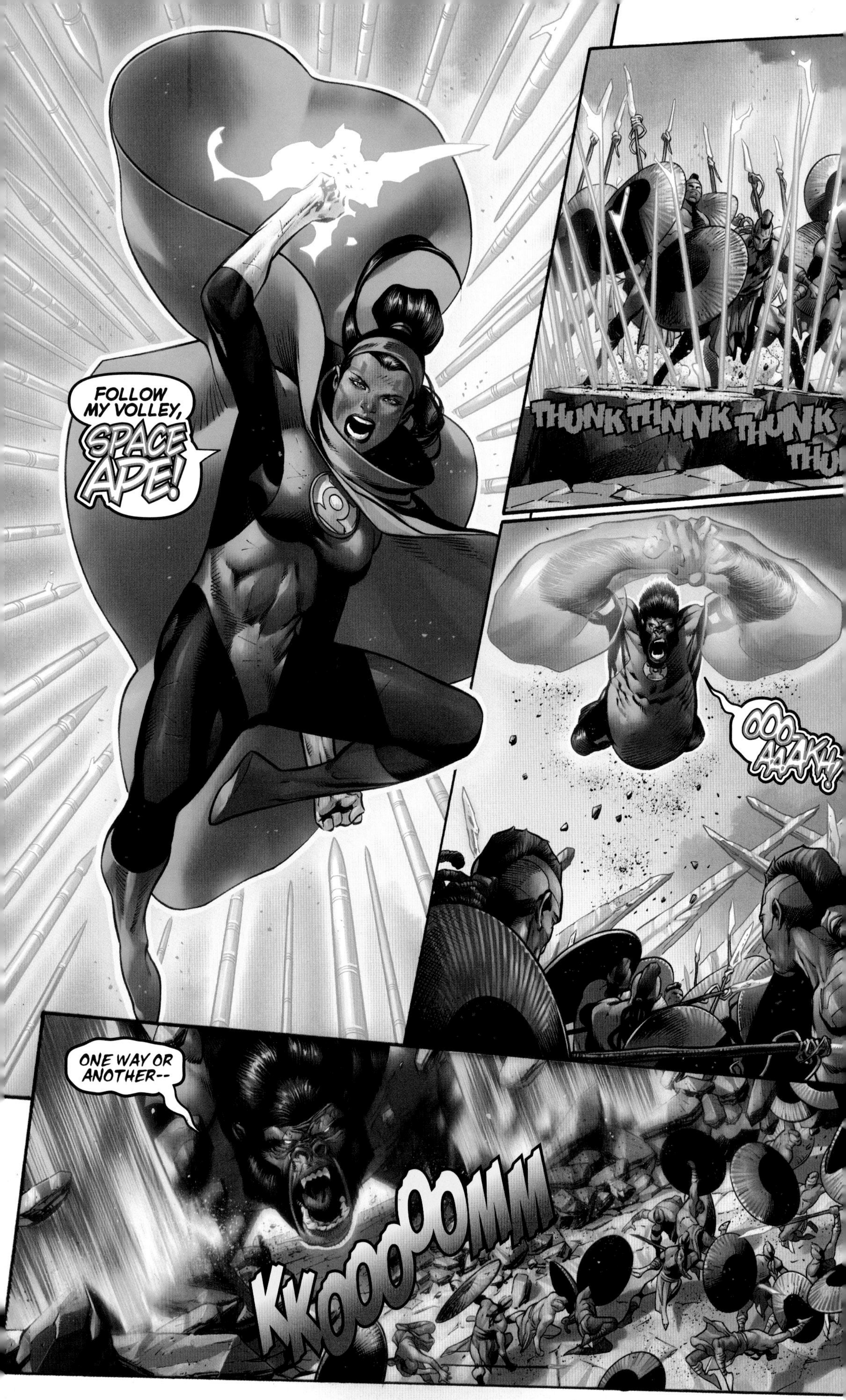
FOLLOW MY VOLLEY, SPACE APE!
THUNK THNNK THUNK THU
OOO-AAAKH!
ONE WAY OR ANOTHER--
KKOOOOOMM

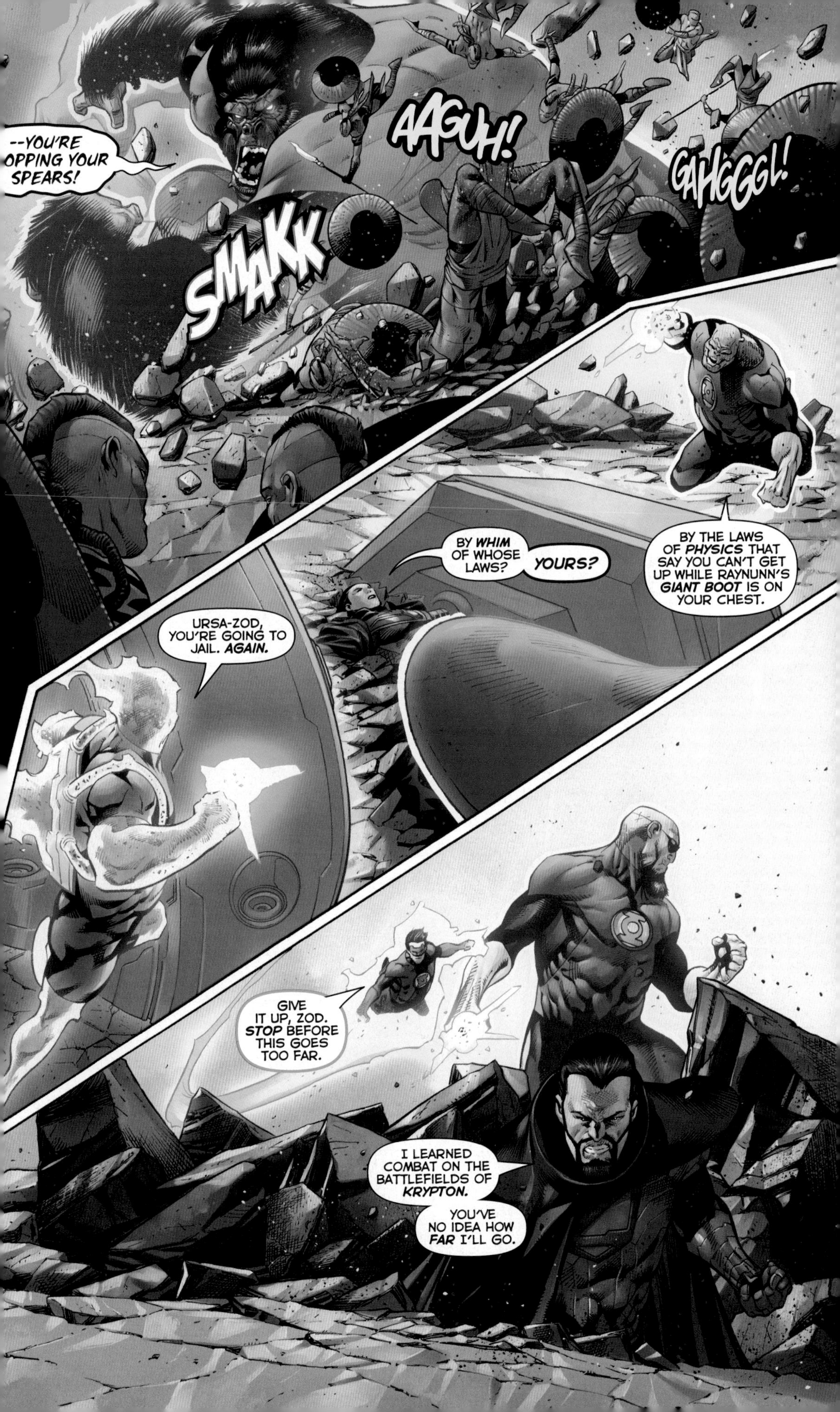
--YOU'RE OPPING YOUR SPEARS!
AAGUH!
GAHGGGL!
SMAKK
BY WHIM OF WHOSE LAWS?
YOURS?
BY THE LAWS OF PHYSICS THAT SAY YOU CAN'T GET UP WHILE RAYNUNN'S GIANT BOOT IS ON YOUR CHEST.
URSA-ZOD, YOU'RE GOING TO JAIL. AGAIN.
GIVE IT UP, ZOD. STOP BEFORE THIS GOES TOO FAR.
I LEARNED COMBAT ON THE BATTLEFIELDS OF KRYPTON.
YOU'VE NO IDEA HOW FAR I'LL GO.

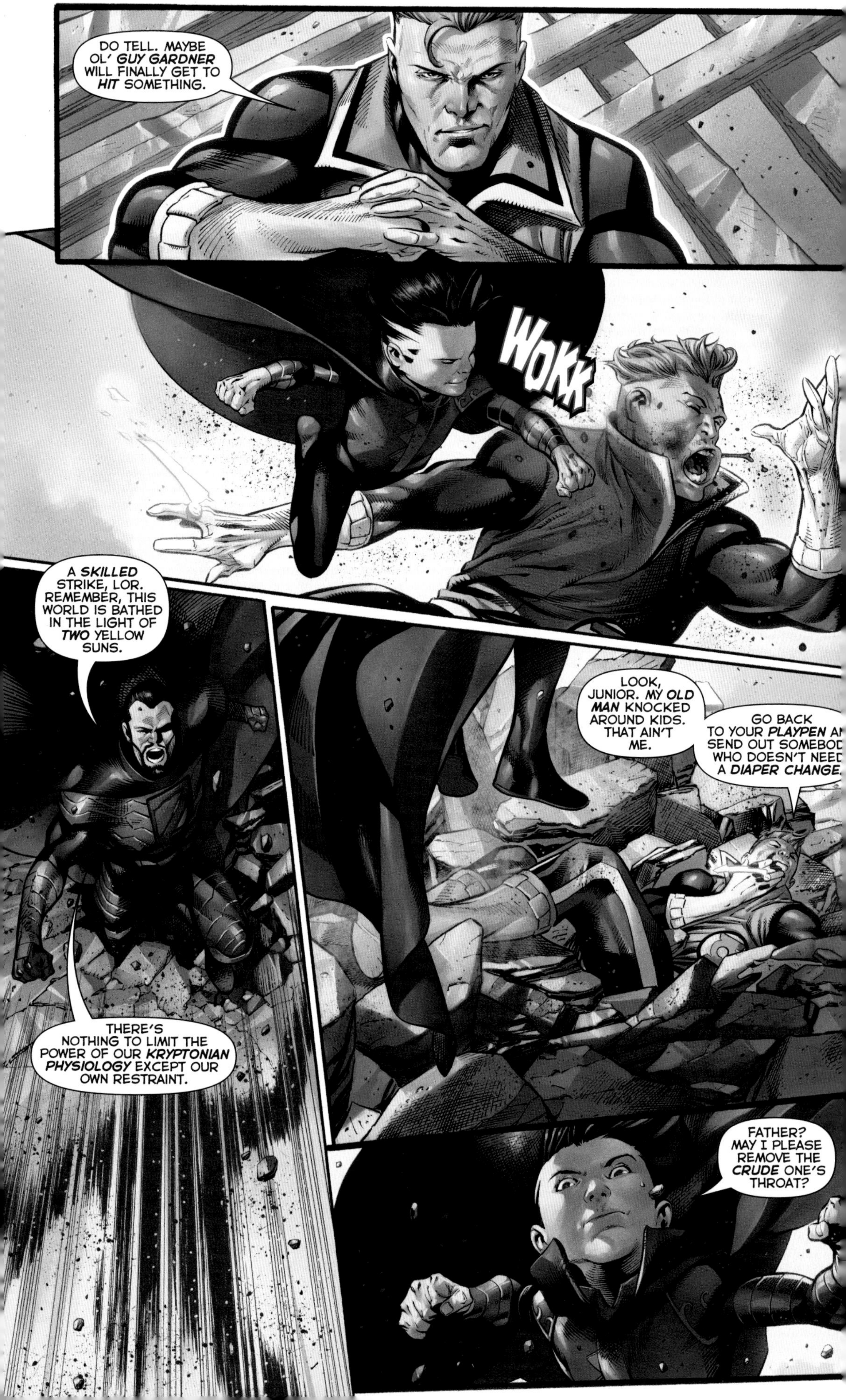
DO TELL. MAYBE OL' GUY GARDNER WILL FINALLY GET TO HIT SOMETHING.
WOKK
A SKILLED STRIKE, LOR. REMEMBER, THIS WORLD IS BATHED IN THE LIGHT OF TWO YELLOW SUNS.
THERE'S NOTHING TO LIMIT THE POWER OF OUR KRYPTONIAN PHYSIOLOGY EXCEPT OUR OWN RESTRAINT.
LOOK, JUNIOR. MY OLD MAN KNOCKED AROUND KIDS. THAT AIN'T ME.
GO BACK TO YOUR PLAYPEN AN SEND OUT SOMEBOD WHO DOESN'T NEED A DIAPER CHANGE.
FATHER? MAY I PLEASE REMOVE THE CRUDE ONE'S THROAT?

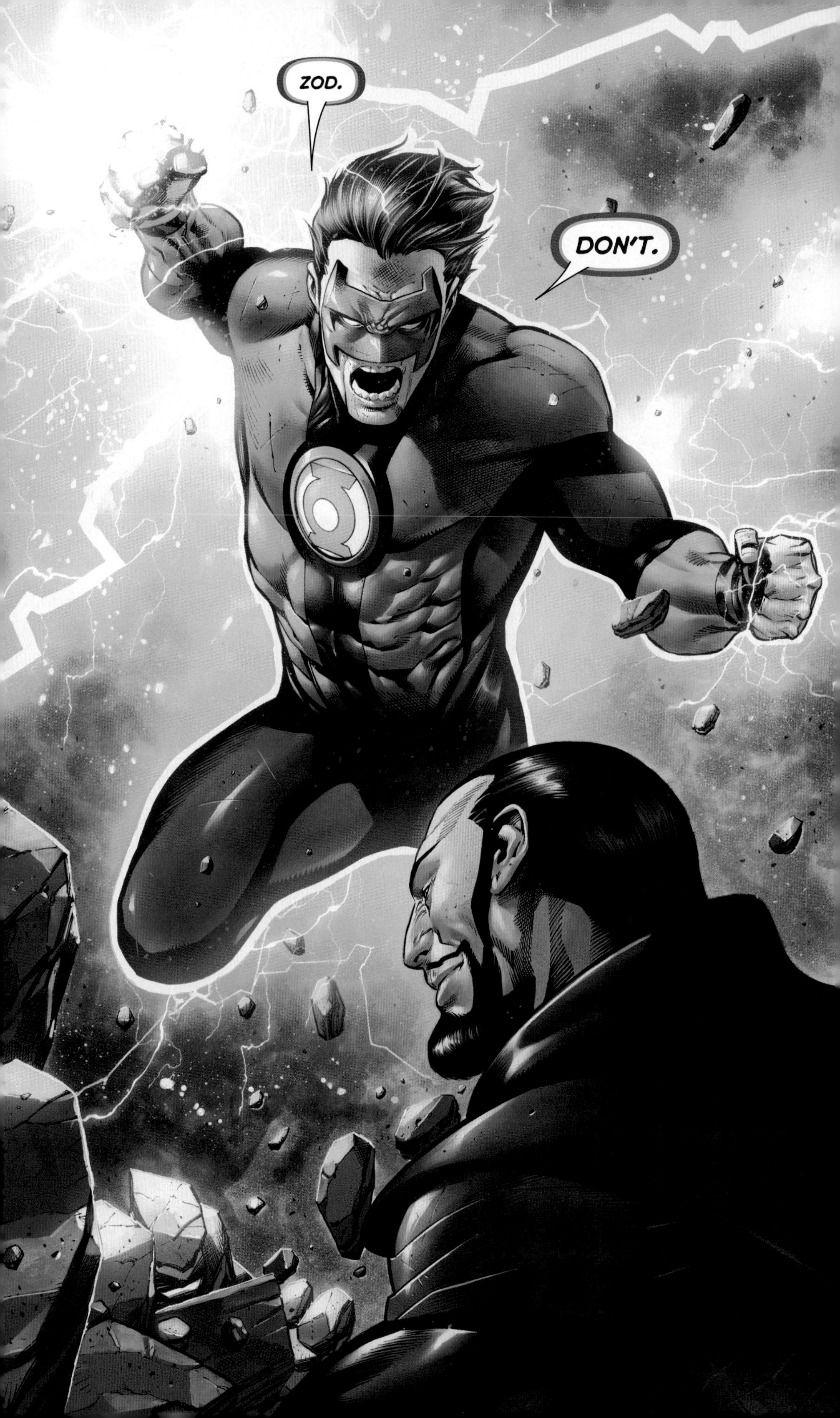
ZOD.
DON'T.

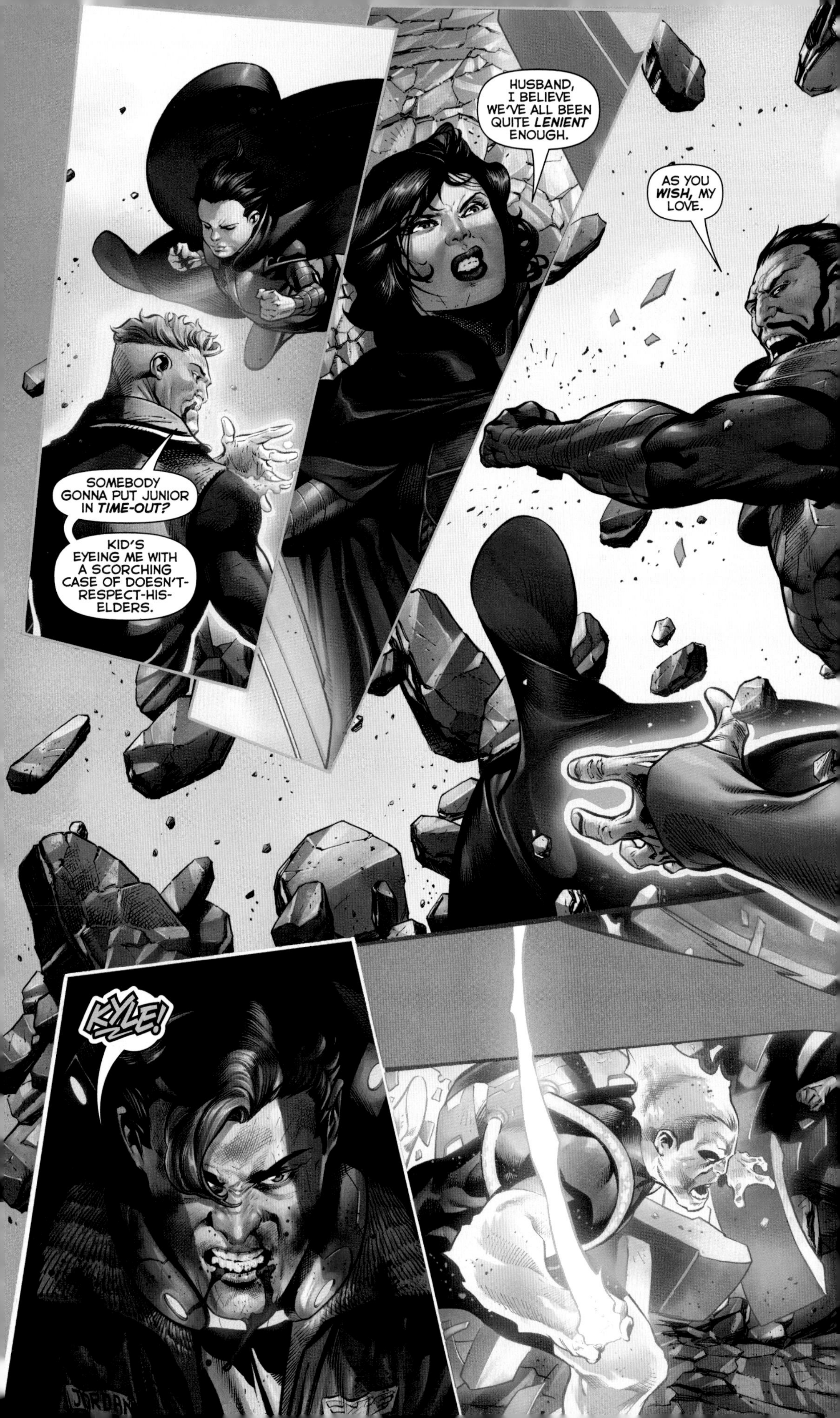
HUSBAND, I BELIEVE WE'VE ALL BEEN QUITE LENIENT ENOUGH.
AS YOU WISH, MY LOVE.
SOMEBODY GONNA PUT JUNIOR IN TIME-OUT?
KID'S EYEING ME WITH A SCORCHING CASE OF DOESN'T-RESPECT-HIS-ELDERS.
KYLE!

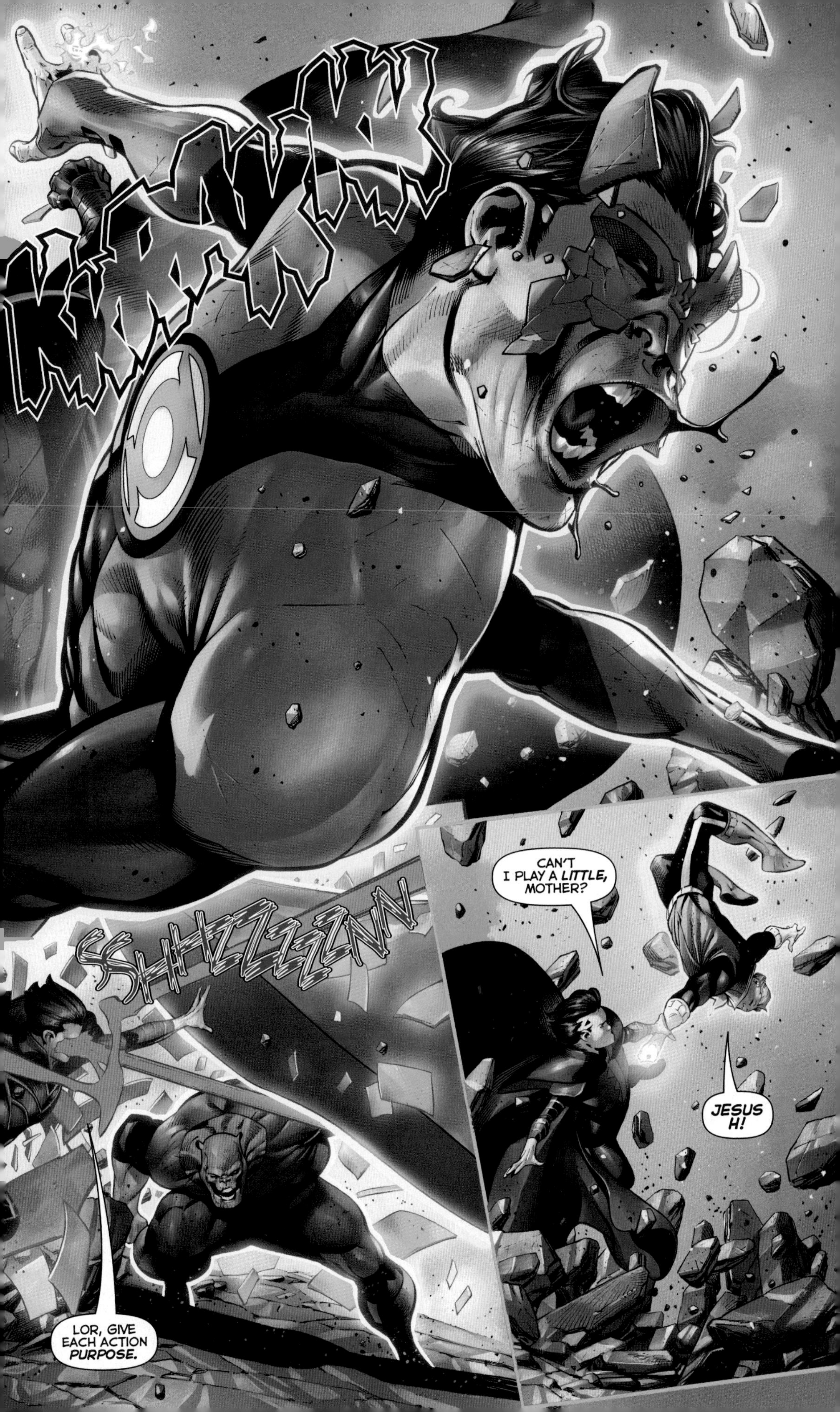
KRAKOW
SSHHZZZZZZNN
LOR, GIVE EACH ACTION PURPOSE.
CAN'T I PLAY A LITTLE, MOTHER?
JESUS H!

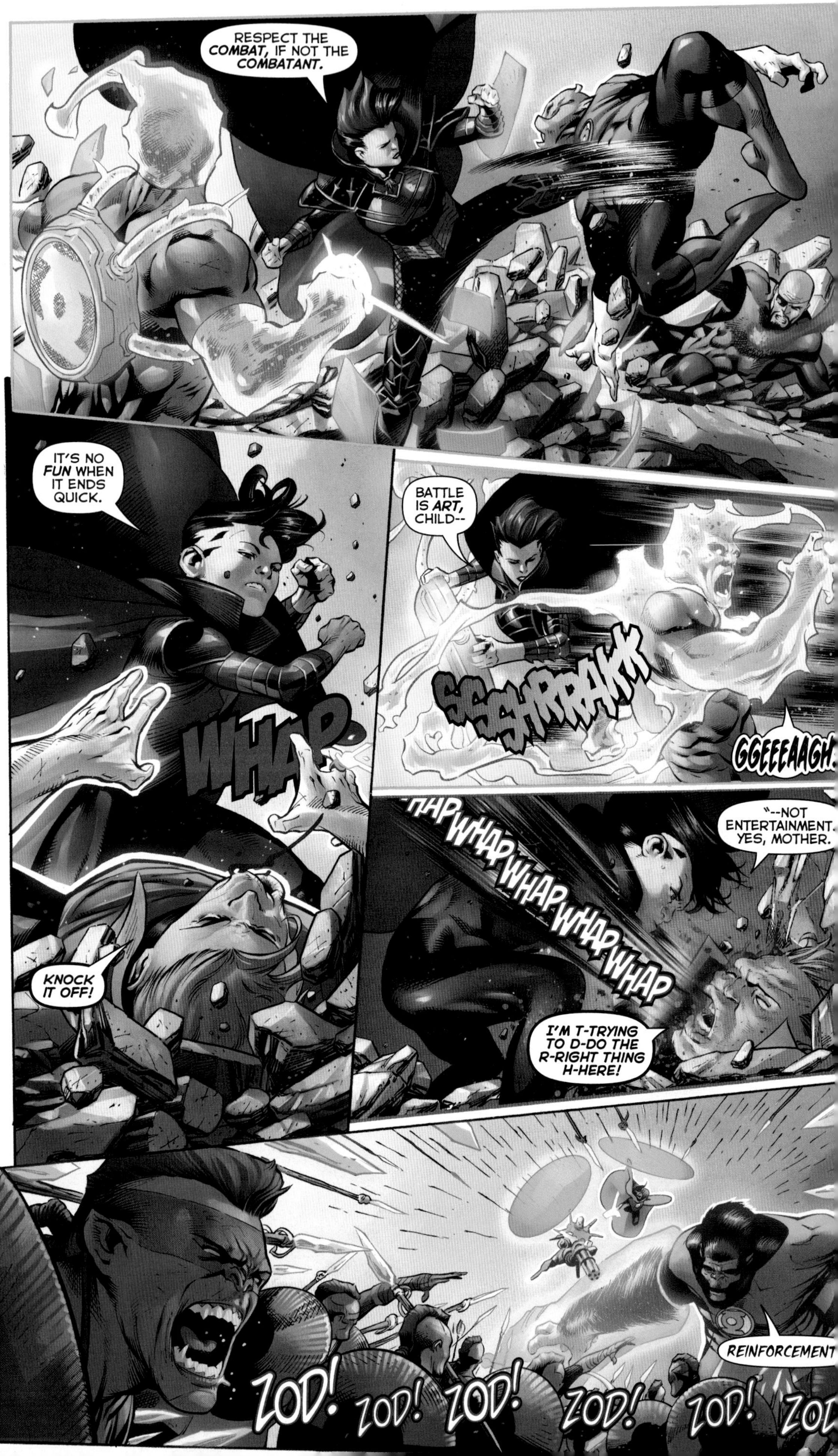

RESPECT THE COMBAT, IF NOT THE COMBATANT.
IT'S NO FUN WHEN IT ENDS QUICK.
WHAP
KNOCK IT OFF!
BATTLE IS ART, CHILD--
SSSHRRAKK
GGEEEAAGH!
WHAP WHAP WHAP WHAP WHAP WHAP
"--NOT ENTERTAINMENT." YES, MOTHER.
I'M T-TRYING TO D-DO THE R-RIGHT THING H-HERE!
REINFORCEMENT
ZOD! ZOD! ZOD! ZOD! ZOD! ZOD

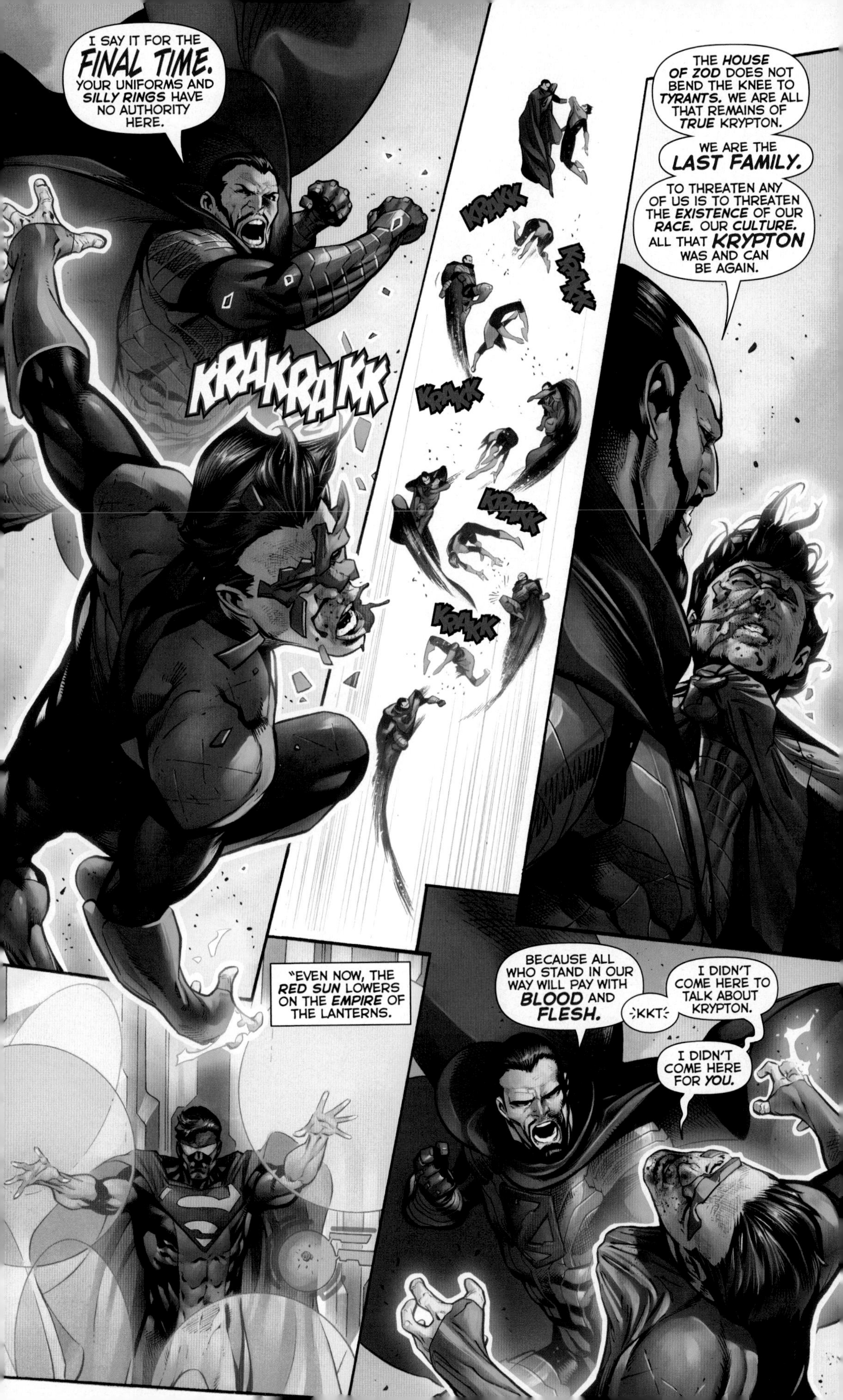

I SAY IT FOR THE FINAL TIME. YOUR UNIFORMS AND SILLY RINGS HAVE NO AUTHORITY HERE.
KRAKRAKRAKK
THE HOUSE OF ZOD DOES NOT BEND THE KNEE TO TYRANTS. WE ARE ALL THAT REMAINS OF TRUE KRYPTON.
WE ARE THE LAST FAMILY.
TO THREATEN ANY OF US IS TO THREATEN THE EXISTENCE OF OUR RACE. OUR CULTURE. ALL THAT KRYPTON WAS AND CAN BE AGAIN.
KRAKK
KRAKK
KRAKK
KRAKK
KRAKK
"EVEN NOW, THE RED SUN LOWERS ON THE EMPIRE OF THE LANTERNS.
BECAUSE ALL WHO STAND IN OUR WAY WILL PAY WITH BLOOD AND FLESH.
KKT
I DIDN'T COME HERE TO TALK ABOUT KRYPTON.
I DIDN'T COME HERE FOR YOU.

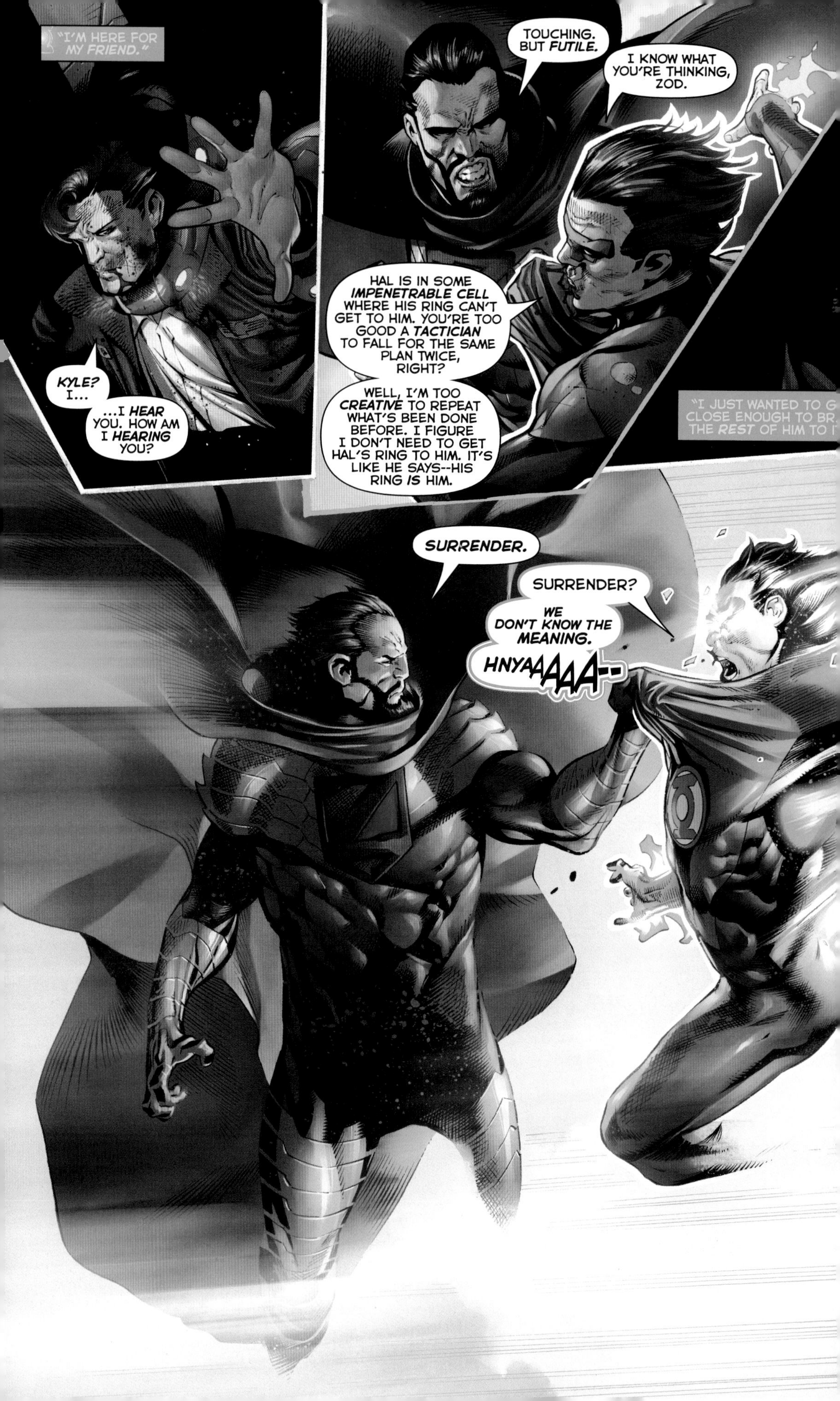
"I'M HERE FOR MY FRIEND."
KYLE? I...
...I HEAR YOU. HOW AM I HEARING YOU?
TOUCHING. BUT FUTILE.
I KNOW WHAT YOU'RE THINKING, ZOD.
HAL IS IN SOME IMPENETRABLE CELL WHERE HIS RING CAN'T GET TO HIM. YOU'RE TOO GOOD A TACTICIAN TO FALL FOR THE SAME PLAN TWICE, RIGHT?
WELL, I'M TOO CREATIVE TO REPEAT WHAT'S BEEN DONE BEFORE. I FIGURE I DON'T NEED TO GET HAL'S RING TO HIM. IT'S LIKE HE SAYS--HIS RING IS HIM.
SURRENDER.
SURRENDER?
WE DON'T KNOW THE MEANING.
HNYAAAAAA--

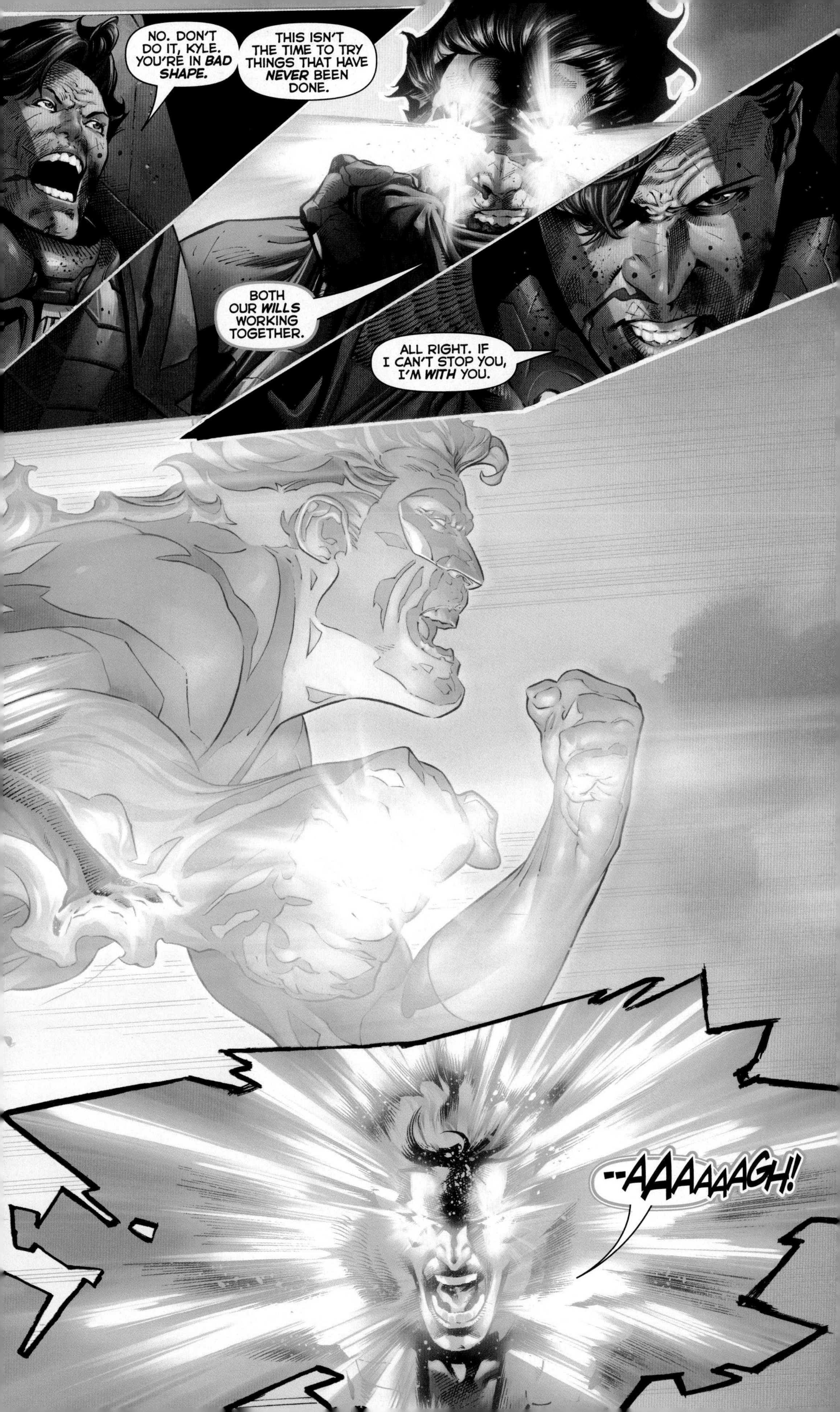
NO. DON'T DO IT, KYLE. YOU'RE IN BAD SHAPE.
THIS ISN'T THE TIME TO TRY THINGS THAT HAVE NEVER BEEN DONE.
BOTH OUR WILLS WORKING TOGETHER.
ALL RIGHT. IF I CAN'T STOP YOU, I'M WITH YOU.
--AAAAAAGH!

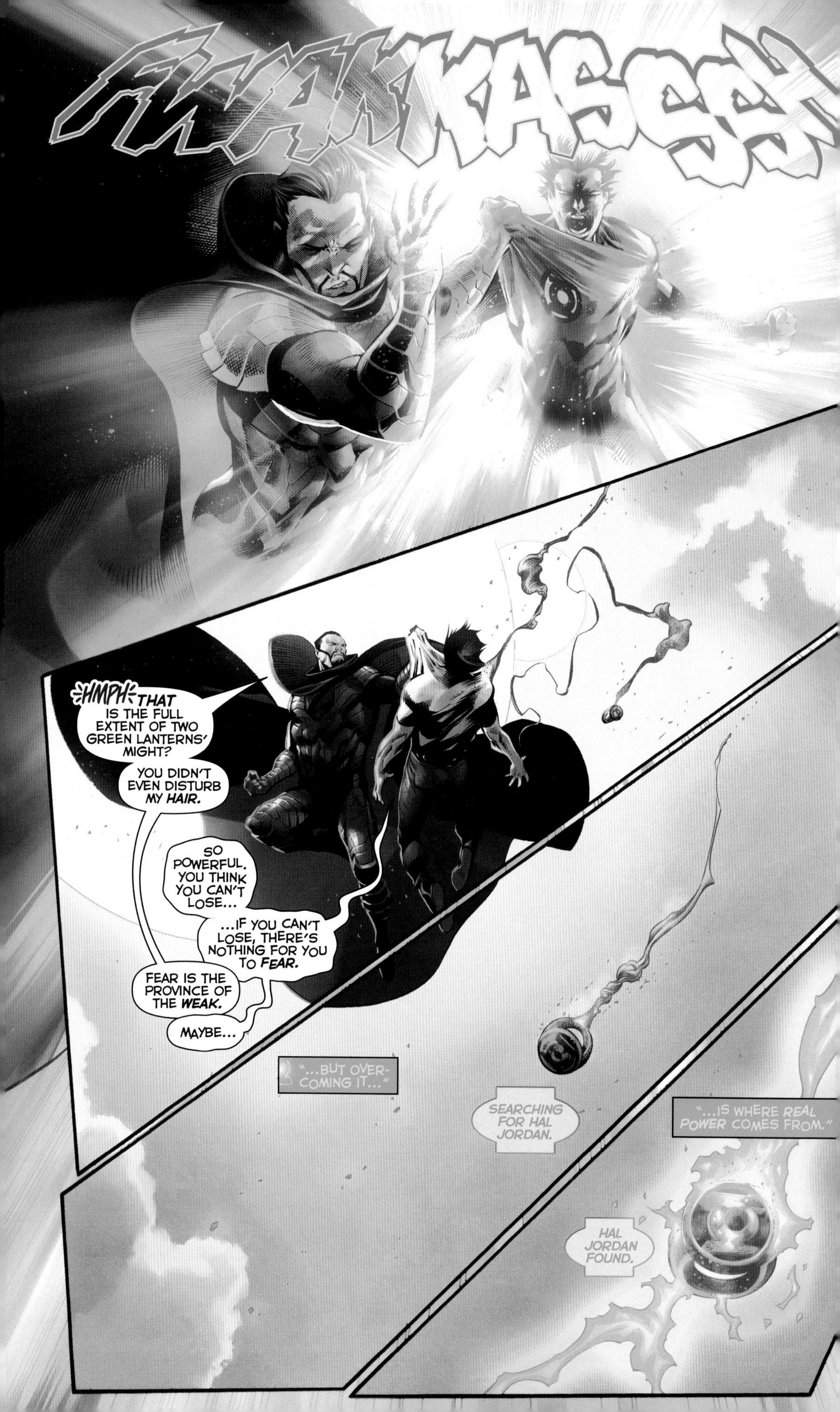
FWAM KASSSS!
HMPH. THAT IS THE FULL EXTENT OF TWO GREEN LANTERNS' MIGHT?
YOU DIDN'T EVEN DISTURB MY HAIR.
SO POWERFUL. YOU THINK YOU CAN'T LOSE...
...IF YOU CAN'T LOSE, THERE'S NOTHING FOR YOU TO FEAR.
FEAR IS THE PROVINCE OF THE WEAK.
MAYBE...
"...BUT OVER-COMING IT..."
SEARCHING FOR HAL JORDAN.
"...IS WHERE REAL POWER COMES FROM."
HAL JORDAN FOUND.

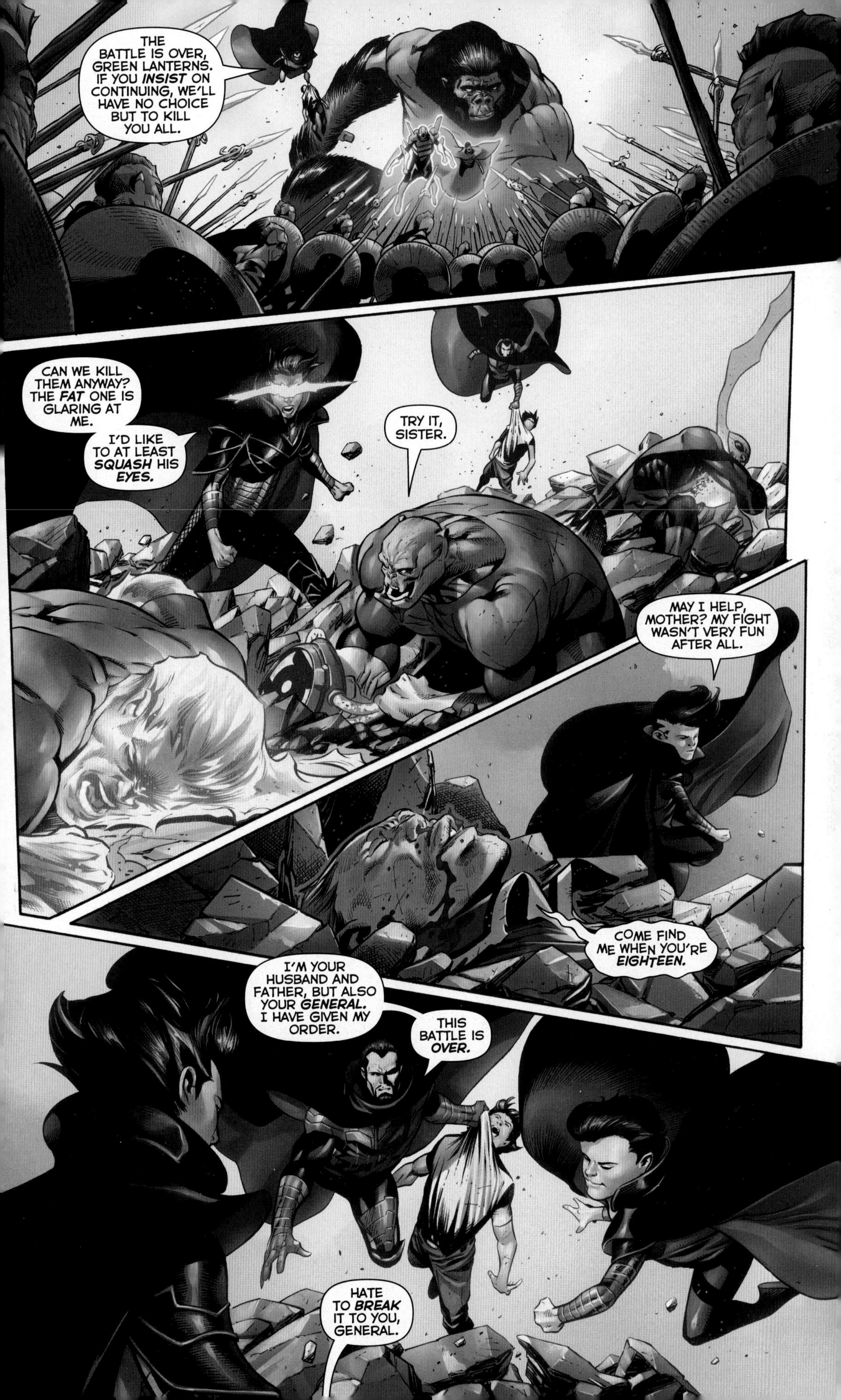
THE BATTLE IS OVER, GREEN LANTERNS. IF YOU INSIST ON CONTINUING, WE'LL HAVE NO CHOICE BUT TO KILL YOU ALL.
CAN WE KILL THEM ANYWAY? THE FAT ONE IS GLARING AT ME.
I'D LIKE TO AT LEAST SQUASH HIS EYES.
TRY IT, SISTER.
MAY I HELP, MOTHER? MY FIGHT WASN'T VERY FUN AFTER ALL.
COME FIND ME WHEN YOU'RE EIGHTEEN.
I'M YOUR HUSBAND AND FATHER, BUT ALSO YOUR GENERAL. I HAVE GIVEN MY ORDER.
THIS BATTLE IS OVER.
HATE TO BREAK IT TO YOU, GENERAL.

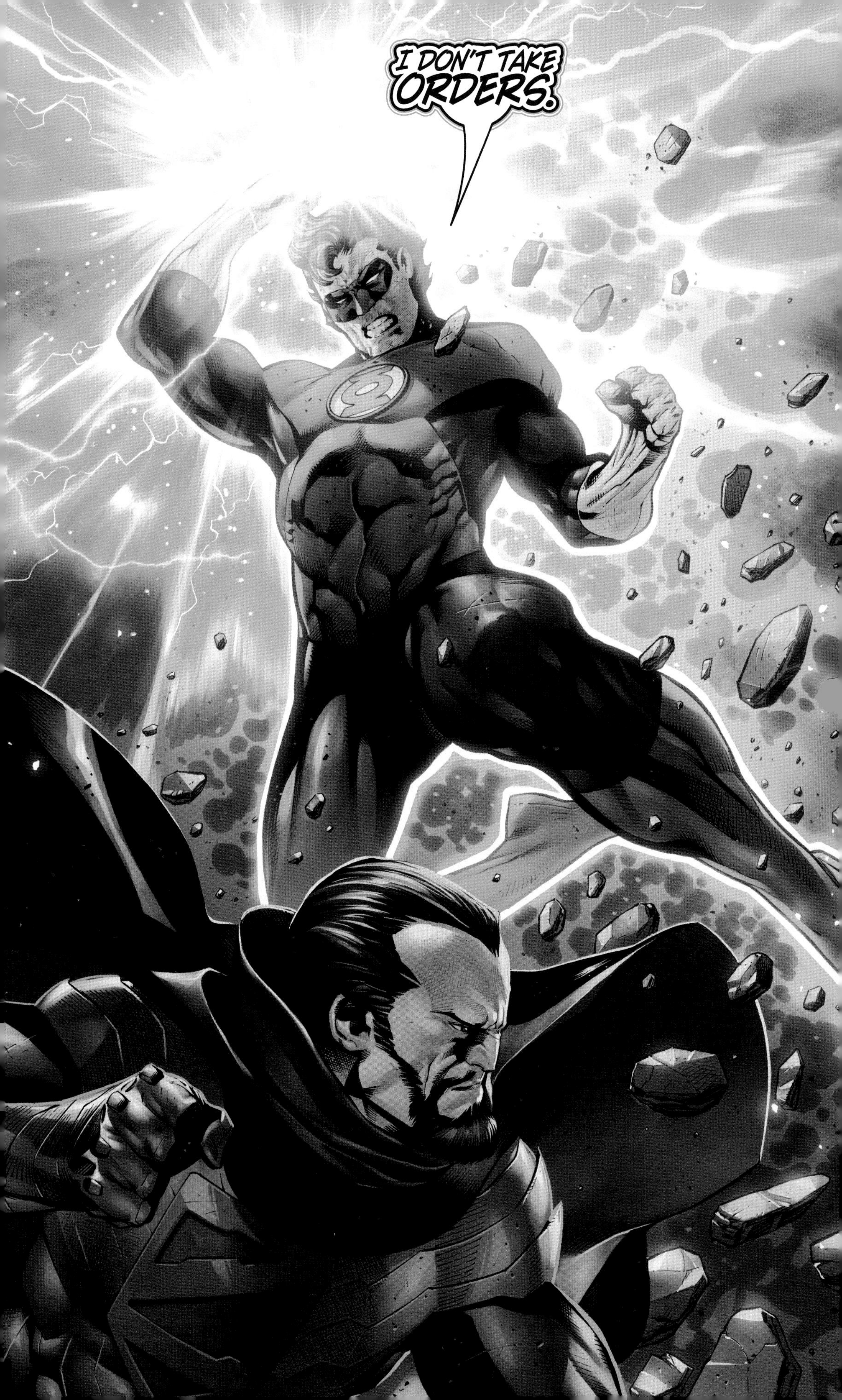
I DON'T TAKE ORDERS.

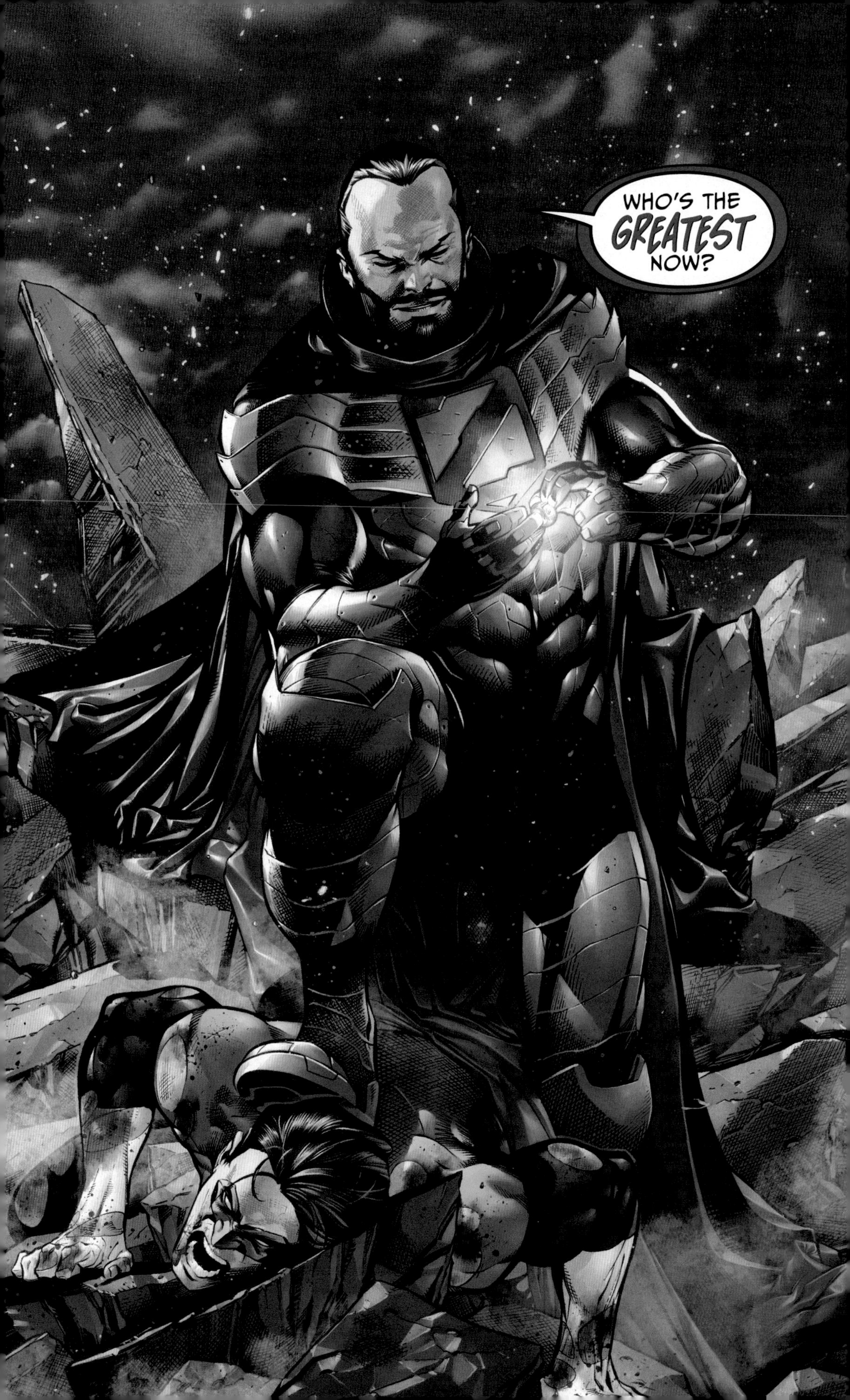
WHO'S THE GREATEST NOW?

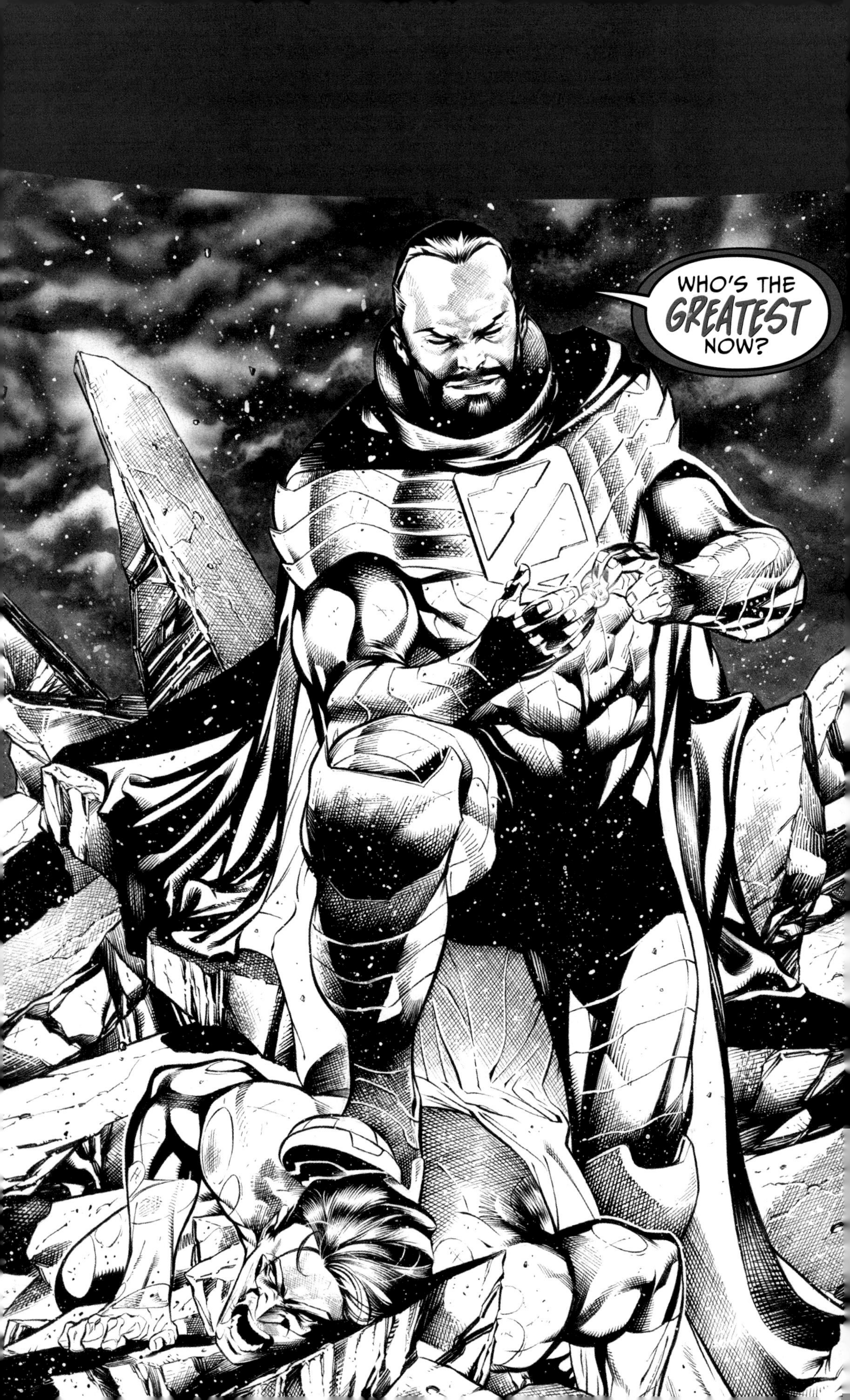
WHO'S THE GREATEST NOW?

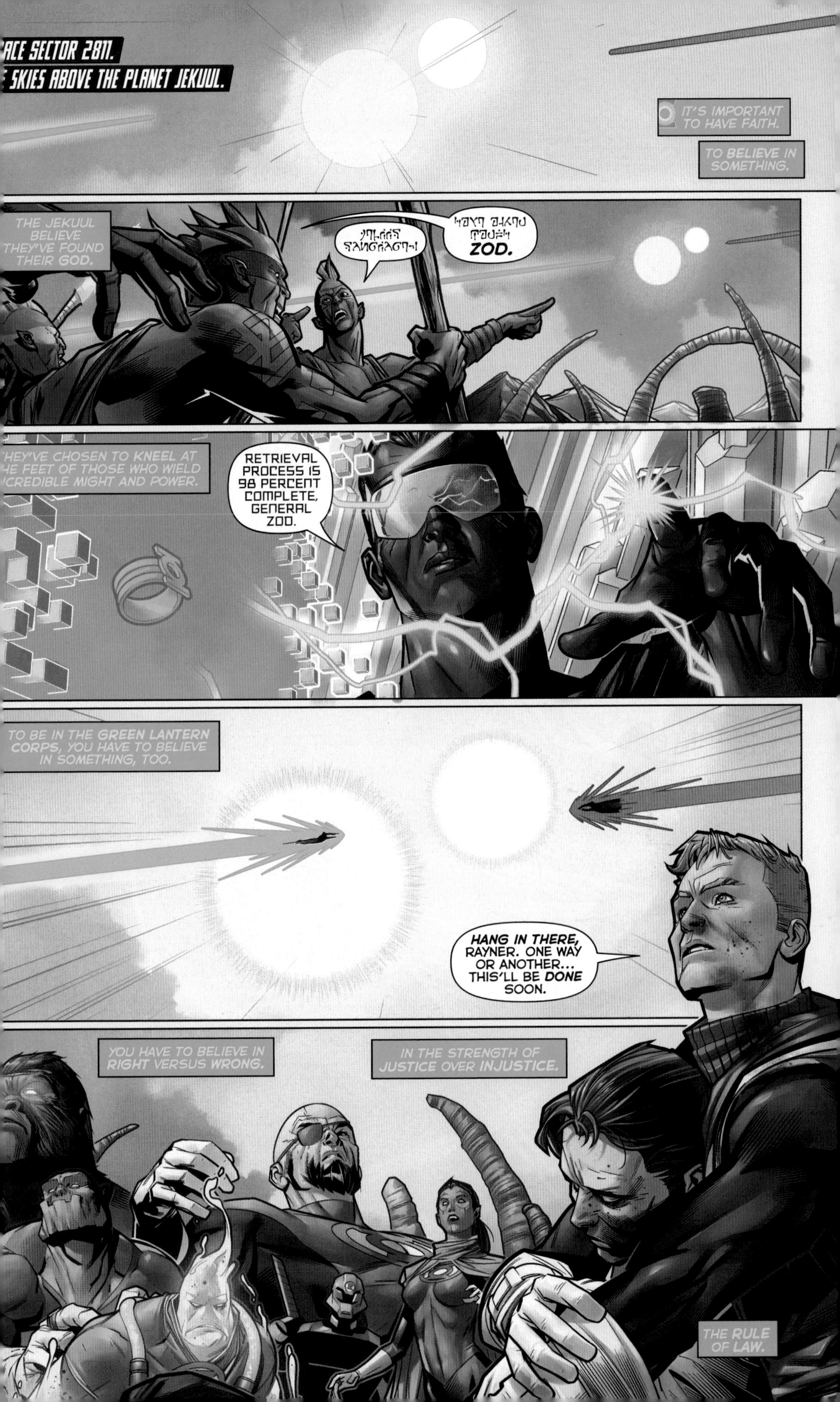

ACE SECTOR 2811.
SKIES ABOVE THE PLANET JEKUUL.
IT'S IMPORTANT TO HAVE FAITH.
TO BELIEVE IN SOMETHING.
THE JEKUUL BELIEVE THEY'VE FOUND THEIR GOD.
ZOD.
HEY'VE CHOSEN TO KNEEL AT HE FEET OF THOSE WHO WIELD NCREDIBLE MIGHT AND POWER.
RETRIEVAL PROCESS IS 98 PERCENT COMPLETE, GENERAL ZOD.
TO BE IN THE GREEN LANTERN CORPS, YOU HAVE TO BELIEVE IN SOMETHING, TOO.
HANG IN THERE, RAYNER. ONE WAY OR ANOTHER... THIS'LL BE DONE SOON.
YOU HAVE TO BELIEVE IN RIGHT VERSUS WRONG.
IN THE STRENGTH OF JUSTICE OVER INJUSTICE.
THE RULE OF LAW.

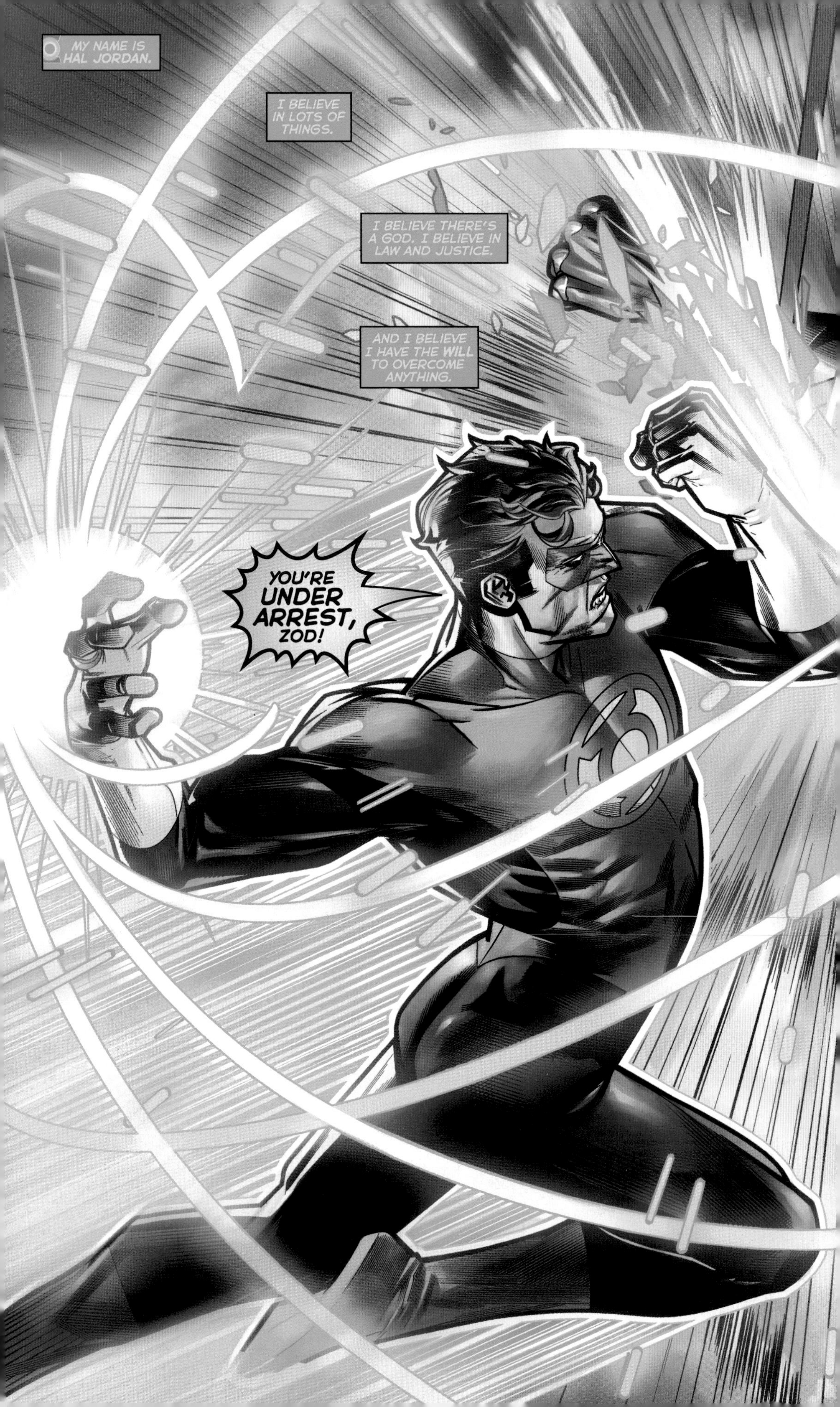
MY NAME IS HAL JORDAN.
I BELIEVE IN LOTS OF THINGS.
I BELIEVE THERE'S A GOD. I BELIEVE IN LAW AND JUSTICE.
AND I BELIEVE I HAVE THE WILL TO OVERCOME ANYTHING.
YOU'RE UNDER ARREST, ZOD!

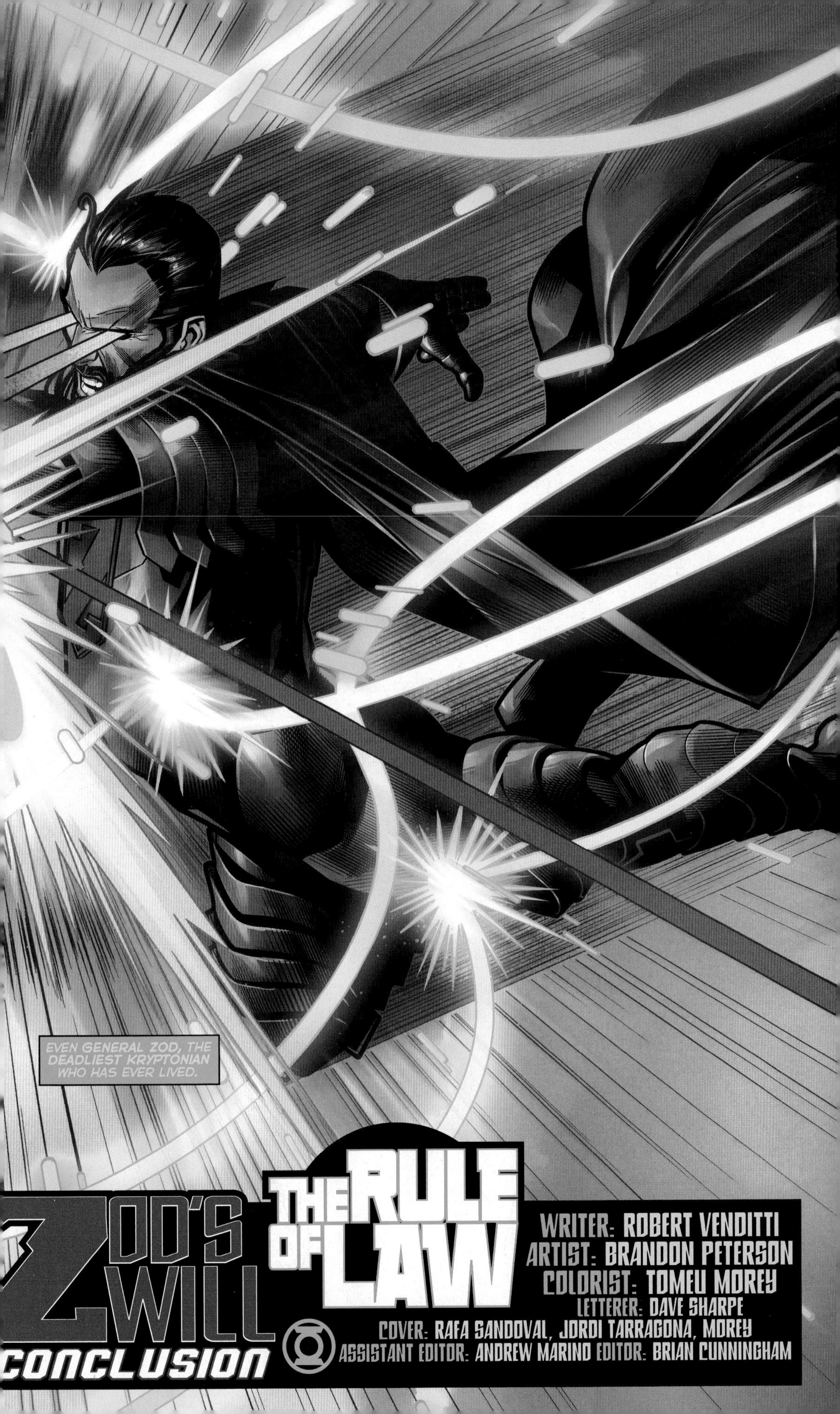
EVEN GENERAL ZOD, THE DEADLIEST KRYPTONIAN WHO HAS EVER LIVED.
ZOD'S WILL CONCLUSION
THE RULE OF LAW
WRITER: ROBERT VENDITTI
ARTIST: BRANDON PETERSON
COLORIST: TOMEU MOREY
LETTERER: DAVE SHARPE
COVER: RAFA SANDOVAL, JORDI TARRAGONA, MOREY
ASSISTANT EDITOR: ANDREW MARINO EDITOR: BRIAN CUNNINGHAM

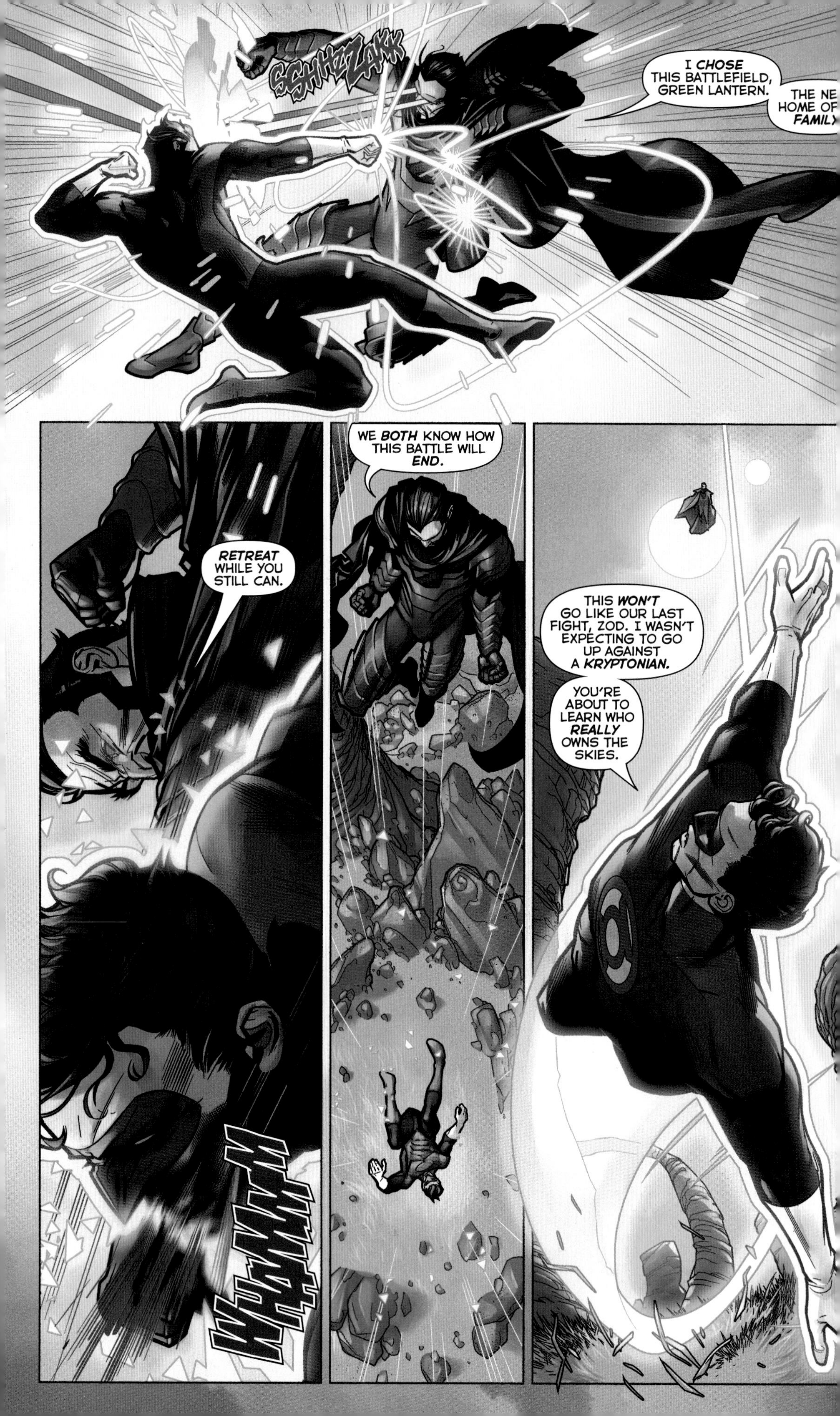
SCHHZAKK
I CHOSE THIS BATTLEFIELD, GREEN LANTERN.
RETREAT WHILE YOU STILL CAN.
WHAMMM
WE BOTH KNOW HOW THIS BATTLE WILL END.
THIS WON'T GO LIKE OUR LAST FIGHT, ZOD. I WASN'T EXPECTING TO GO UP AGAINST A KRYPTONIAN.
YOU'RE ABOUT TO LEARN WHO REALLY OWNS THE SKIES.

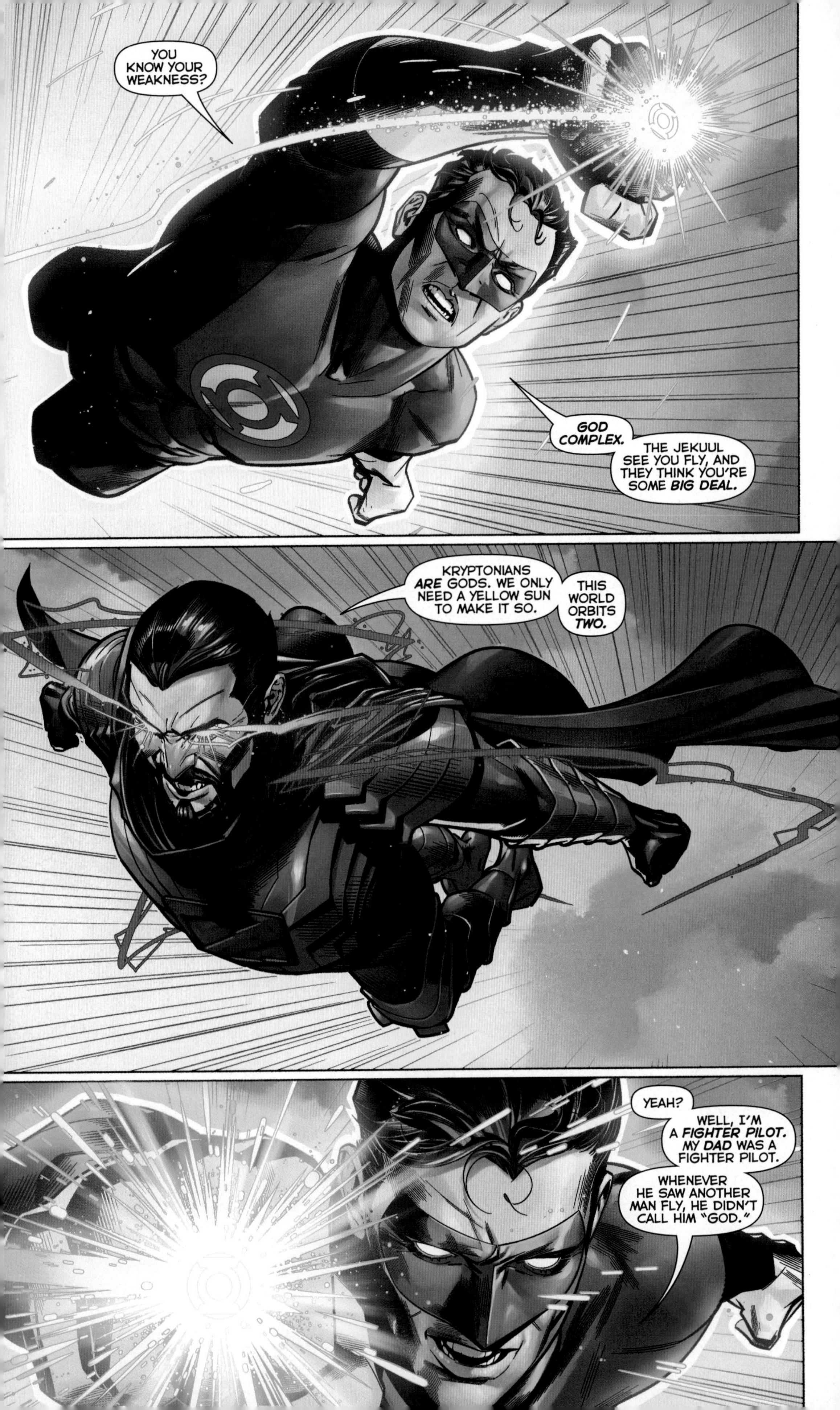
YOU KNOW YOUR WEAKNESS?
GOD COMPLEX.
THE JEKUUL SEE YOU FLY, AND THEY THINK YOU'RE SOME BIG DEAL.
KRYPTONIANS ARE GODS. WE ONLY NEED A YELLOW SUN TO MAKE IT SO.
THIS WORLD ORBITS TWO.
YEAH?
WELL, I'M A FIGHTER PILOT. MY DAD WAS A FIGHTER PILOT.
WHENEVER HE SAW ANOTHER MAN FLY, HE DIDN'T CALL HIM "GOD."

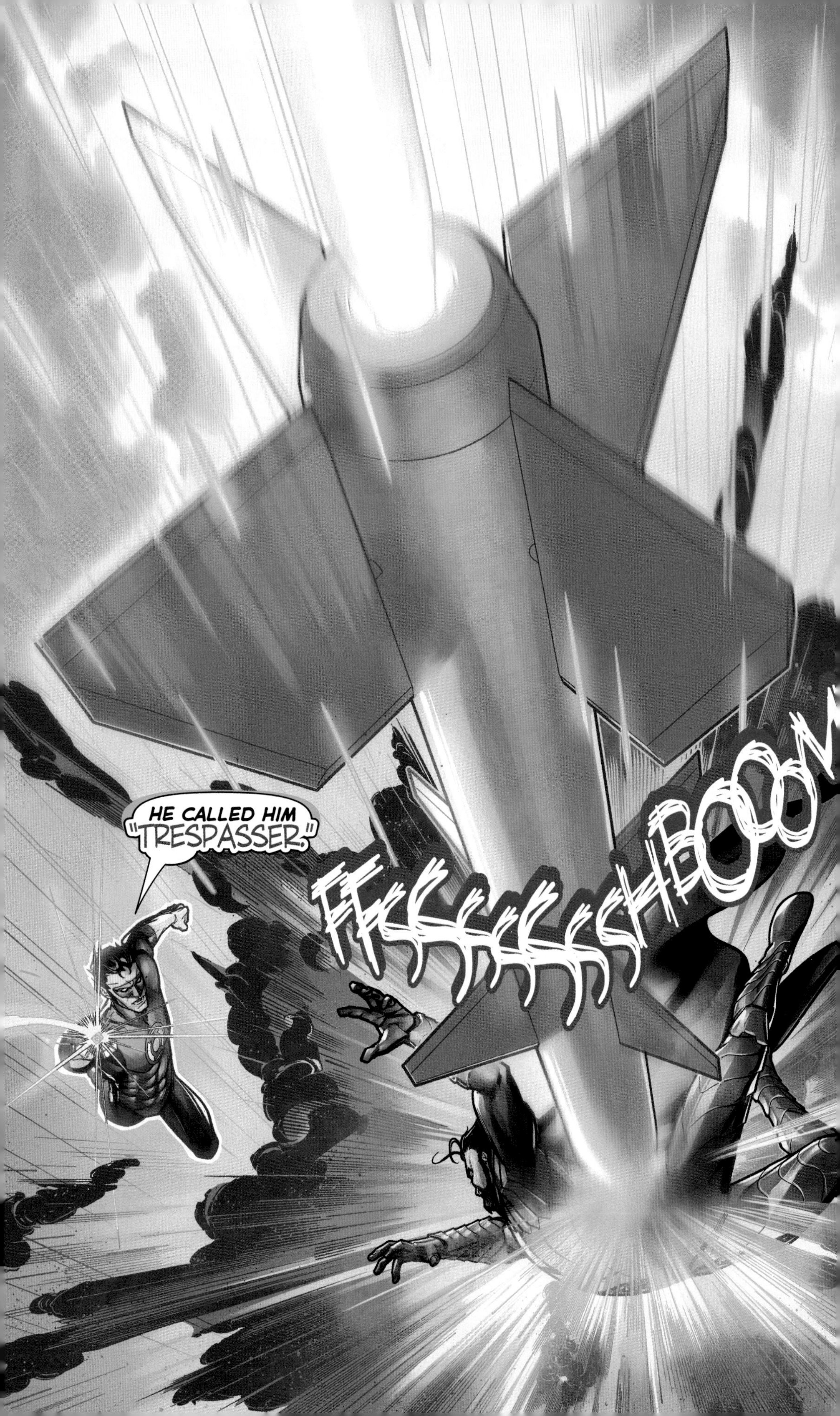
HE CALLED HIM "TRESPASSER."
FFSSSSSSSHBOOOM

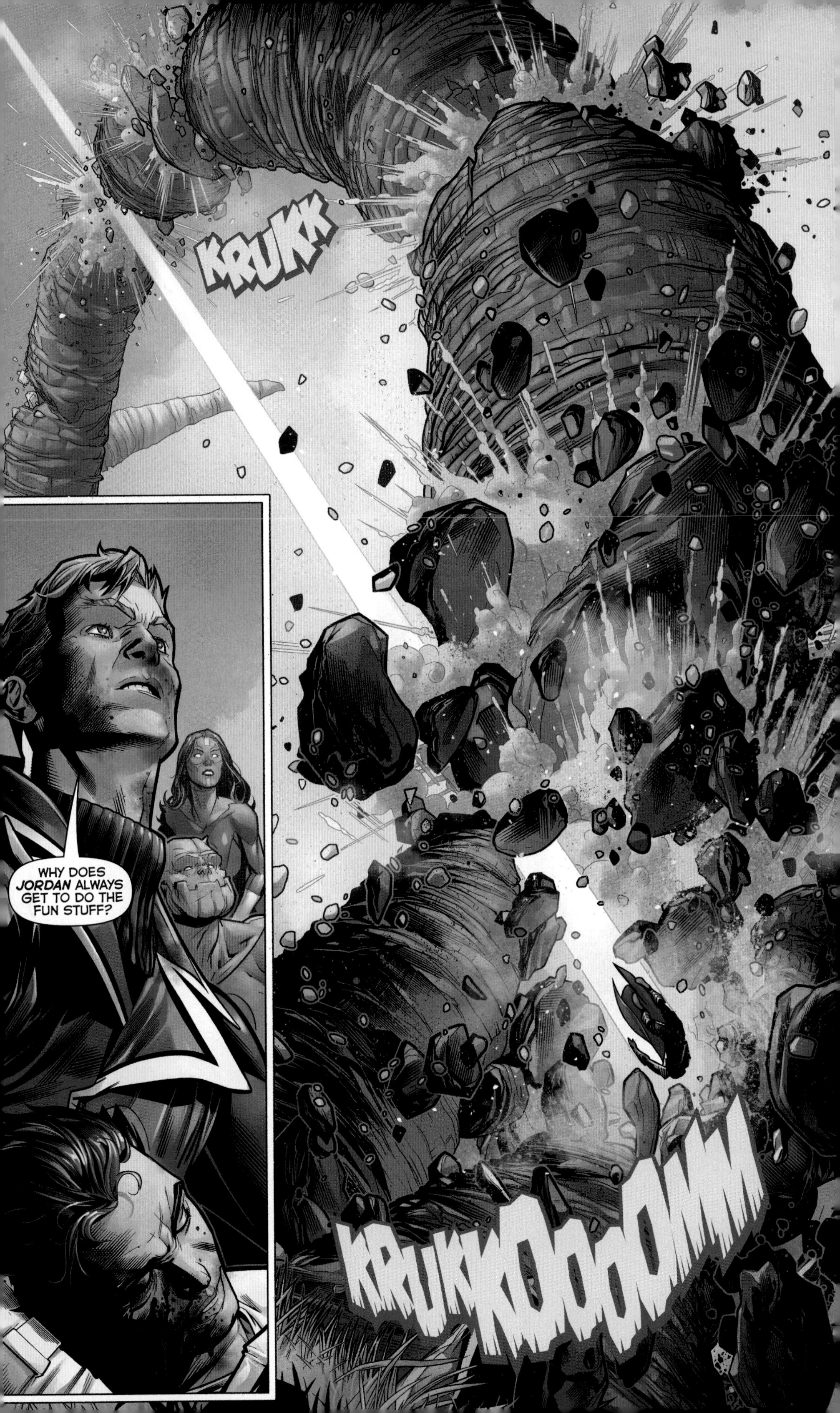
KRUKK
WHY DOES JORDAN ALWAYS GET TO DO THE FUN STUFF?
KRUKKOOOOMM

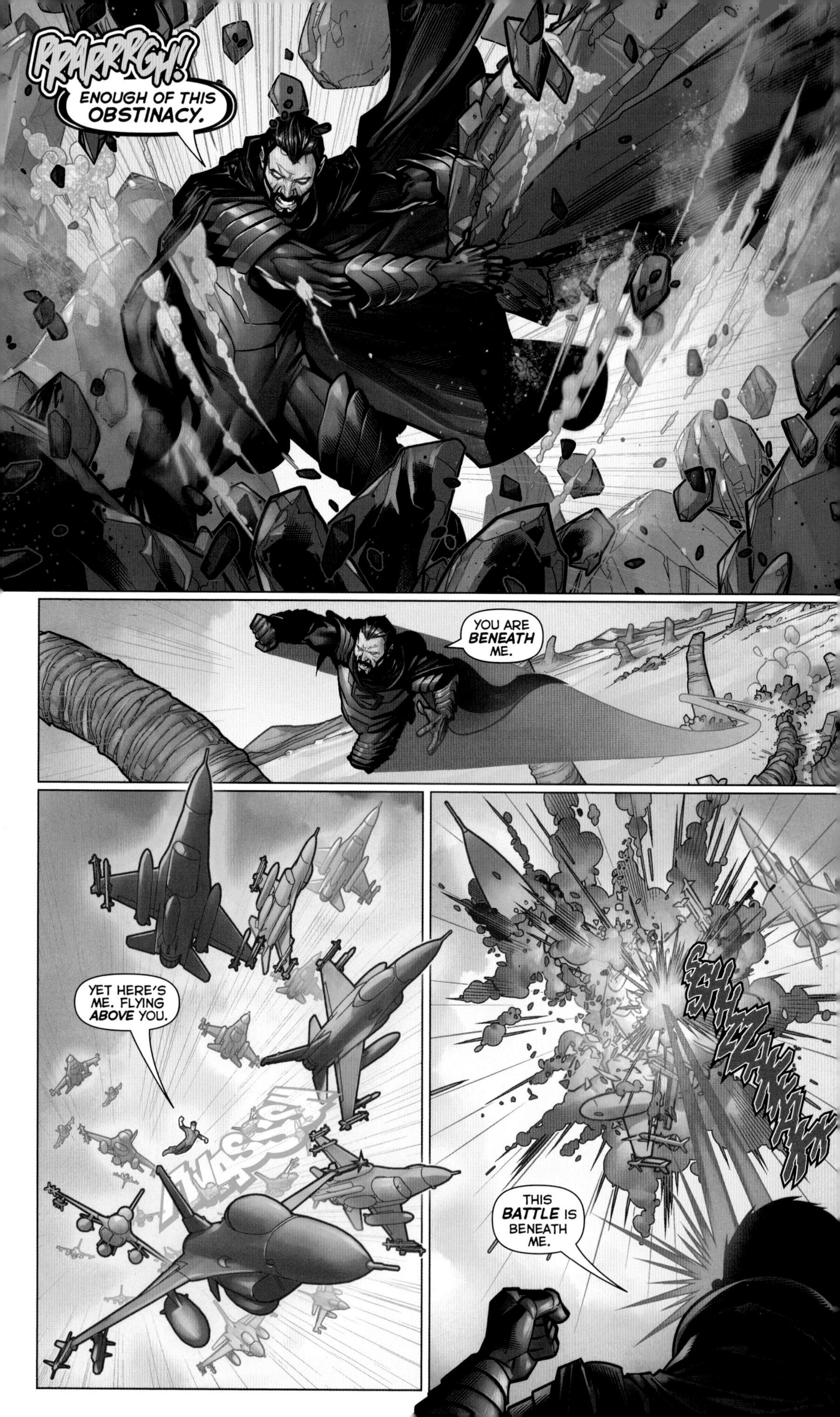
RRARRRGH!!
ENOUGH OF THIS OBSTINACY.
YOU ARE BENEATH ME.
YET HERE'S ME. FLYING ABOVE YOU.
THIS BATTLE IS BENEATH ME.

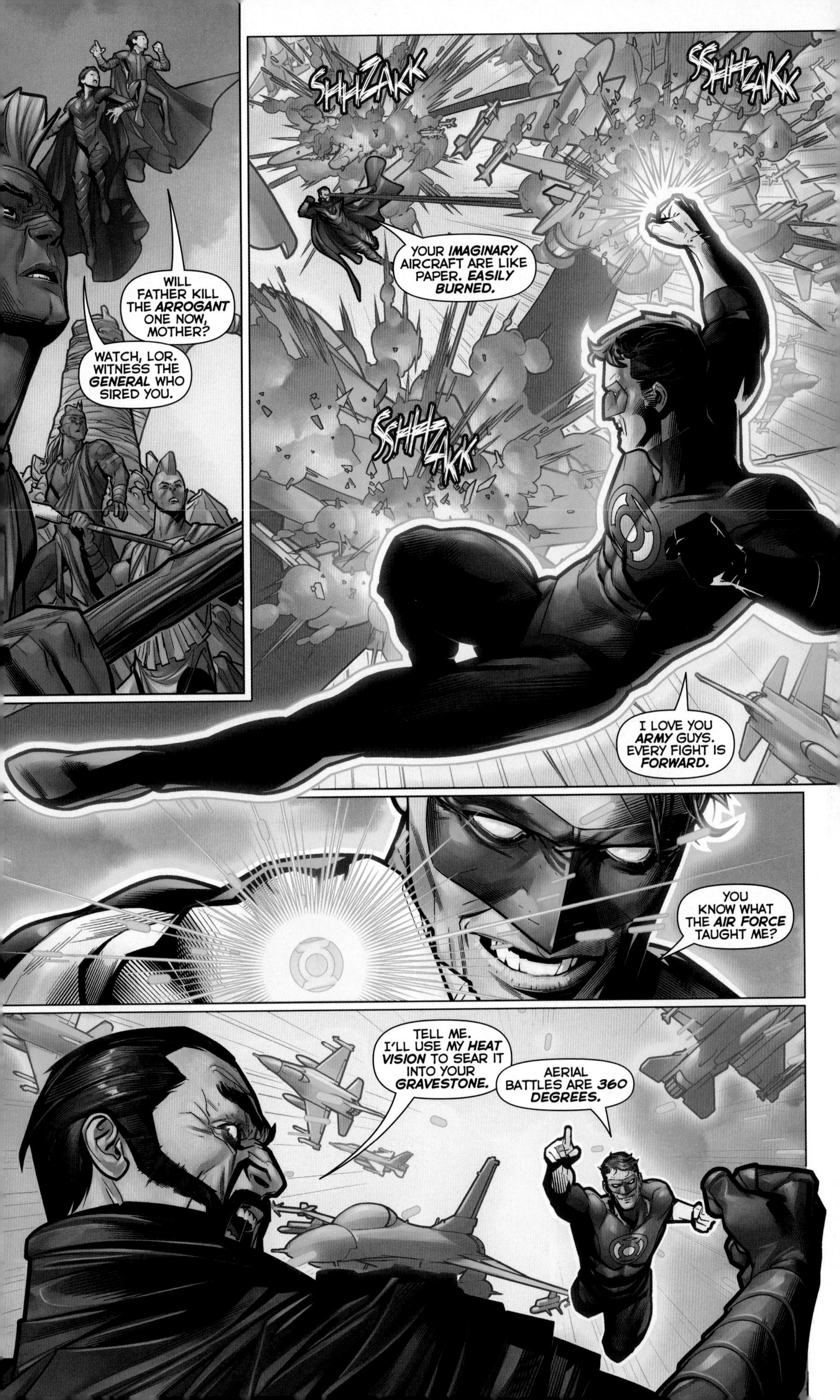

WILL FATHER KILL THE ARROGANT ONE NOW, MOTHER?
WATCH, LOR. WITNESS THE GENERAL WHO SIRED YOU.
SHHZAKK
SSHHZAKK
YOUR IMAGINARY AIRCRAFT ARE LIKE PAPER. EASILY BURNED.
SSHHZAKK
I LOVE YOU ARMY GUYS. EVERY FIGHT IS FORWARD.
YOU KNOW WHAT THE AIR FORCE TAUGHT ME?
TELL ME. I'LL USE MY HEAT VISION TO SEAR IT INTO YOUR GRAVESTONE.
AERIAL BATTLES ARE 360 DEGREES.

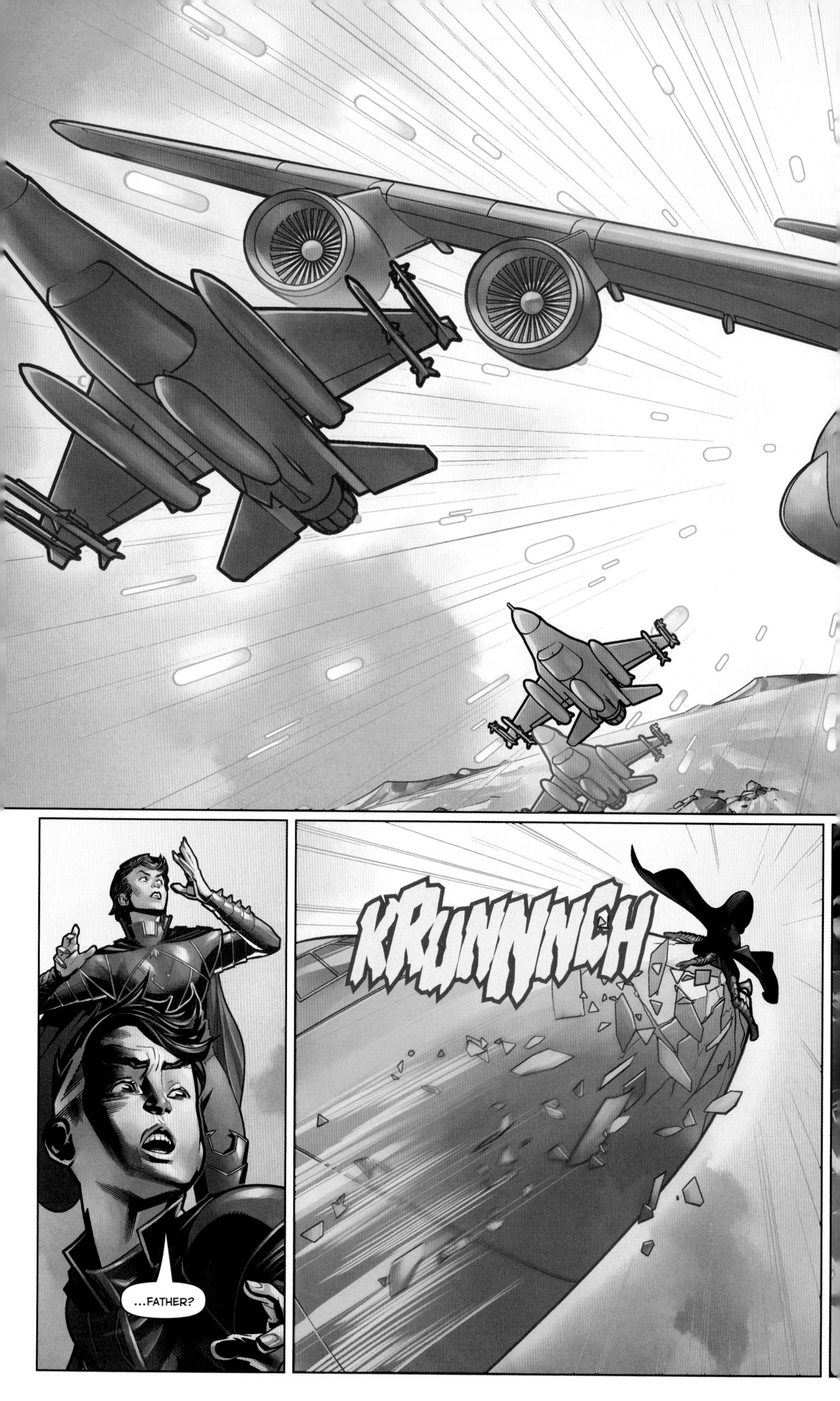
...FATHER?
KRUNNNCH

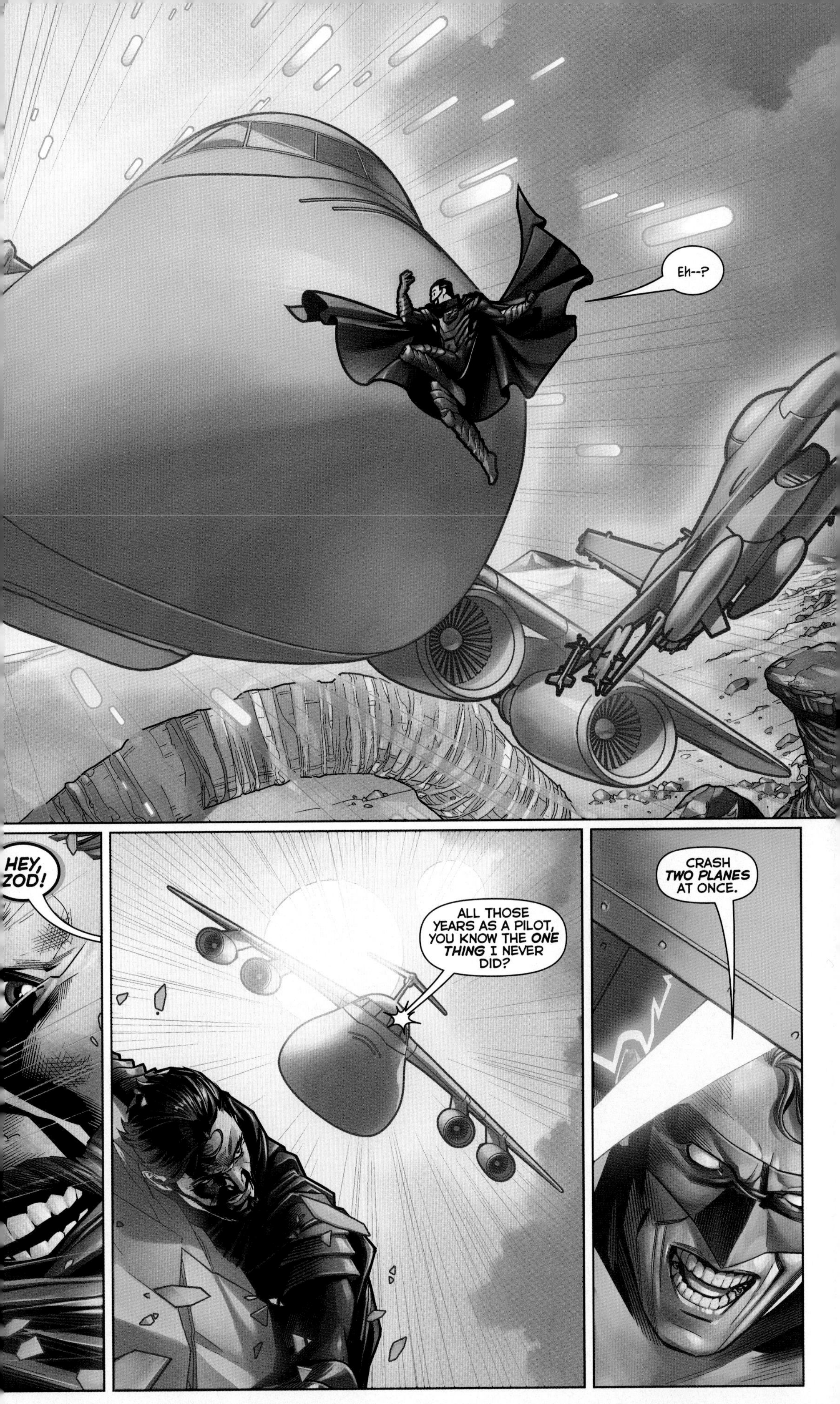
Eh--?
HEY, ZOD!
ALL THOSE YEARS AS A PILOT, YOU KNOW THE *ONE THING* I NEVER DID?
CRASH *TWO PLANES* AT ONCE.

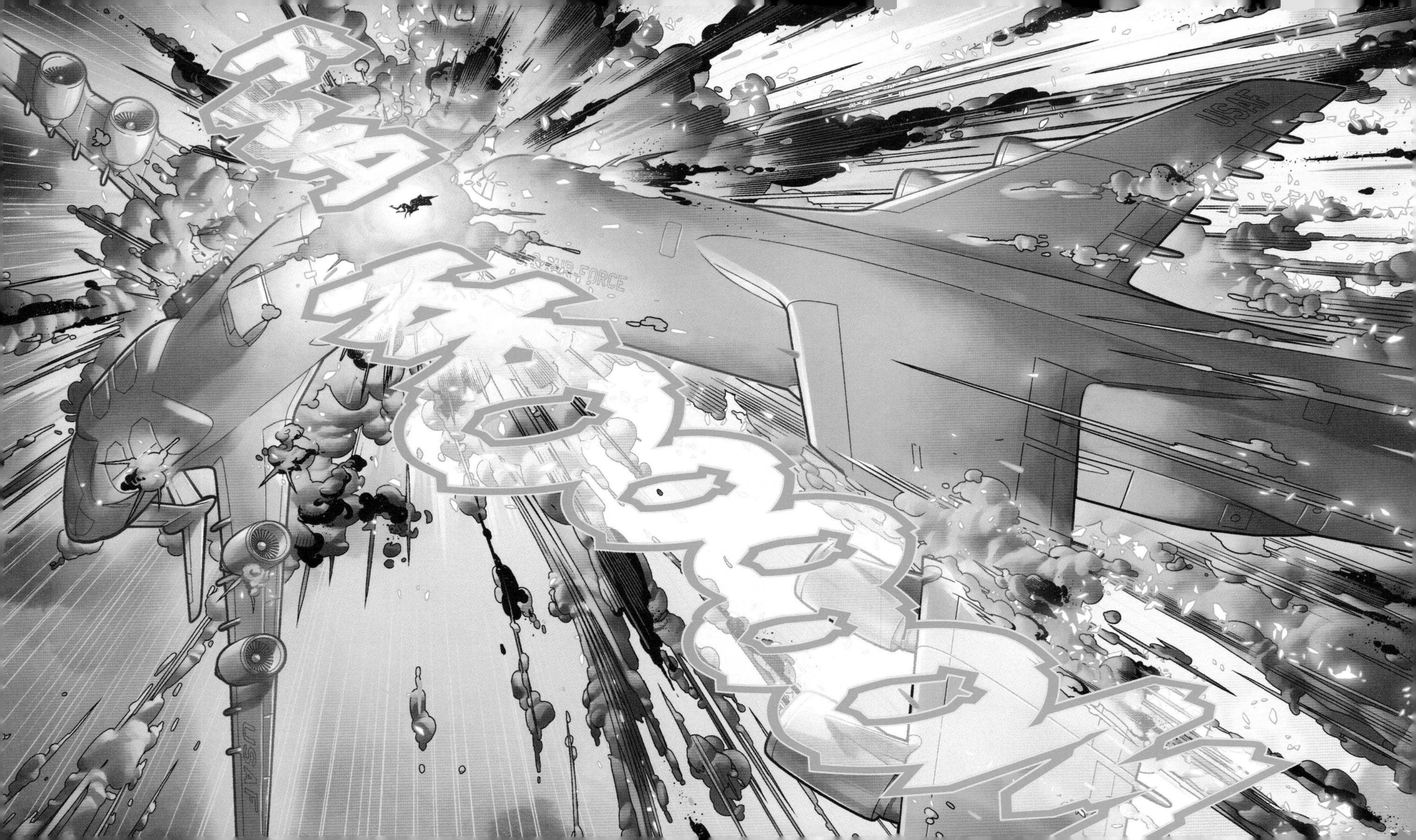
KA-KROOOOM
U.S. AIR FORCE
USAF
USAF

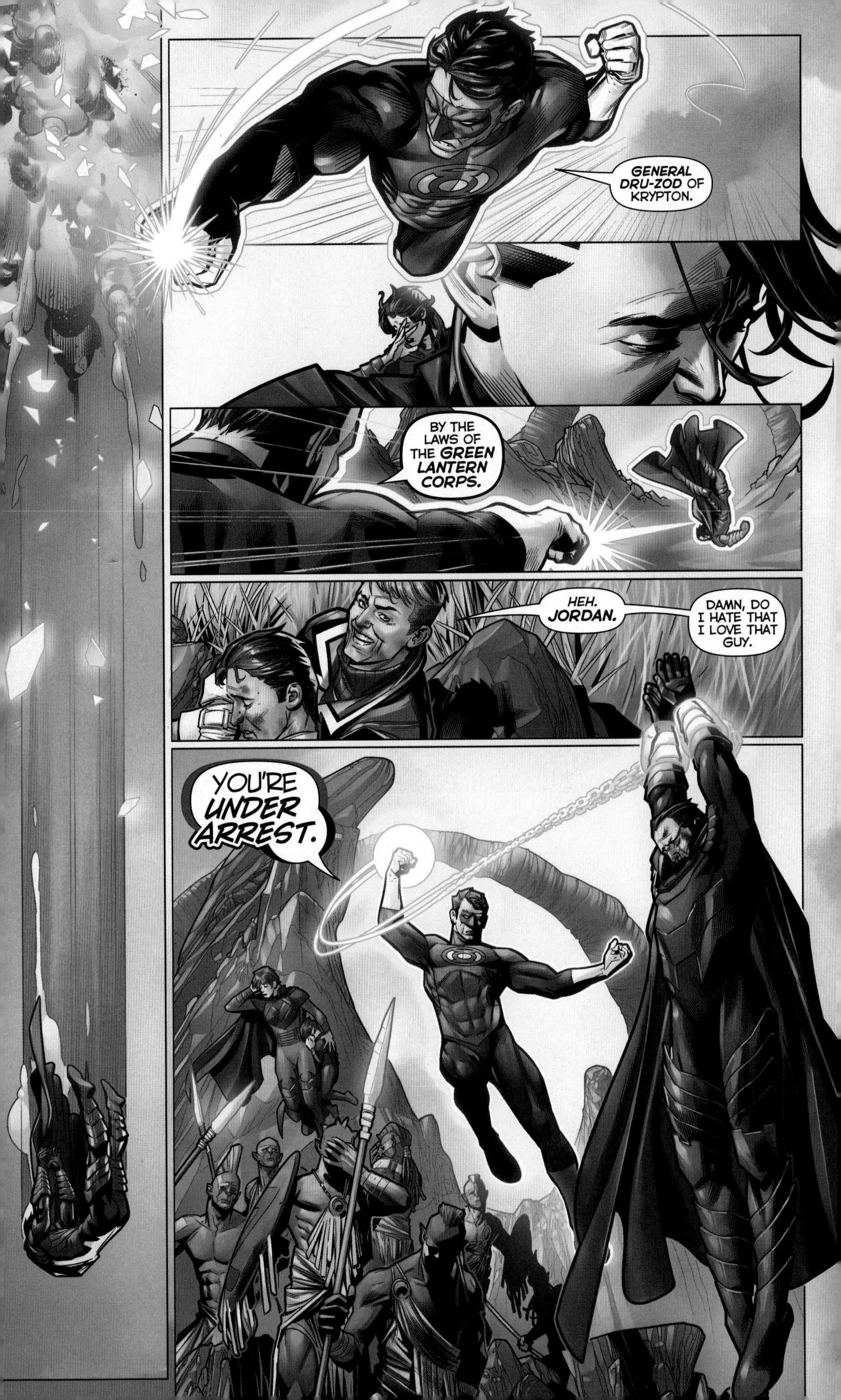

GENERAL DRU-ZOD OF KRYPTON.
BY THE LAWS OF THE GREEN LANTERN CORPS.
HEH. JORDAN.
DAMN, DO I HATE THAT I LOVE THAT GUY.
YOU'RE UNDER ARREST.

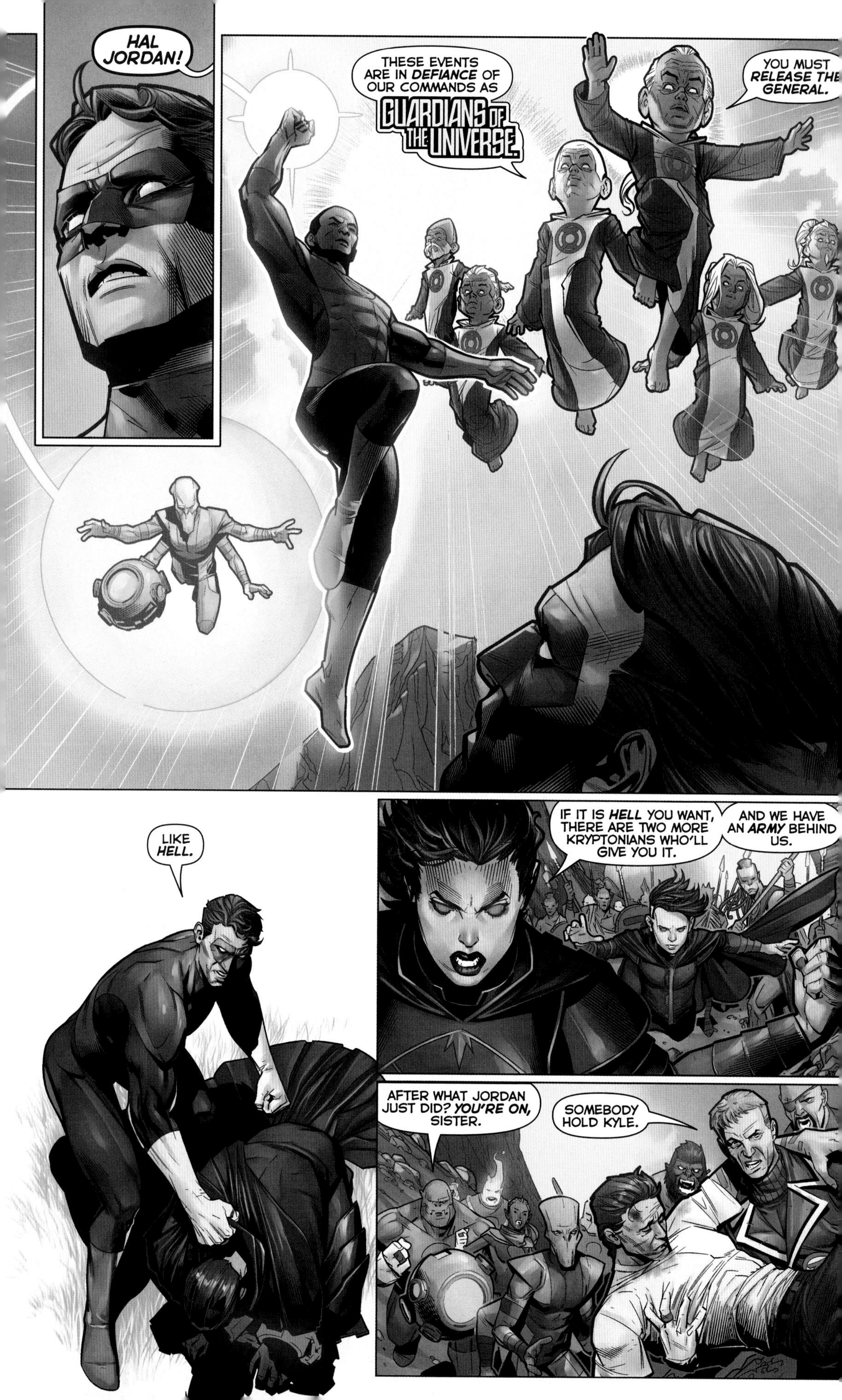
HAL JORDAN!
THESE EVENTS ARE IN DEFIANCE OF OUR COMMANDS AS GUARDIANS OF THE UNIVERSE.
YOU MUST RELEASE THE GENERAL.
LIKE HELL.
IF IT IS HELL YOU WANT, THERE ARE TWO MORE KRYPTONIANS WHO'LL GIVE YOU IT.
AND WE HAVE AN ARMY BEHIND US.
AFTER WHAT JORDAN JUST DID? YOU'RE ON, SISTER.
SOMEBODY HOLD KYLE.

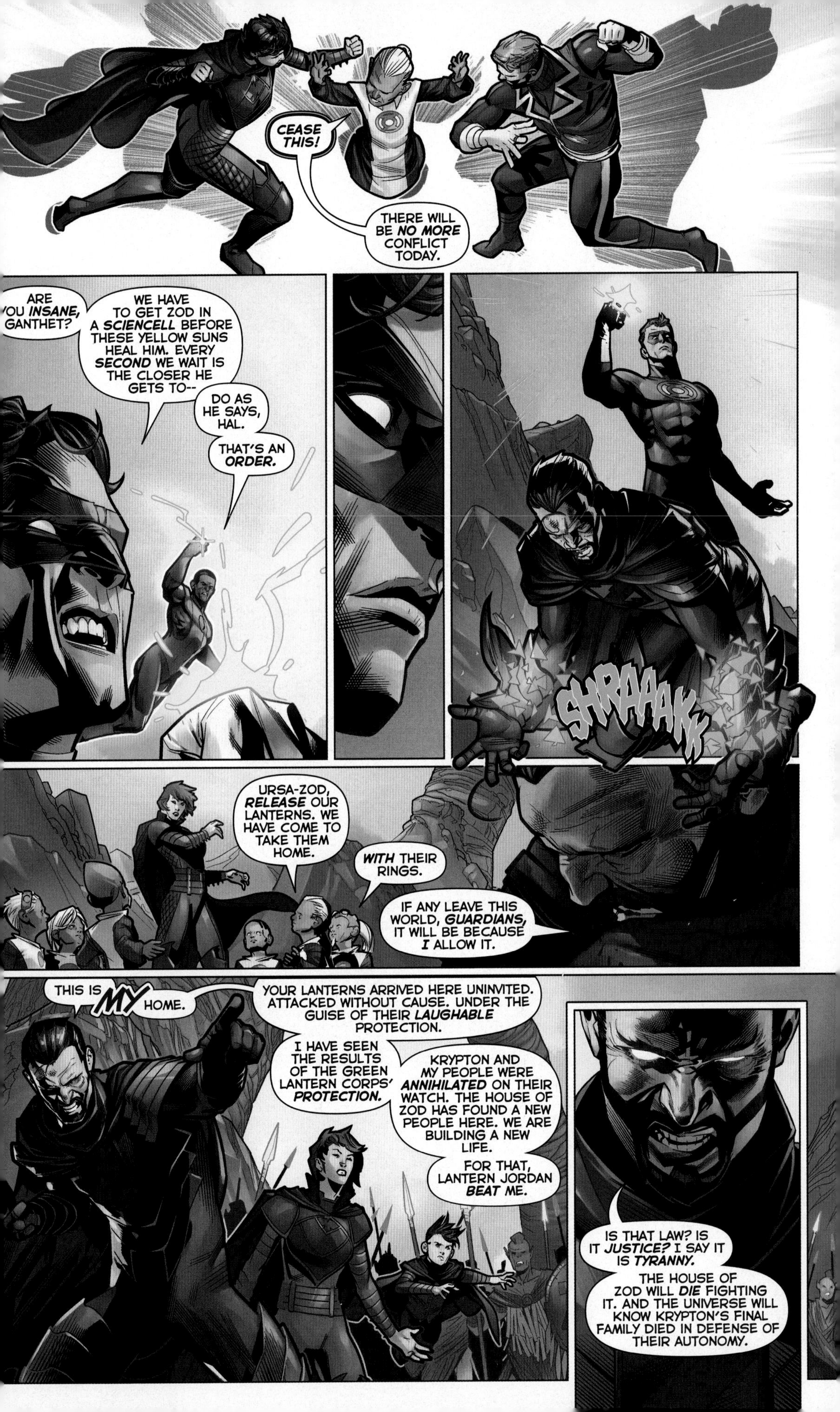
CEASE THIS!
THERE WILL BE NO MORE CONFLICT TODAY.
ARE YOU INSANE, GANTHET?
WE HAVE TO GET ZOD IN A SCIENCELL BEFORE THESE YELLOW SUNS HEAL HIM. EVERY SECOND WE WAIT IS THE CLOSER HE GETS TO--
DO AS HE SAYS, HAL.
THAT'S AN ORDER.
SHRAAAKK
URSA-ZOD, RELEASE OUR LANTERNS. WE HAVE COME TO TAKE THEM HOME.
WITH THEIR RINGS.
IF ANY LEAVE THIS WORLD, GUARDIANS, IT WILL BE BECAUSE I ALLOW IT.
THIS IS MY HOME.
YOUR LANTERNS ARRIVED HERE UNINVITED. ATTACKED WITHOUT CAUSE. UNDER THE GUISE OF THEIR LAUGHABLE PROTECTION.
I HAVE SEEN THE RESULTS OF THE GREEN LANTERN CORPS' PROTECTION.
KRYPTON AND MY PEOPLE WERE ANNIHILATED ON THEIR WATCH. THE HOUSE OF ZOD HAS FOUND A NEW PEOPLE HERE. WE ARE BUILDING A NEW LIFE.
FOR THAT, LANTERN JORDAN BEAT ME.
IS THAT LAW? IS IT JUSTICE? I SAY IT IS TYRANNY.
THE HOUSE OF ZOD WILL DIE FIGHTING IT. AND THE UNIVERSE WILL KNOW KRYPTON'S FINAL FAMILY DIED IN DEFENSE OF THEIR AUTONOMY.

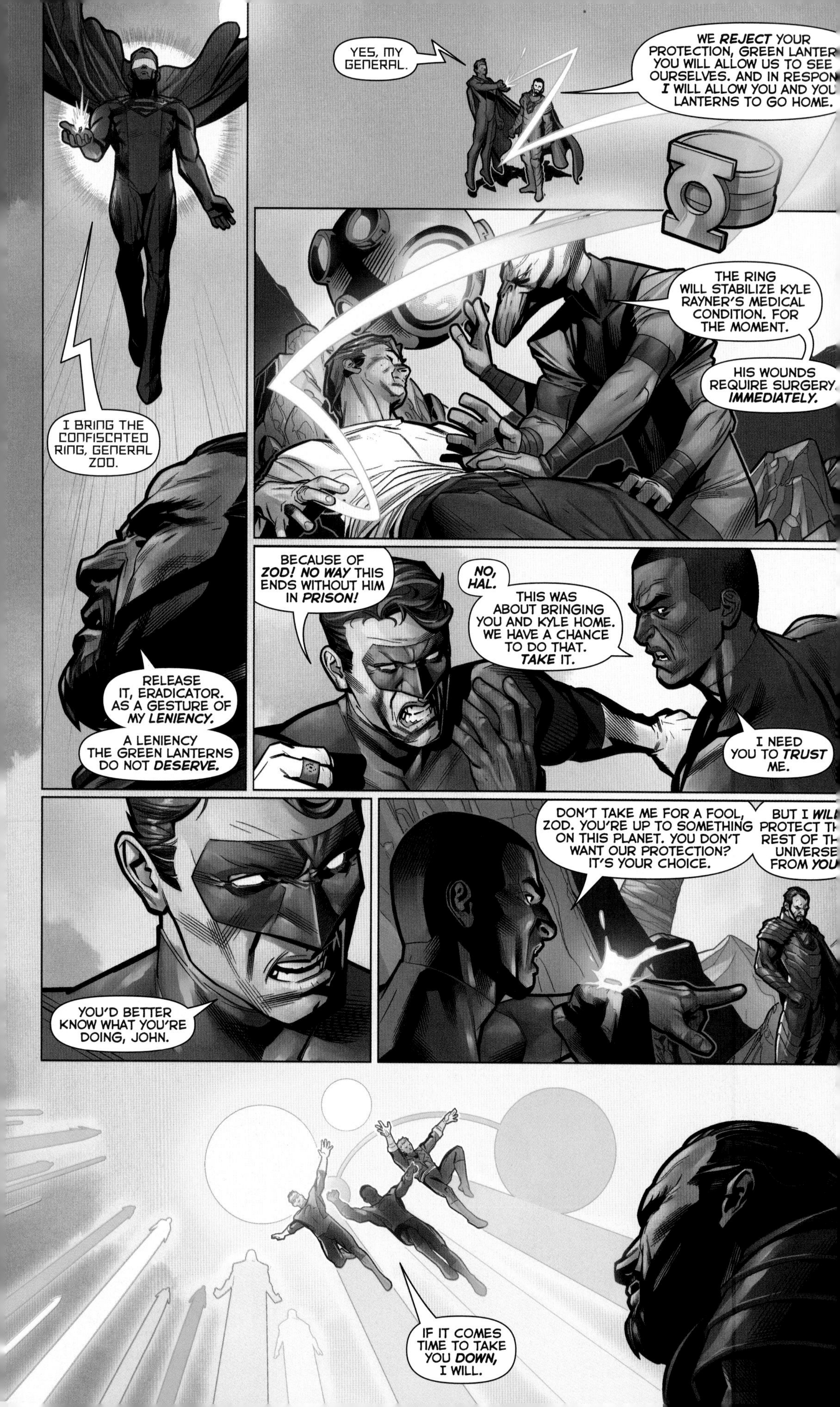

YES, MY GENERAL.
WE REJECT YOUR PROTECTION, GREEN LANTER YOU WILL ALLOW US TO SEE OURSELVES. AND IN RESPON I WILL ALLOW YOU AND YOU LANTERNS TO GO HOME.
I BRING THE CONFISCATED RING, GENERAL ZOD.
THE RING WILL STABILIZE KYLE RAYNER'S MEDICAL CONDITION. FOR THE MOMENT.
HIS WOUNDS REQUIRE SURGERY. IMMEDIATELY.
RELEASE IT, ERADICATOR. AS A GESTURE OF MY LENIENCY.
A LENIENCY THE GREEN LANTERNS DO NOT DESERVE.
BECAUSE OF ZOD! NO WAY THIS ENDS WITHOUT HIM IN PRISON!
NO, HAL.
THIS WAS ABOUT BRINGING YOU AND KYLE HOME. WE HAVE A CHANCE TO DO THAT. TAKE IT.
I NEED YOU TO TRUST ME.
YOU'D BETTER KNOW WHAT YOU'RE DOING, JOHN.
DON'T TAKE ME FOR A FOOL, ZOD. YOU'RE UP TO SOMETHING ON THIS PLANET. YOU DON'T WANT OUR PROTECTION? IT'S YOUR CHOICE.
BUT I WIL PROTECT TH REST OF TH UNIVERSE FROM YOU
IF IT COMES TIME TO TAKE YOU DOWN, I WILL.

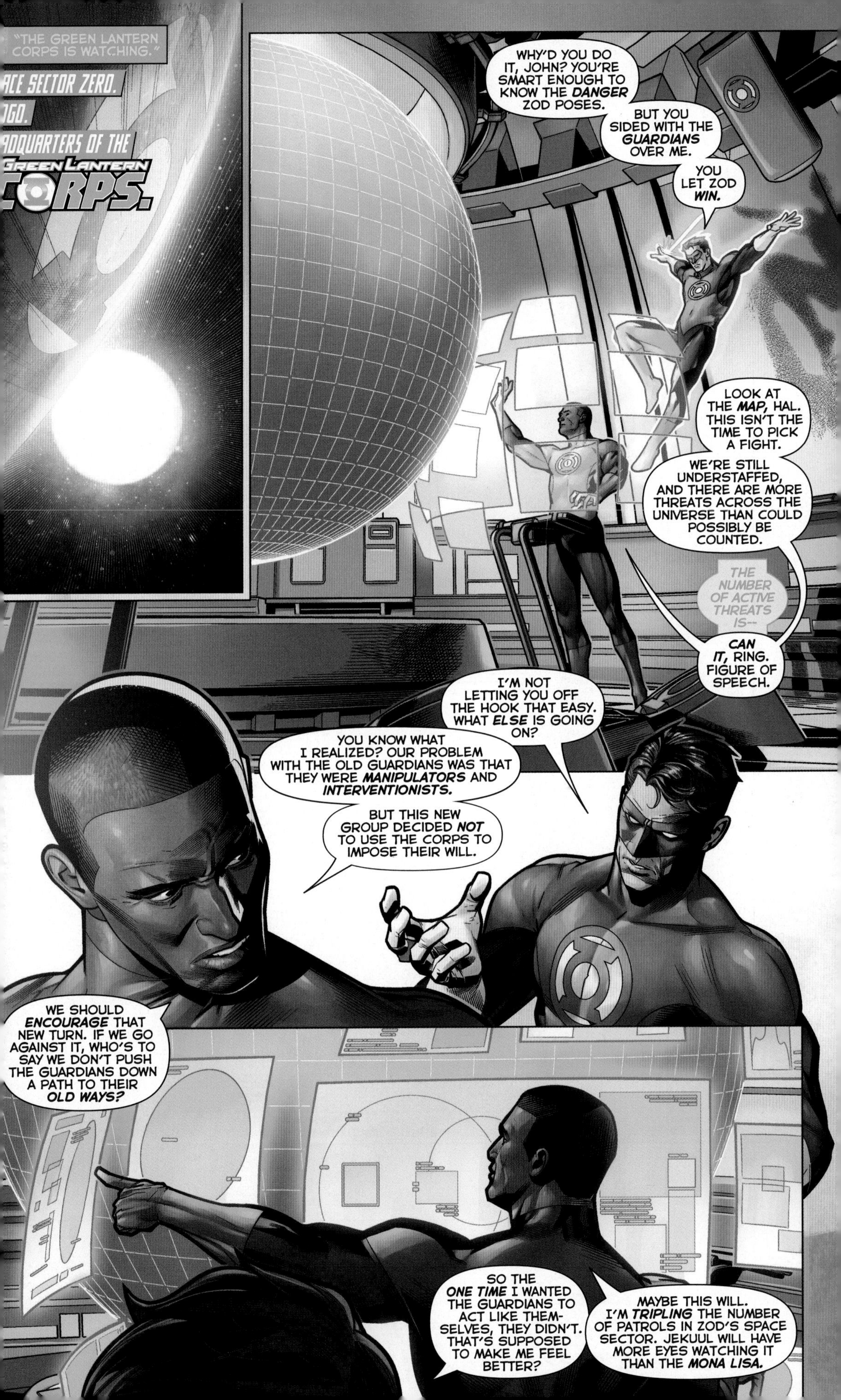
"THE GREEN LANTERN CORPS IS WATCHING."
ACE SECTOR ZERO.
OGO.
ADQUARTERS OF THE GREEN LANTERN CORPS.
WHY'D YOU DO IT, JOHN? YOU'RE SMART ENOUGH TO KNOW THE DANGER ZOD POSES.
BUT YOU SIDED WITH THE GUARDIANS OVER ME.
YOU LET ZOD WIN.
LOOK AT THE MAP, HAL. THIS ISN'T THE TIME TO PICK A FIGHT.
WE'RE STILL UNDERSTAFFED, AND THERE ARE MORE THREATS ACROSS THE UNIVERSE THAN COULD POSSIBLY BE COUNTED.
THE NUMBER OF ACTIVE THREATS IS--
CAN IT, RING. FIGURE OF SPEECH.
I'M NOT LETTING YOU OFF THE HOOK THAT EASY. WHAT ELSE IS GOING ON?
YOU KNOW WHAT I REALIZED? OUR PROBLEM WITH THE OLD GUARDIANS WAS THAT THEY WERE MANIPULATORS AND INTERVENTIONISTS.
BUT THIS NEW GROUP DECIDED NOT TO USE THE CORPS TO IMPOSE THEIR WILL.
WE SHOULD ENCOURAGE THAT NEW TURN. IF WE GO AGAINST IT, WHO'S TO SAY WE DON'T PUSH THE GUARDIANS DOWN A PATH TO THEIR OLD WAYS?
SO THE ONE TIME I WANTED THE GUARDIANS TO ACT LIKE THEMSELVES, THEY DIDN'T. THAT'S SUPPOSED TO MAKE ME FEEL BETTER?
MAYBE THIS WILL. I'M TRIPLING THE NUMBER OF PATROLS IN ZOD'S SPACE SECTOR. JEKUUL WILL HAVE MORE EYES WATCHING IT THAN THE MONA LISA.

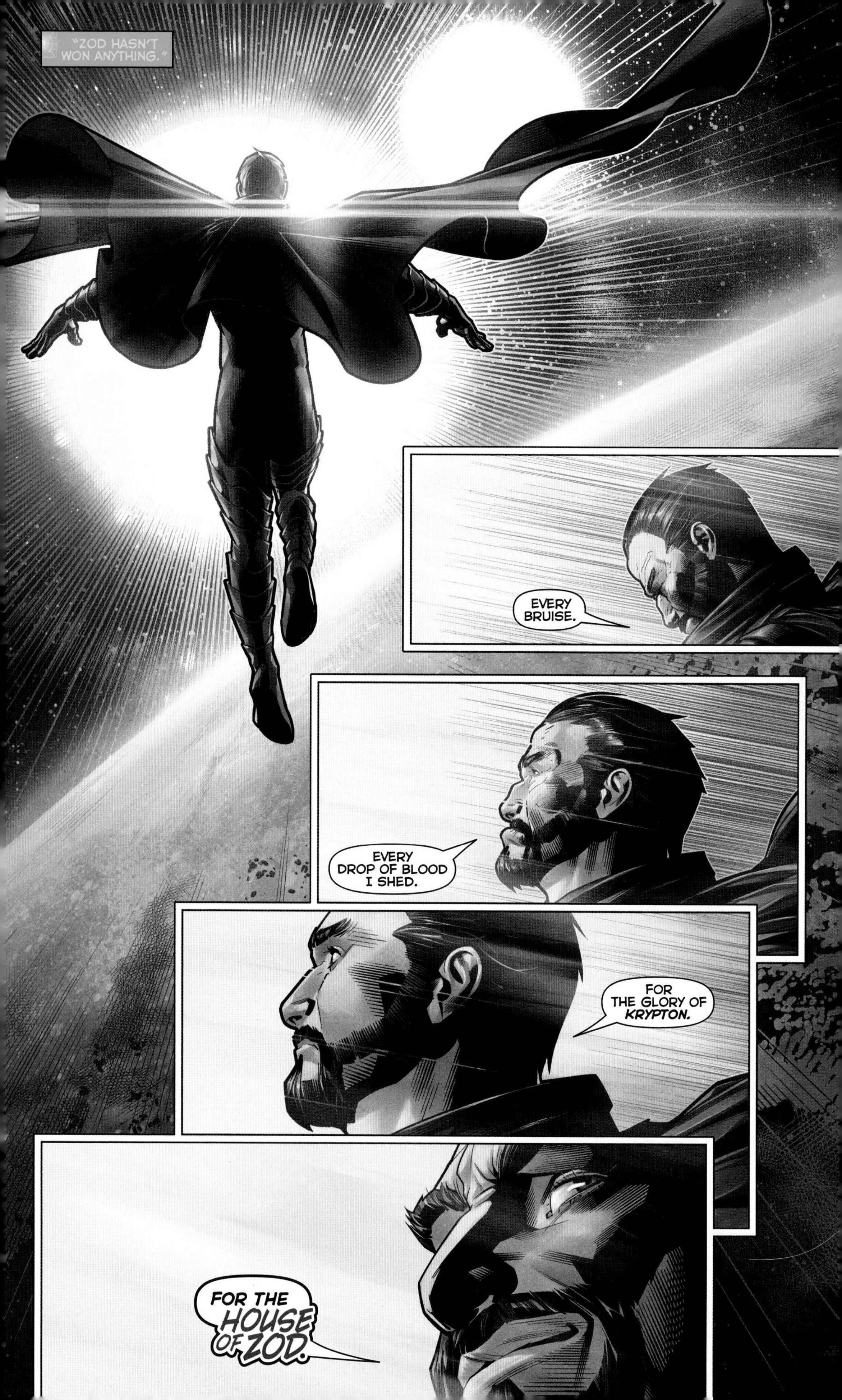
"ZOD HASN'T WON ANYTHING."
EVERY BRUISE.
EVERY DROP OF BLOOD I SHED.
FOR THE GLORY OF *KRYPTON.*
FOR THE *HOUSE OF ZOD.*

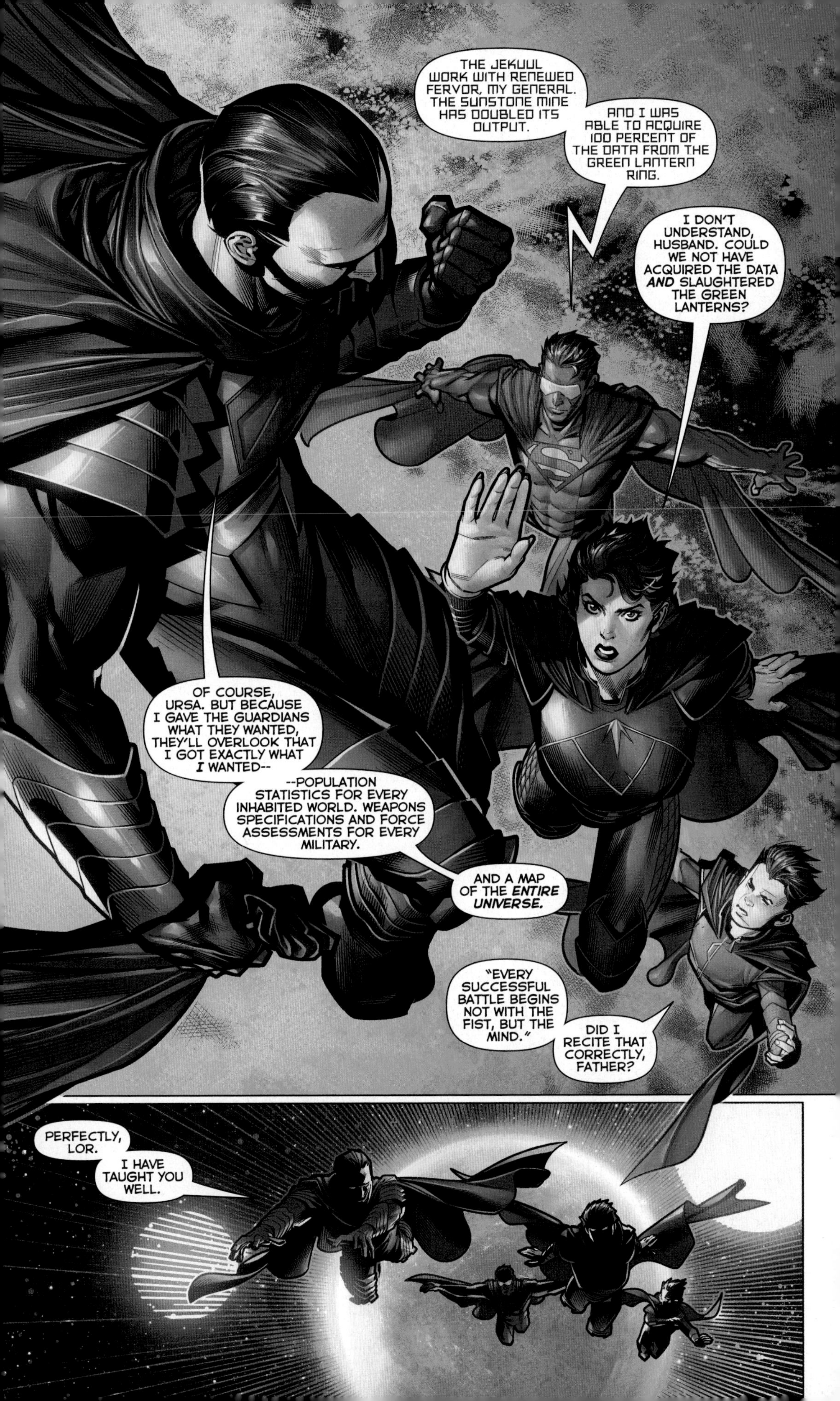
THE JEKUUL WORK WITH RENEWED FERVOR, MY GENERAL. THE SUNSTONE MINE HAS DOUBLED ITS OUTPUT.
AND I WAS ABLE TO ACQUIRE 100 PERCENT OF THE DATA FROM THE GREEN LANTERN RING.
I DON'T UNDERSTAND, HUSBAND. COULD WE NOT HAVE ACQUIRED THE DATA AND SLAUGHTERED THE GREEN LANTERNS?
OF COURSE, URSA. BUT BECAUSE I GAVE THE GUARDIANS WHAT THEY WANTED, THEY'LL OVERLOOK THAT I GOT EXACTLY WHAT I WANTED--
--POPULATION STATISTICS FOR EVERY INHABITED WORLD. WEAPONS SPECIFICATIONS AND FORCE ASSESSMENTS FOR EVERY MILITARY.
AND A MAP OF THE ENTIRE UNIVERSE.
"EVERY SUCCESSFUL BATTLE BEGINS NOT WITH THE FIST, BUT THE MIND."
DID I RECITE THAT CORRECTLY, FATHER?
PERFECTLY, LOR.
I HAVE TAUGHT YOU WELL.

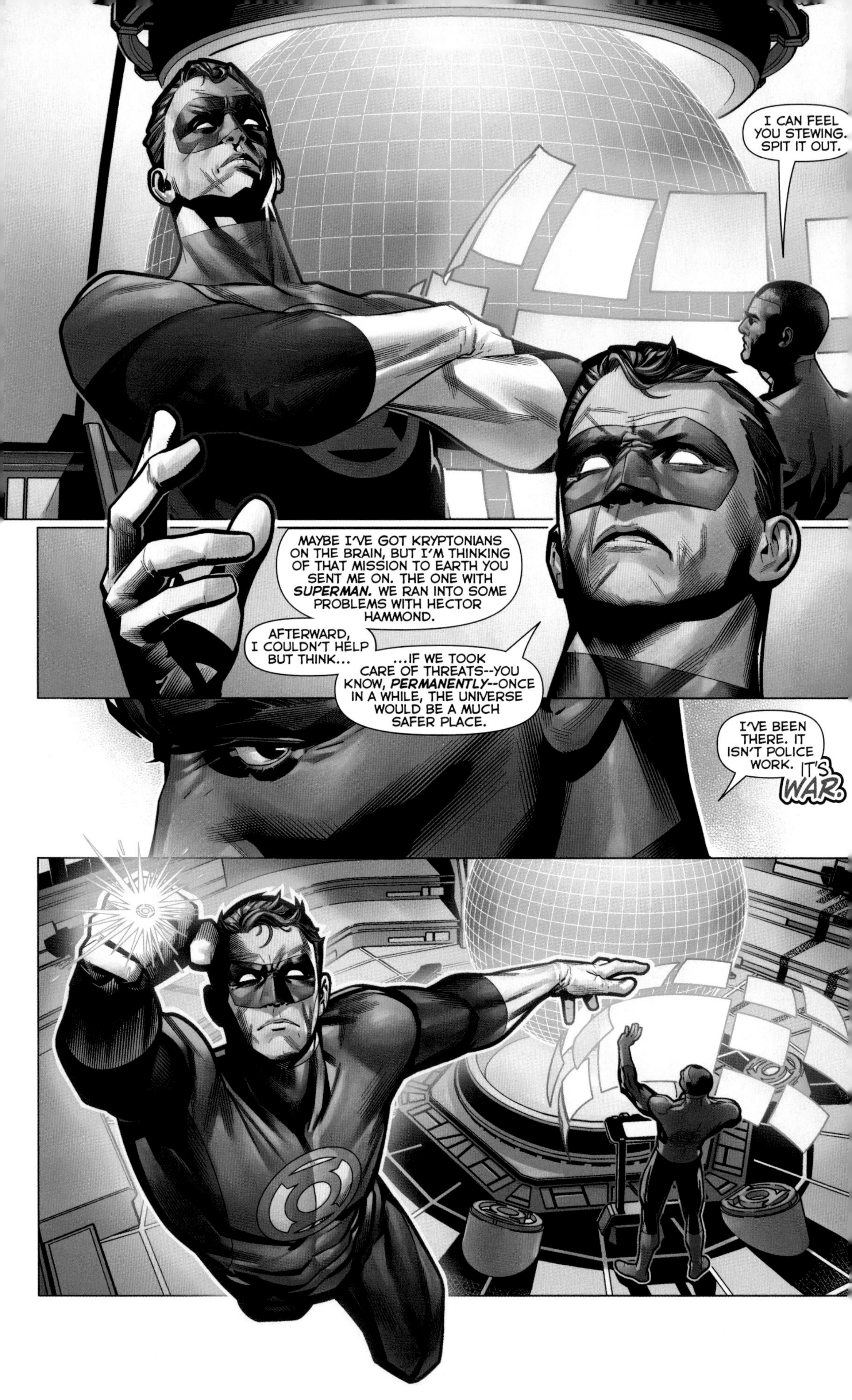
I CAN FEEL YOU STEWING. SPIT IT OUT.
MAYBE I'VE GOT KRYPTONIANS ON THE BRAIN, BUT I'M THINKING OF THAT MISSION TO EARTH YOU SENT ME ON. THE ONE WITH SUPERMAN. WE RAN INTO SOME PROBLEMS WITH HECTOR HAMMOND.
AFTERWARD, I COULDN'T HELP BUT THINK...
...IF WE TOOK CARE OF THREATS--YOU KNOW, PERMANENTLY--ONCE IN A WHILE, THE UNIVERSE WOULD BE A MUCH SAFER PLACE.
I'VE BEEN THERE. IT ISN'T POLICE WORK. IT'S WAR.

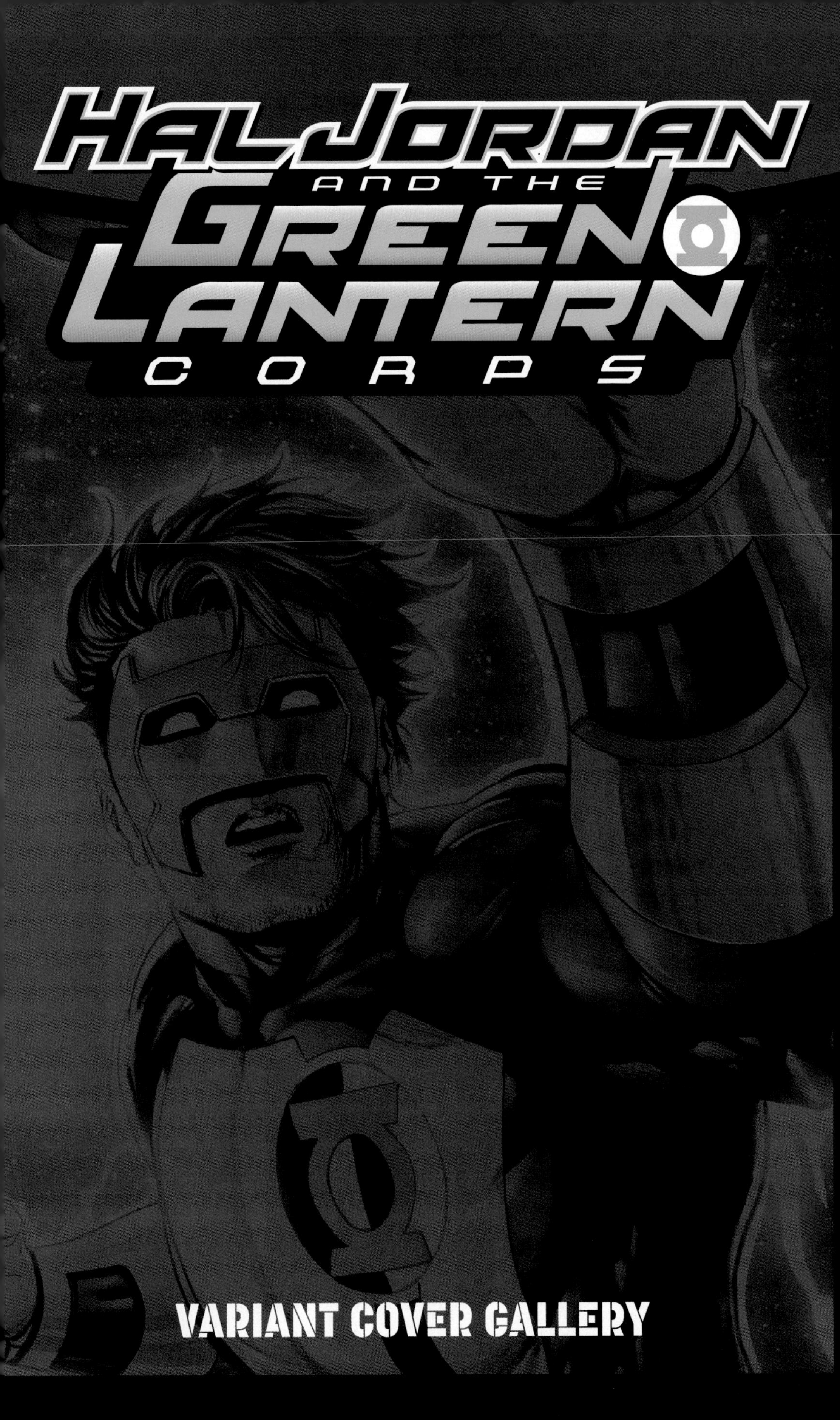
HAL JORDAN AND THE GREEN LANTERN CORPS
VARIANT COVER GALLERY

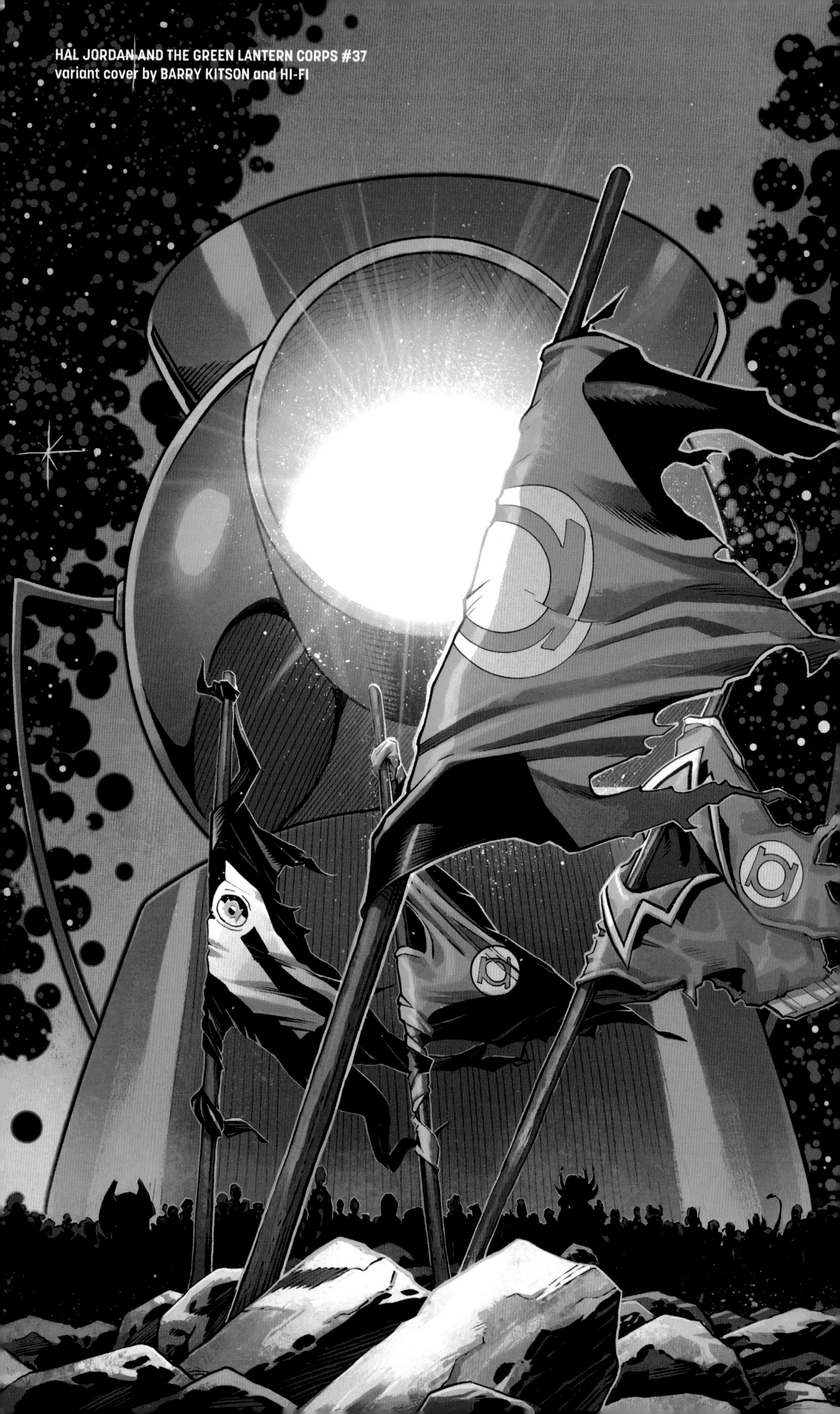

HAL JORDAN AND THE GREEN LANTERN CORPS #37
variant cover by BARRY KITSON and HI-FI

HAL JORDAN AND THE GREEN LANTERN CORPS #38
variant cover by TYLER KIRKHAM and TOMEU MOREY

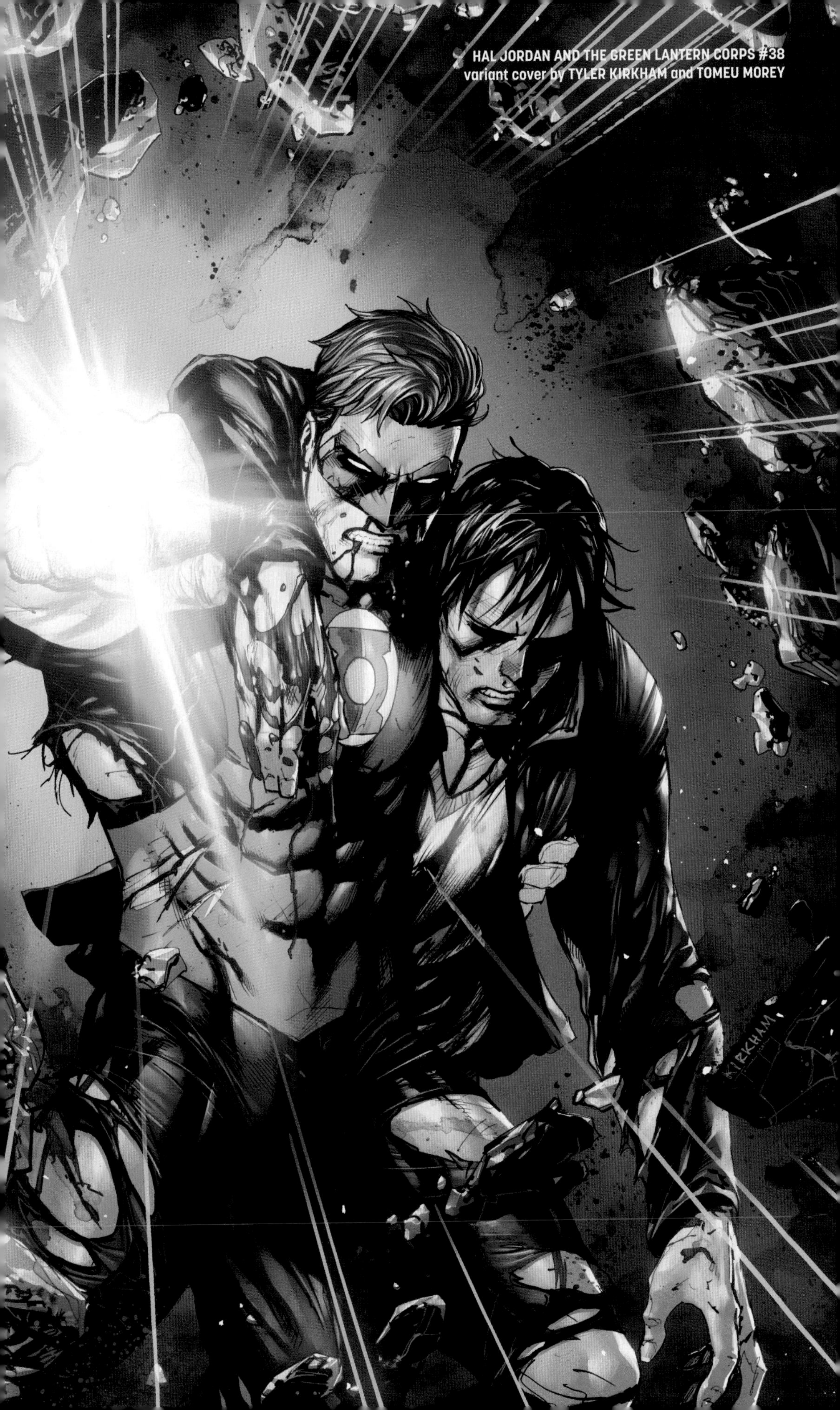
KIRKHAM

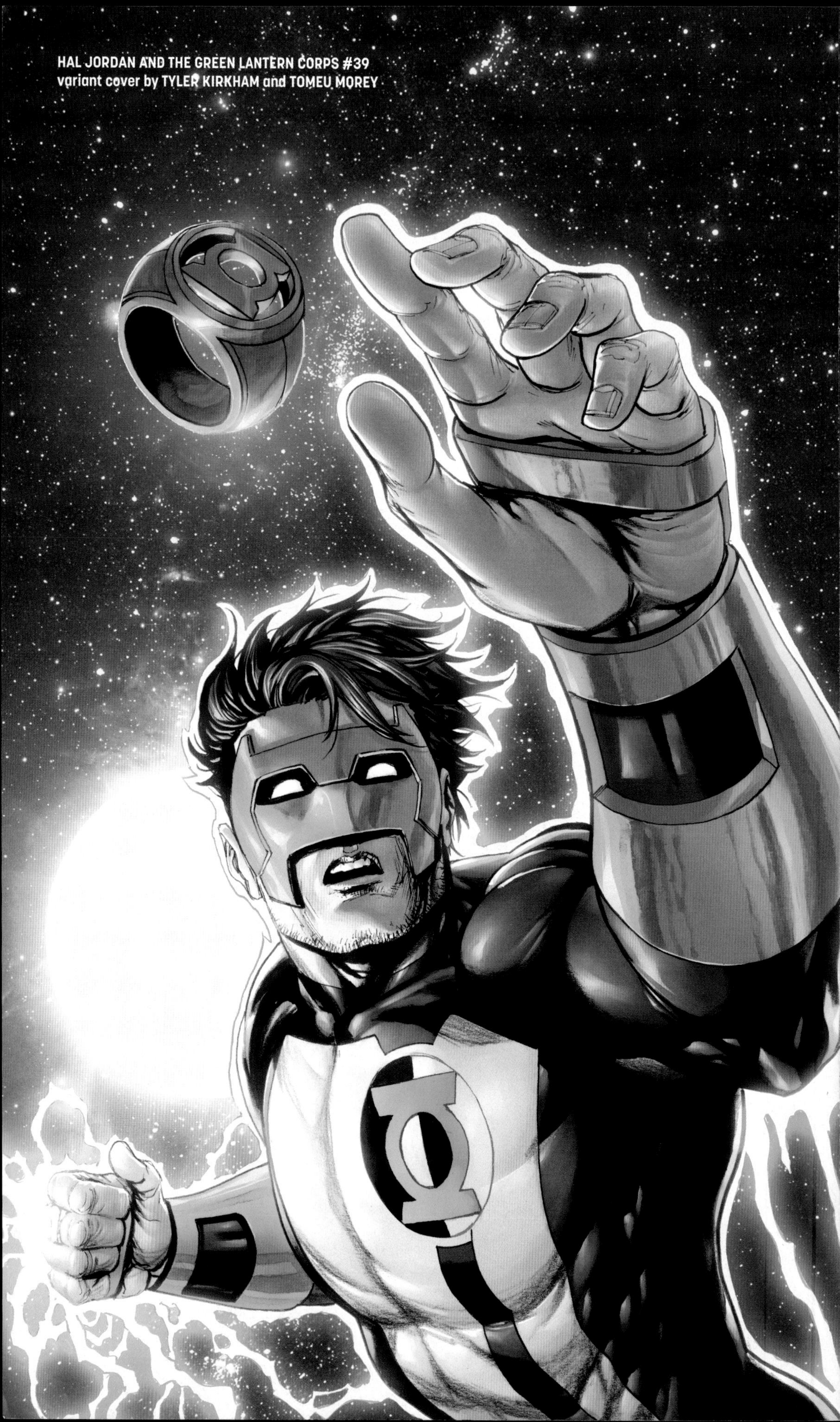

HAL JORDAN AND THE GREEN LANTERN CORPS #39
variant cover by TYLER KIRKHAM and TOMEU MOREY

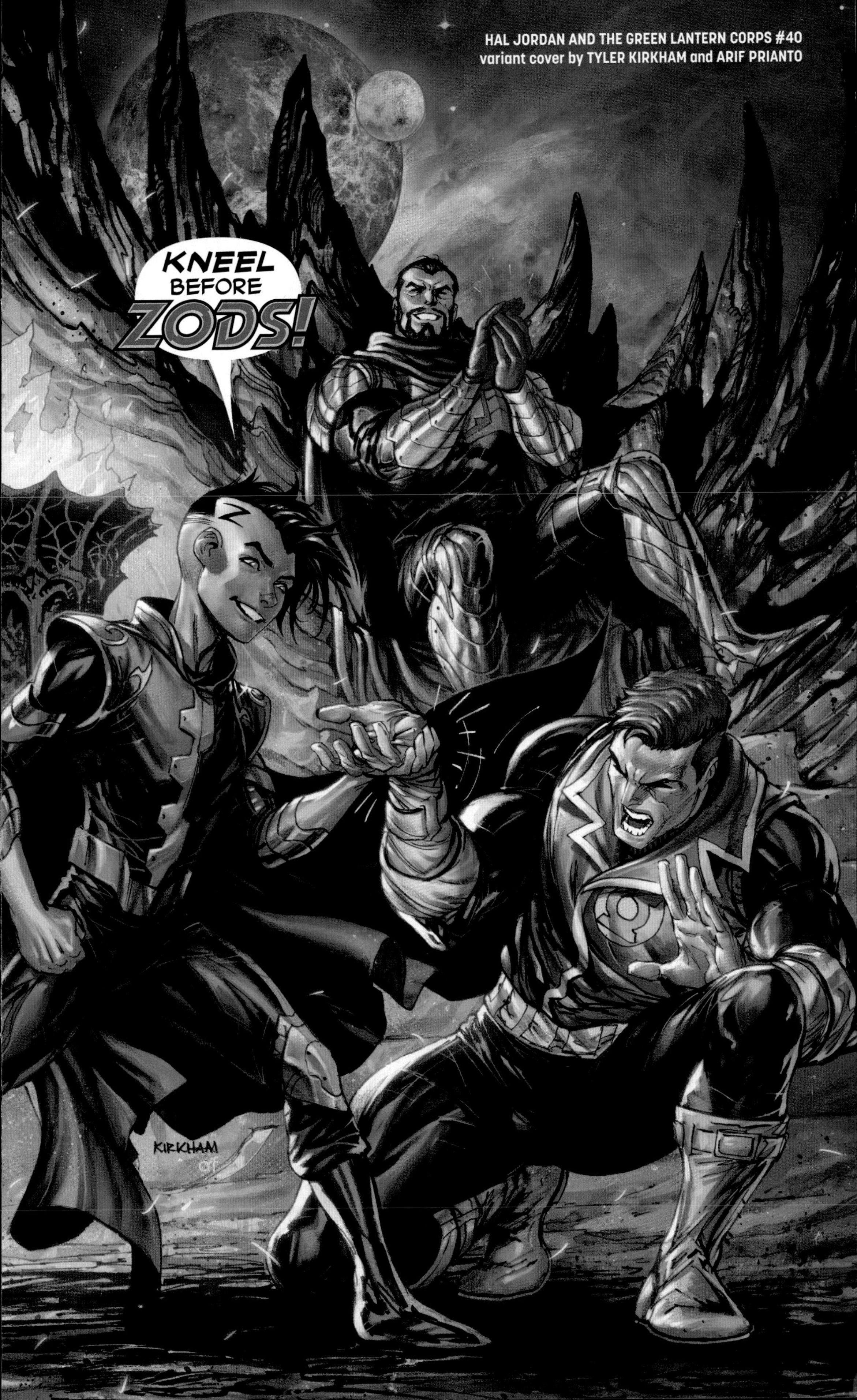
KNEEL BEFORE ZODS!
KIRKHAM
arf

HAL JORDAN AND THE GREEN LANTERN CORPS #40
variant cover by TYLER KIRKHAM and ARIF PRIANTO

HAL JORDAN AND THE GREEN LANTERN CORPS #41
variant cover by TYLER KIRKHAM and ARIF PRIANTO

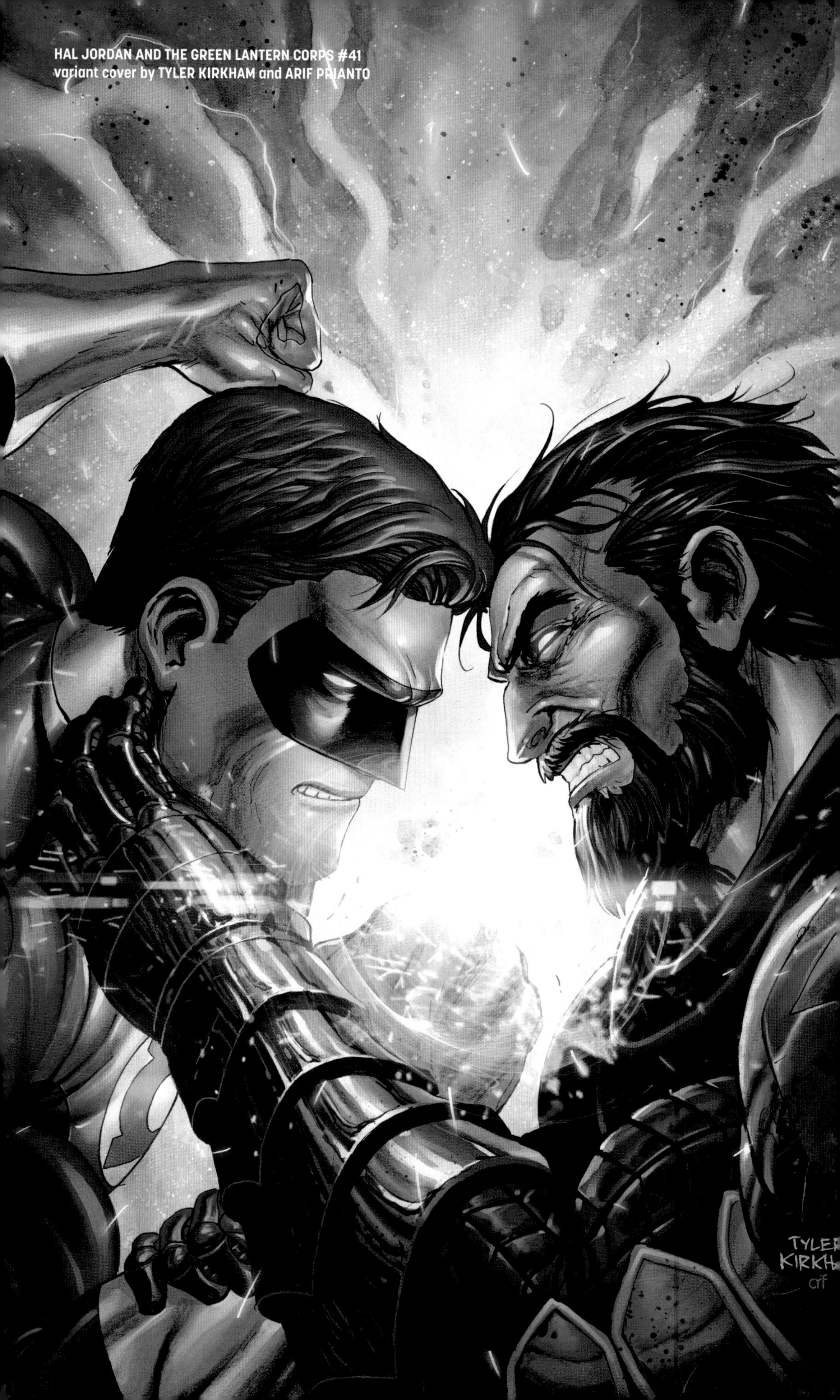

JEKUUL HAY CHARACTER SKETCH
by RAFA SANDOVAL

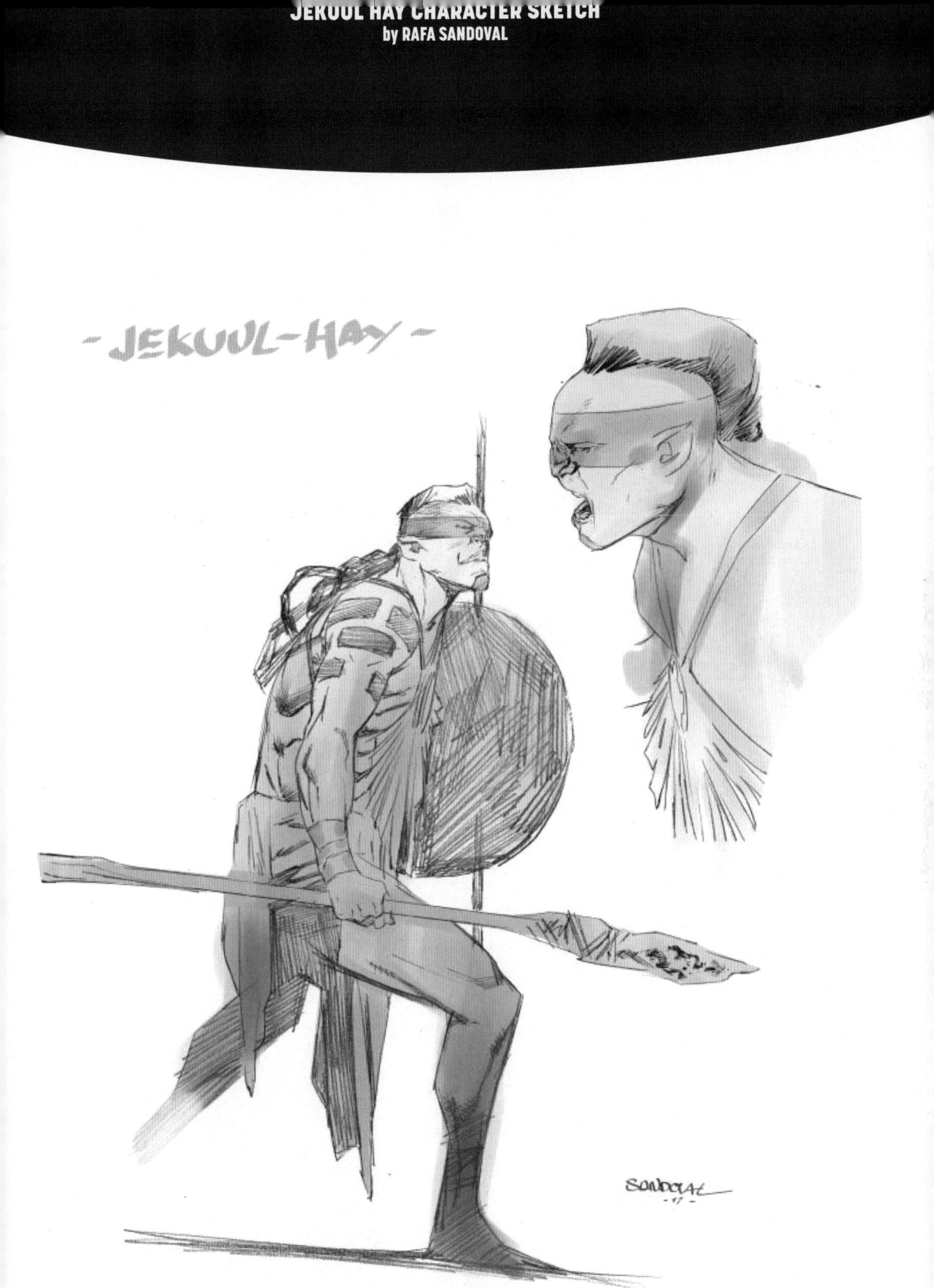
-JEKUUL-HAY-
SANDOVAL
-17-

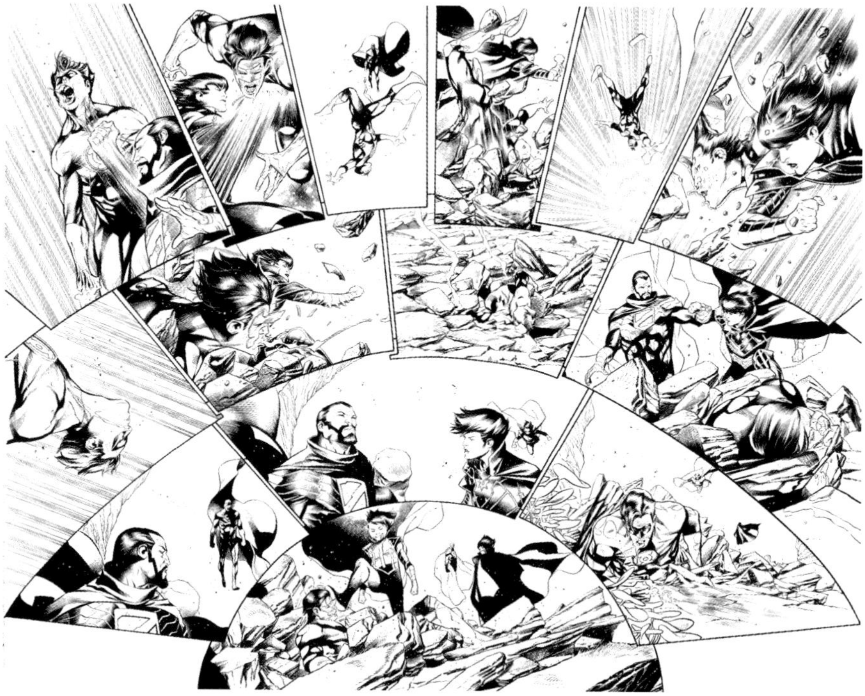

INKS FOR HAL JORDAN AND THE GREEN LANTERN CORPS #37 PAGES 18-19
by RAFA SANDOVAL and JORDI TARRAGONA

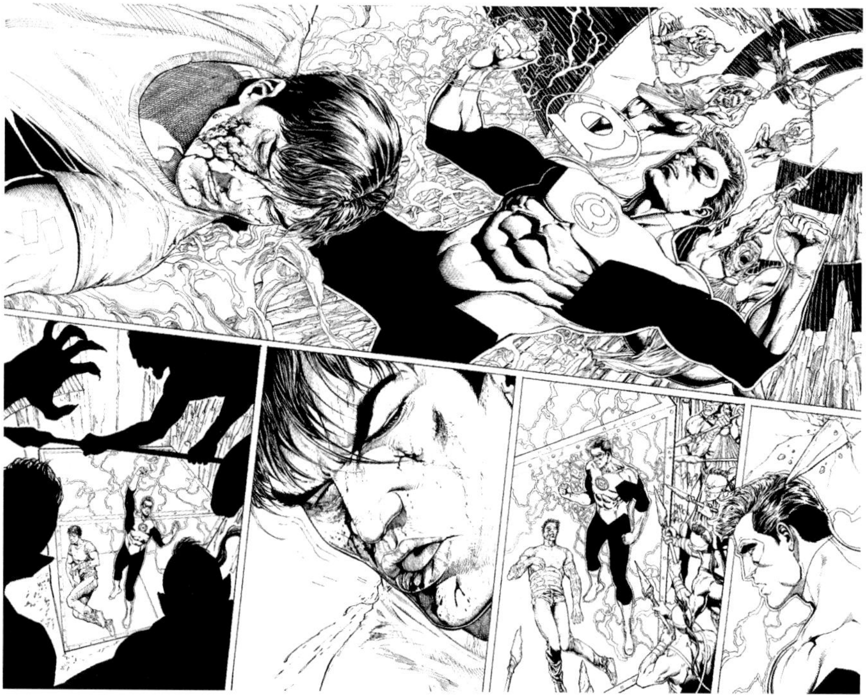

INKS FOR HAL JORDAN AND THE GREEN LANTERN CORPS #38 PAGES 12-13
by ETHAN VAN SCIVER

INKS FOR HAL JORDAN AND THE GREEN LANTERN CORPS #38 PAGE 2
by ETHAN VAN SCIVER

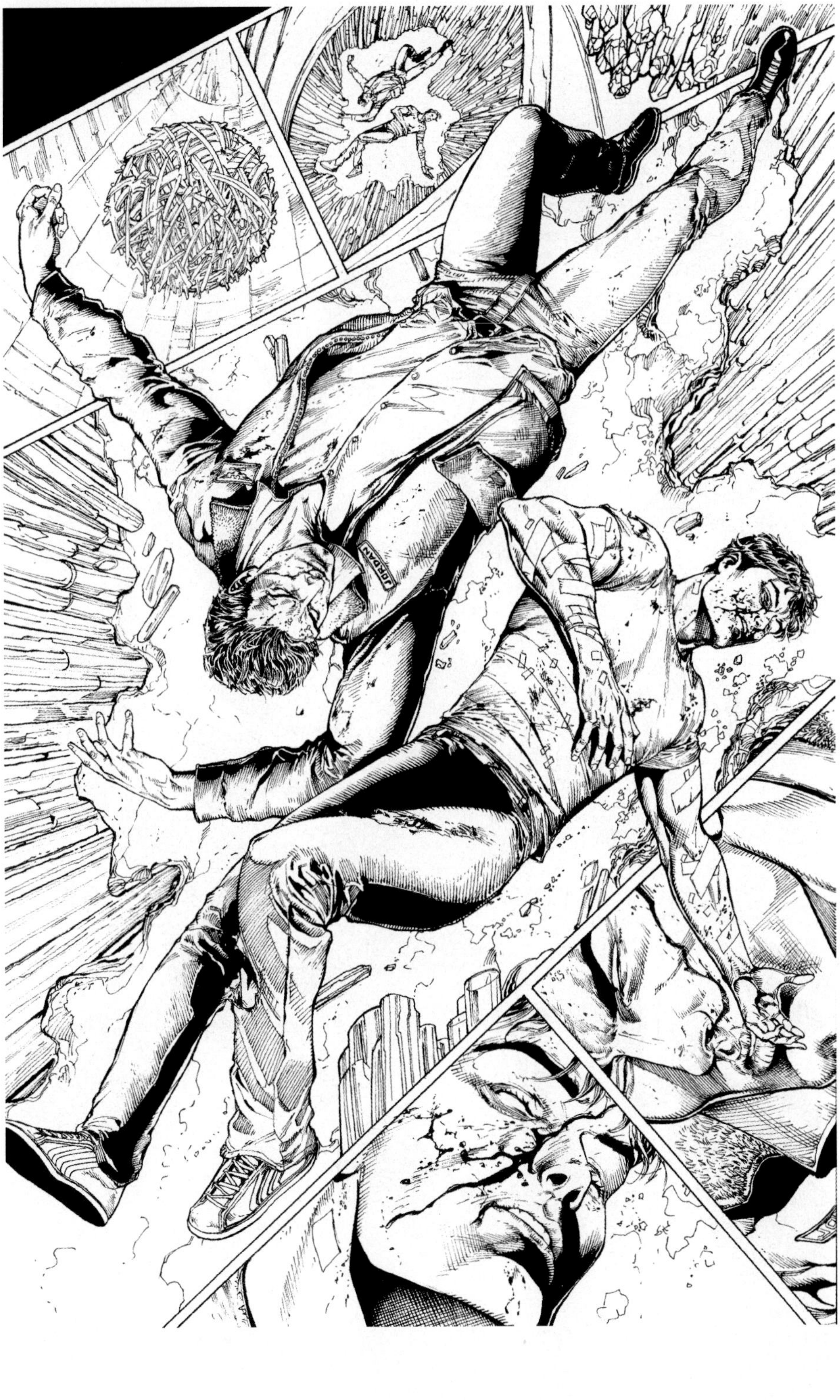
JORDAN

INKS FOR HAL JORDAN AND THE GREEN LANTERN CORPS #39 PAGE 4
by RAFA SANDOVAL and JORDI TARRAGONA

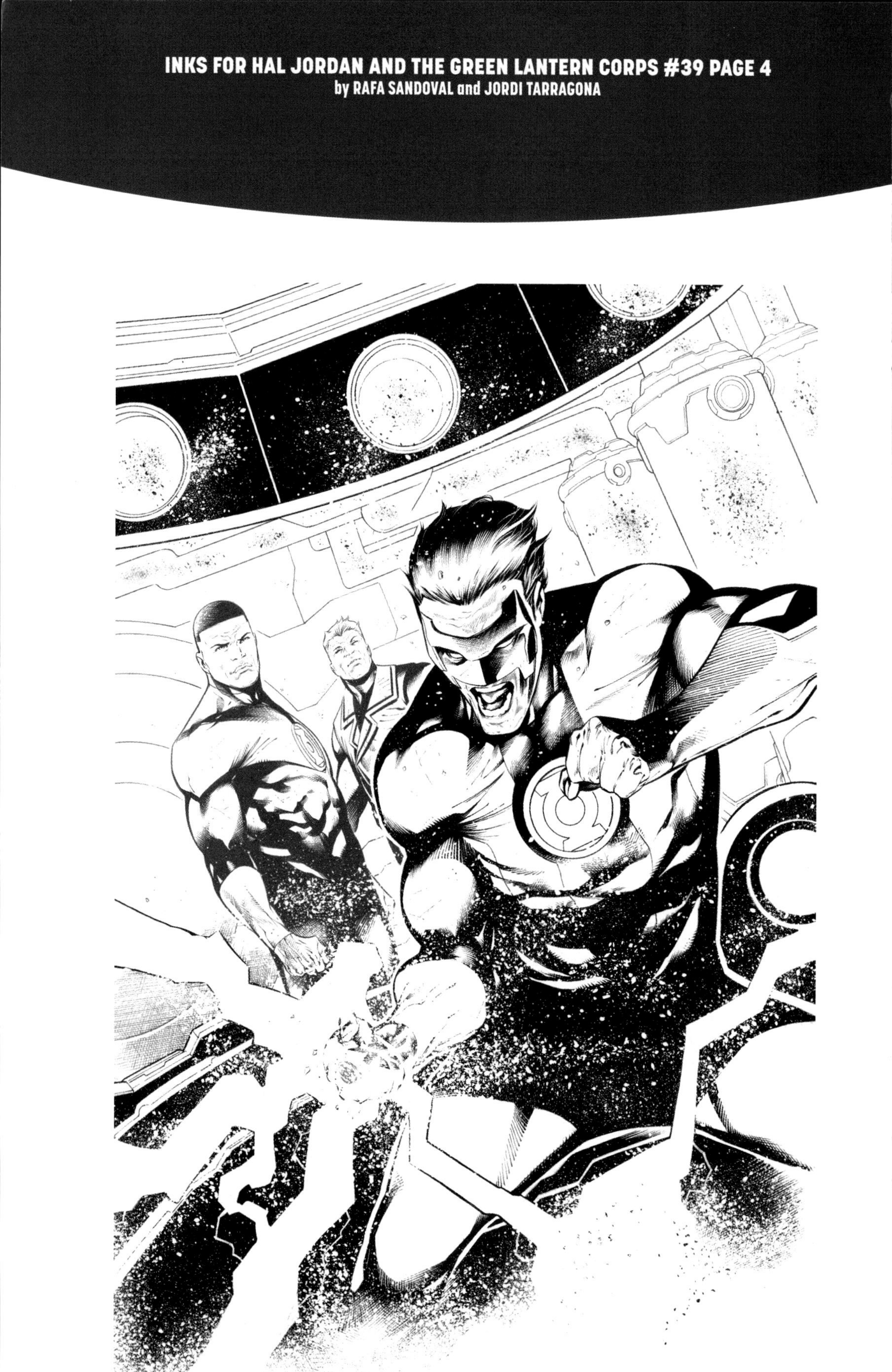

INKS FOR HAL JORDAN AND THE GREEN LANTERN CORPS #40 PAGE 11
by RAFA SANDOVAL and JORDI TARRAGONA

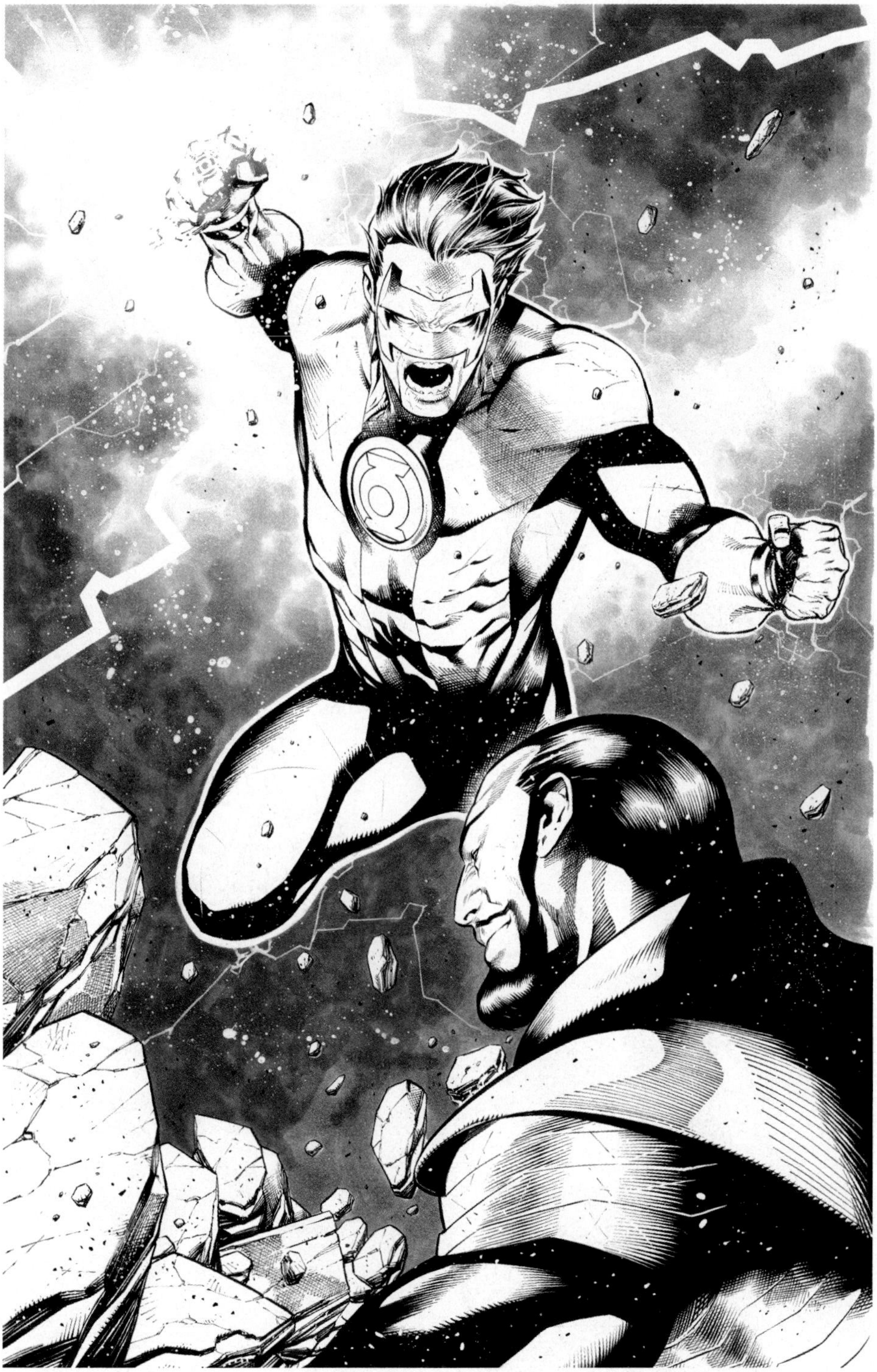

INKS FOR HAL JORDAN AND THE GREEN LANTERN CORPS #40 PAGES 12-13
by RAFA SANDOVAL and JORDI TARRAGONA

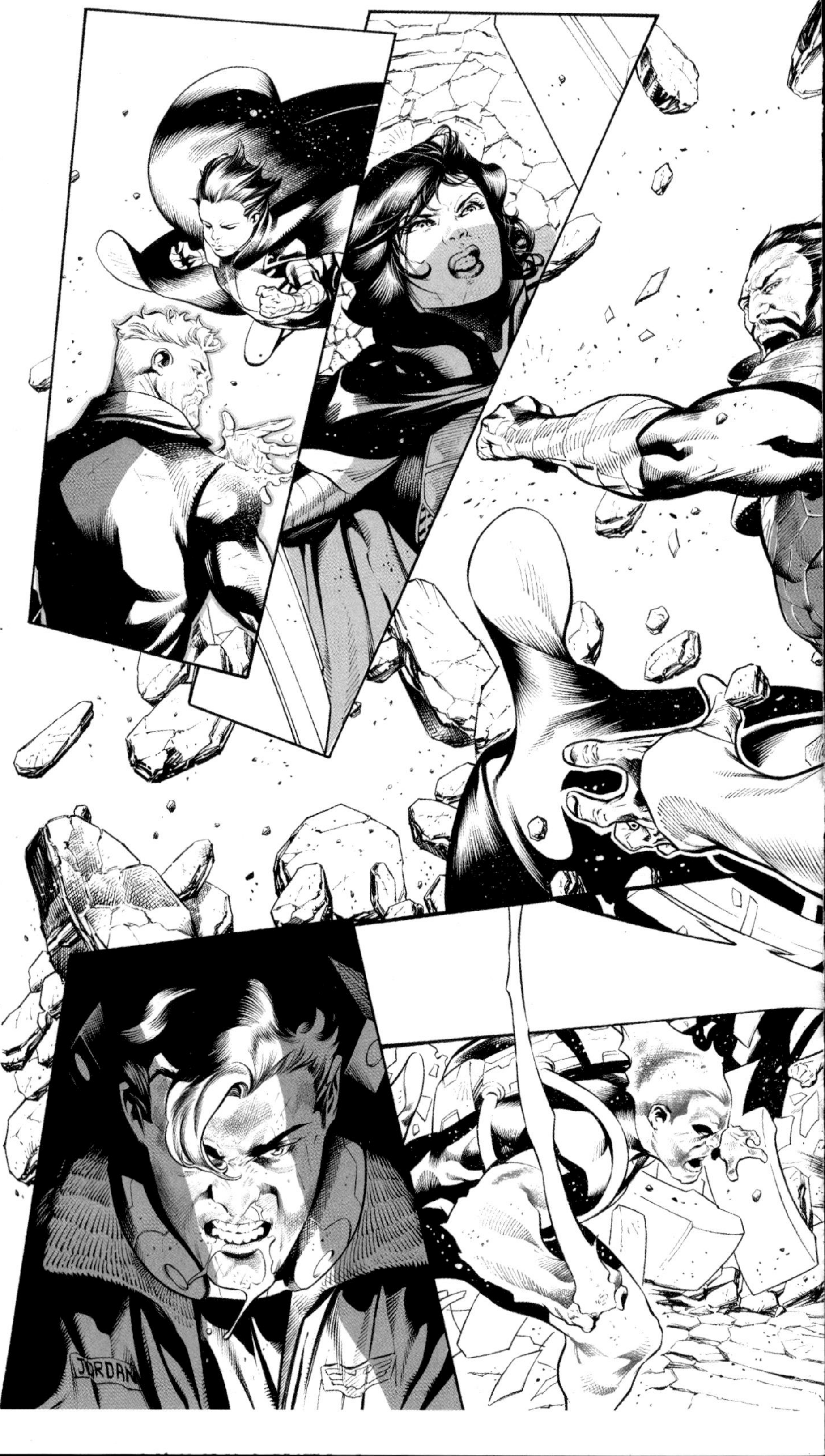
JORDAN

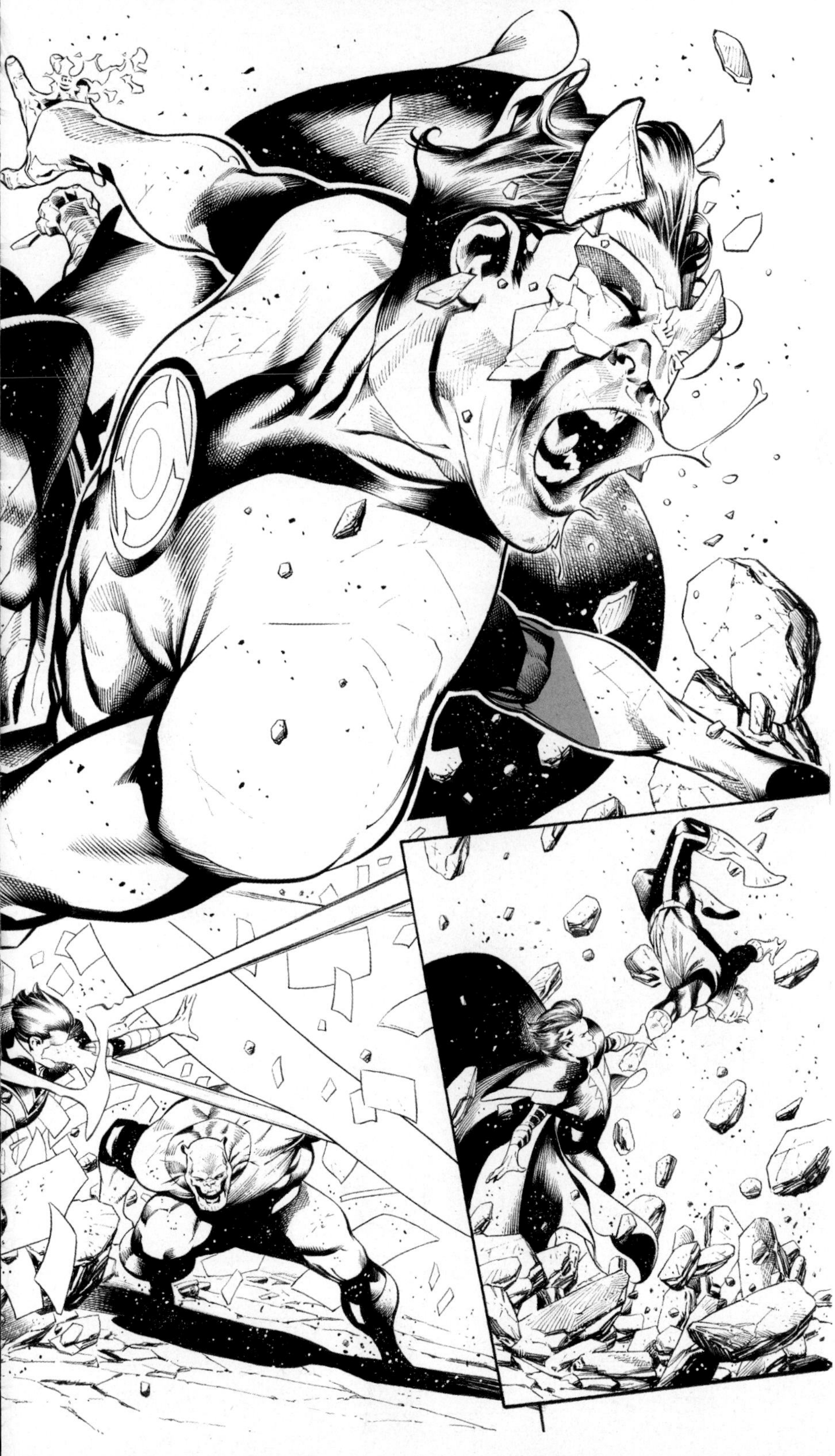

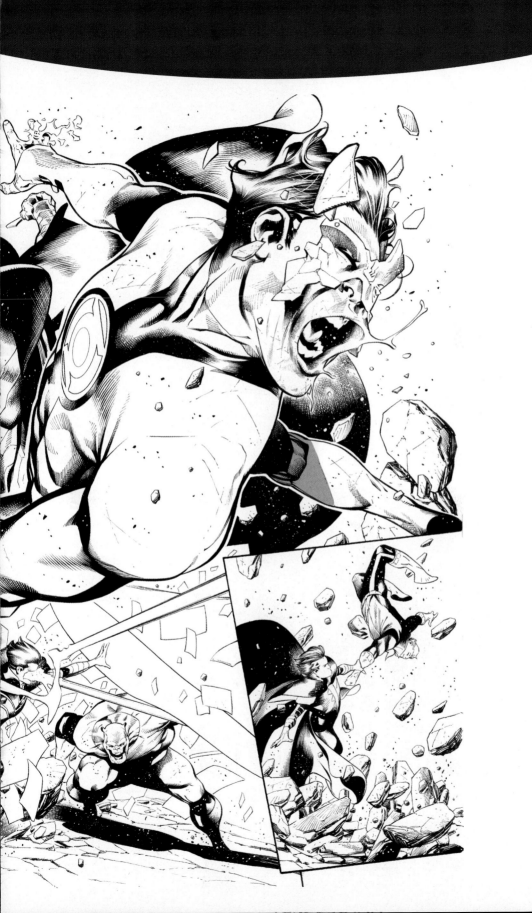

"Thrilling and shocking in equal measure."
–IGN

"Geoff Johns is a master storyteller."
–NEWSARAMA

"High energy adventure, huge stakes, great characters, a dastardly foe, and great creative talent."
–COMIC BOOK RESOURCES

"The #1 New York Times bestseller."
BLACKEST NIGHT
"The talk of the comic book world." —USA WEEKEND
GEOFF JOHNS
IVAN REIS
OCLAIR ALBERT
JOE PRADO

BLACKEST NIGHT
GEOFF JOHNS with IVAN REIS

BLACKEST NIGHT
GEOFF JOHNS
DOUG MAHNKE
GREEN LANTERN

BLACKEST NIGHT: GREEN LANTERN

"The talk of the comic book world." —USA WEEKEND
BLACKEST NIGHT
PETER J. TOMASI
PATRICK GLEASON
GREEN LANTERN CORPS

BLACKEST NIGHT: GREEN LANTERN CORPS

READ THE ENTIRE EPIC!

BLACKEST NIGHT

BLACKEST NIGHT: GREEN LANTERN

BLACKEST NIGHT: GREEN LANTERN CORPS

BLACKEST NIGHT: BLACK LANTERN CORPS VOL. 1

BLACKEST NIGHT: BLACK LANTERN CORPS VOL. 2

BLACKEST NIGHT: RISE OF THE BLACK LANTERNS

BLACKEST NIGHT: TALES OF THE CORPS

Get more DC graphic novels wherever comics and books are sold!

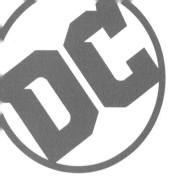

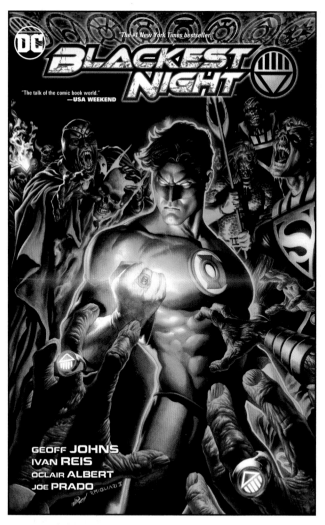

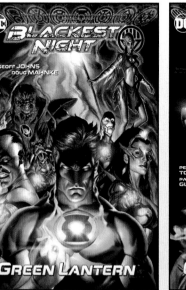

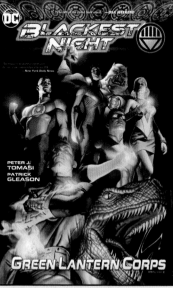

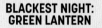